An Overture to Geofinance

Global Finance, Geopolitics, and the Wielding of Power: Theory and Praxis

An Overture to Geofinance

Global Finance, Geopolitics, and the Wielding of Power: Theory and Praxis

Pascal vander Straeten

Value4Risk LLC

Dallas

First published 2018
by Value4Risk LLC

ISBN: 0692102639
ISBN-13: 9780692102633 (Value4Risk LLC)
e-book ISBN: 1984393170
e-book ISBN-13: 9781984393173

Value4Risk LLC, Prosper, Texas

An Overture to Geofinance

Geofinance is about a way of seeing the world. As a true introduction, this work aims at commencing a journey that very few have undertaken: namely, witnessing the pioneering of a brand-new interdisciplinary theory. Indeed, the world of today can no longer be analyzed and understood solely from the perspective of finance, economics, political sciences, or geography. This silo mentality is no longer compatible with the complex world in which we are living. We need a holistic approach that builds bridges among various research fields and helps us understand the complex nature of a phenomenon. That phenomenon is geofinance, as it combines the world of global finance with the realm of geopolitics.

Intuitively, many among you already perceive not only how geopolitics affect the world of global finance but also how international finance affects world events and their stakeholders, be they governments, businesses, or individuals. This introductory textbook shepherds practitioners, cognoscenti, scholars, and students through their first encounter with geofinance. It aims to offer a clear framework for exploring contemporary power conflicts by illustrating how the world of geopolitics and the realm of global finance mutually shape and interact with each other. The overarching theme of geofinancial structures (contexts) and geofinancial agents (institutions, organizations, countries, markets, and individuals wielding financial power) is accessible and requires no previous understanding of theory or current financial affairs. Throughout the book, case studies, including those of the influence of financial markets on geopolitics, the contagion effects between sovereign and banking risks, the influence of geopolitical "black swans" on the world of international finance, the impact of geofinance on business, et cetera, emphasize the multifaceted nature of the complex relationship between global finance and geopolitics in its broadest sense. These examples aid *An Overture to Geofinance* in explaining contemporary global power struggles, the global-finance actions of the Great Powers, the persistence of nationalist conflicts fueled by finance, the changing influence of borders on finance, the impact of the financialization of the global economy on world events, and the new geopolitics of finance.

The book also explains how the realm of global finance bears a lot of similarities to geography in the strictest meaning of the word: namely, with Mother Nature. The book explores how both spheres (i.e., the financial sphere and the biosphere) are complex and dynamic but also chaotic, and it proposes paths to understand and apprehend this complex nexus between geopolitics and global finance. But, prior to going over the applications of geofinance, the book introduces readers to the vectors that drive the existence of the concept of geofinance as both the practice and representation of geofinance are discussed. *An Overture to Geofinance* is illustrated with figures and richly referenced. Reading this book will provide a deeper and more critical understanding of the current world of global finance and facilitate access to higher-level course work and essays on geofinance. Students of finance, geography, and international relations and mainstream readers alike will find this book an essential stepping-stone to a fuller understanding of contemporary financially driven conflicts.

Pascal vander Straeten is a senior risk executive with Value4Risk. His research interests include financial markets, risk management, and geopolitics. He is the author of *Tail Risk Management: Building a Resilient Financial Business in a Volatile World* (published in July 2017).[1]

---

[1] Pascal vander Straeten, *Tail Risk Management: Building a Resilient Financial Business in a Volatile World* (Dallas: Value4Risk LLC, 2017).

For the first time we can perceive something of the real proportion of features and events on the stage of the whole world, and may seek a formula which shall express certain aspects, at any rate, of geographical and financial causation in universal history.

Sir Halford John Mackinder

Contents

12

List of Figures

*To the love of my life, Barbara, without whose support
I would not have been able to reach my goals.*

Acknowledgments

This book project began in the summer of 2012. I was already in my sixth month of expatriation in Canberra, the capital of Australia, discussing the growing influence of global finance on the world of geopolitics with a fellow scholar who had just moved there from South Africa. Our discussions were mostly about the value, if any, of the discipline of geopolitics and the limited usefulness of neoclassical economics and modern political science for trying to explain current global events, including the financialization of the world economy and how it affects the rise of regional powers such as China and Russia but also Turkey and Iran.

The project of writing this book, however, gave way to other priorities, particularly speaking engagements and presentations I made on geofinancial intelligence to the local business community as well as to some foreign government agencies. Eventually, though, I felt a strong obligation—encouraged also by some of my clients—to complete the book. I also wanted to offer the material to a larger audience without compromising the book's attempt to deliver theoretical content.

Over recent years, I have received numerous constructive comments on my notes from several pundits, such as university professors, entrepreneurs, and government officials as well as former colleagues. I am deeply thankful to them. This has not only helped me improve successive versions of the compendium but also given me an in-depth opportunity to learn how different organizations and professionals think about the issues presented here.

I would like to thank the New South Wales Business Chamber for giving me the opportunity to produce a first complete draft of the manuscript as a visiting speaker at the chamber's premises in Sydney and Canberra. Many thanks also to the staff at the

National Library of Australia and the Belgian and German embassies in Canberra. Furthermore, I should like to thank the Dallas Regional Chamber for the speaking opportunities on the subject. Finally, it goes without saying that all opinions and all faults found here are my own.

Dallas, Texas, April 2018

Abbreviations

AKP: *Adalet ve Kalkınma Partisi* (translated here as "Justice and Development Party")
BAT: Baidu, Alibaba, and Tencent
BIS: Bank for International Settlements
BRICS: the countries in a group consisting of Brazil, Russia, India, China, and South Africa
CBOE: Chicago Board Options Exchange
CDO: collateralized debt obligation
CFIUS: Committee for Foreign Investments in the United States
CLS bank: continuous linked settlement bank
DJI: Dow Jones Index
ETF: exchange-traded funds
ETIM: East Turkistan Islamic Movement
EU BRRD: European Union Bank Recovery and Resolution Directive
EU: European Union
FDI: foreign direct investments
Fintech: financial technology, describing a business that aims to provide financial services by making use of software and modern technology
FSB: Financial Stability Board
FSF: Financial Stability Forum
FX: foreign exchange
G20: the twenty major advanced and emerging economies—Argentina, Australia, Brazil, Canada, China, France, Germany, India, Indonesia, Italy, Japan, Republic of Korea, Mexico, Russia, Saudi Arabia, South Africa, Turkey, the United Kingdom, the United States, and the European Union

G7: group consisting of the finance ministers of seven industrialized nations—the United States, the United Kingdom, France, Germany, Italy, Canada, and Japan

G8: a group consisting of the G7 plus the EU

GDP: gross domestic product

GFC: global financial crisis

GM: General Motors

GMAC: General Motors Acceptance Corporation

GPS: Global Positioning System

Grexit: Greece exit from the EU

ICC: International Criminal Court

IMF: International Monetary Fund

KGB: *Komitet gosudarstvennoy bezopasnosti* (translated as "Committee for State Security")

MBS: mortgage-backed securities

MGI: McKinsey Global Institute

MM: money market

NASDAQ: National Association of Securities Dealers Automated Quotations

NATO: North Atlantic Treaty Organization

NGO: nongovernmental agency

NIRP: negative interest-rate policy

NKVD: *Narodnyi Komissariat Vnutrennikh Del* (translated as "People's Commissariat for Internal Affairs")

NTB: nontariff barrier

NYSE: New York Stock Exchange

OECD: Organisation of Economic Cooperation and Development

OFAC: Office of Foreign Assets Control, a department of the US Treasury that enforces economic and trade sanctions against countries and groups of individuals involved in terrorism, narcotics, and other disreputable activities

OTC: over the counter

PDVSA: *Petróleos de Venezuela*

PLA: People's Liberation Army

QE: quantitative easing

RXMSM: a benchmark index to track the performance of a hypothetical risk-reversal strategy that buys Treasury bills to cover the liability from the short S&P 500 (SPX) put-option position

SEPT: science, education, production, and trade

SKEW: a measure of potential risk in financial markets; much like the VIX index, a proxy for investor sentiment and volatility

SWIFT: Society for Worldwide Interbank Financial Telecommunication

TNP: Treaty on the Non-Proliferation of Nuclear Weapons

US AID: United States Agency for International Development

USSR: Union of Soviet Socialist Republics (a.k.a. the former Soviet Union)

VIX: trademarked ticker symbol for the Chicago Board Options Exchange Market Volatility Index, a popular measure of the implied volatility of S&P 500 Index options

WEU: Western European Union

WMD: weapons of mass destruction

WTO: World Trade Organization

WWI: World War I

WWII: World War II

ZIRP: zero interest-rate policy

Prologue

What is in this book, and what will you get out of reading it? The objectives of this book are numerous. They are to:

- introduce an academic understanding of geofinance;

- relate real-world events and development to theoretical perspectives;

- provide a framework for interpreting current foreign affairs through the prism of global finance;

- understand geofinance as an interaction between global finance and geopolitics; and

- explore contemporary geopolitics as an investigation of how global finance is inseparable from world events.

The book is an outgrowth of my work in a company I established six years ago in Australia: Value4Risk Geofinancial Risk Consulting.[2] I have continued to remain passionate (and conduct research) about geofinance. The professional services I offered, together with this work, aim to assist organizations in achieving a better comprehension of current events by placing them in a context of global finance. I try to accomplish this goal by introducing an overarching framework, borrowing different theoretical definitions from the world of geopolitics as well as finance. The main frame is one of structure and agency or, put simply, that organizations try to achieve particular financial goals within specific situations. These situations can, to some degree, help organizations achieve their goals and/or frustrate them or limit their options. Using a geographic perspective, I define

---

[2] The company Value4Risk Geofinancial Risk Consulting was based in Canberra, Australia, until 2015. https://addr.ws/value4risk-geofinancial-risk-consulting-business-consultant--canberra-au.html.

structures as both the situations within particular places and how global finance has an impact on actions taken within these countries and markets.

Though I may have labeled this book an *overture*, I have tried to write it in a way that is useful for both scholars and nonscholars who seek a mastery of contemporary events and how they relate to one another. With that goal in mind, I have attempted to balance the introduction of new concepts with examples that have contemporary meaning, brief case studies of what are likely to be persistent conflicts, and guidelines and questions for you to pursue your own inquiries.

The book consists of several sections that map a road toward a gradual understanding of what geofinance really is. In the first section—"The Genesis of Geofinance as a Concept"—I go over the history of the use of the term *geofinance*, its intricate relationship with geopolitics, the distinction between geofinance and financial geography, and geo-economics, with the ultimate objective of coming up with a definition of *geofinance*.

In the second section of the book, "The Theory of Geofinance," I trace the four vectors that have driven the birth of geofinance: namely, the increasing financialization of the economy, liberalization, the trend of globalization, and the importance of international financial markets in an environment of deregulation and liberalization.

In the third section, I look at how geofinance used as a tool can bring added value to organizations. In the fourth section, about how we should manage geofinance, I state that we can learn a lot from nature when looking at geofinancial events—namely, that while these events may seem chaotic, we should actually embrace the randomness and dynamism of their systems just like nature does (with, for example, the biosphere).

In the fifth section, I go over the main current geofinancial environment that affects the atlas of the world. In the sixth section, I explore the interplay between financial markets and geopolitics, explaining with concrete examples how financial markets and geopolitics influence each other. In the seventh part, related to the nexus between geofinance and business, I explore how companies can gain from looking at events from a geofinancial perspective. In the eighth part, I talk about a couple of practical cases that apply to geofinance. And in the final section, I come up with an outlook about future geofinancial events.

With this overture to geofinance, my goal has been to provide an introduction to the subject. I am fully aware that since there are (almost) no research studies about this topic and this field is relatively new, I am exposing myself to potential theoretical mishaps and wrong postulations. While I am not an academic, I feel that my vast professional experience backed by more than twenty-five years as a senior risk executive in commercial banking, coupled with a very diverse international exposure, allows me to be among the first to jump into the water and pioneer the establishment of this new concept. I have tried to put together the first theoretical building blocks that hopefully will allow for this idea of geofinance to fly out and conquer this brave new world.

The relatively recent upsurge of academic interest in financial crises and how geopolitics and global finance interact have produced many excellent books designed for graduate students, academics, professionals, and advanced undergraduates. This book provides an introduction to geofinance and a stepping-stone to more theoretical approaches, complemented with practical case studies. I aim to ease and promote the concept of geofinance and provide access so that more students and professionals are equipped with a critical understanding of it. I feel lucky and privileged to have had the opportunity to train and write on these topics. I hope that you find my way of looking at current events and geofinance helpful, and I wish you the best in your pursuit of greater understanding of our troubled world. To that end, I hope that this overture is of some help to you.

After reading this book, you will:

- understand how global finance is shaped by geopolitical circumstances;

- understand how global finance can cause geopolitical tensions;

- be able to use theoretical perspectives to develop a deeper and more critical understanding of current events than what you can gain by merely reading online news or watching TV news; and

- have a basic knowledge of essential persistent global conflicts from the perspective of finance.

Foreword

This book shows how the study of global finance can be an alternative approach for the study of geopolitics when the aim is to understand the competitive advantage of organizations as well as of nations. We will describe the study of geofinance as a part of normative intelligence analysis, written in the tradition of critical theory and based methodologically in the evolutionary sciences.

This introduction aims to show the relationships among the disciplines of finance, international politics, geopolitics, economics, strategy, intelligence studies, strategic intelligence, business intelligence, economic intelligence, critical theory, and the historical method.

In other words, this overture to geofinance will combine the evolving fields of geopolitics, financial markets, and business intelligence. The objective of this book is to instill a greater awareness of the role of global finance prevalent in the world of international politics and business decisions.

By walking you through those concepts, I do hope that you will start asking yourself the right questions—and if you already have, that you'll take the next step to shield your organization or country by understanding the realm through which any future organization or nation will have to navigate.

As I write this, no book has yet managed to cover the full range of methods that analyze the nexus of geopolitics and financial markets and how it applies to both organizations and nations.

[3] To avoid any confusion, the book does not refer to and has no link with any company bearing a similar name.

This gap in the literature is the driving force behind the present overture as it relates to a new field of study called geofinance.[3]

The applicable methods are sketched out, providing the reader with the range of ideas underlying them and giving sufficient background for further empirical work. The treatment can also be used as an initiation for a course on applied geopolitics and global finance.

A Word about the Author

Pascal has a passion for financial risk management and geopolitics, and over the years he has specialized in the risk management of extreme events, institutional banking, and capital markets activities as well as corporate finance, with a particular focus on initiating and enhancing efficiencies in relation to risk processes that focus on proactive risk management and economic capital savings.

He has more than twenty-five years of professional experience, with assignments in Australia, Belgium, France, Germany, Italy, Luxembourg, Spain, the United Kingdom, and the United States. Most recently, Pascal ran the credit-risk management of the financial markets activities of a large global commercial bank.

Currently managing his own financial- and political-risk advisory and research firm, he aims to assist businesses and financial organizations in weathering extreme (tail) risk events as well as in creating a risk-aware corporate culture with business resiliency. He has a proven track record of setting up, building, and expanding risk-management frameworks and processes.

Pascal's expertise includes day-to-day management of large credit-risk and underwriting departments, drafting and executing risk policies, regulatory-change management, developing and implementing training modules in relation to enterprise risk management as well as financial and political tail-risk management, and designing risk-mapping, early-warning, and reverse stress-testing tools.

In July 2017, Pascal published *Tail Risk Management: Building a Resilient Financial Business in a Volatile World.*

Introduction

In the Western world, the logic of geofinance is a process that the nation-state does not control since it is driven chiefly by private-sector financial initiatives on a global scale. In other parts of the globe, the state is more heavily involved in economic activities. Thus, in Beijing or Moscow, for instance, it is the Chinese or Russian government itself that is in the driver's seat when Chinese or Russian companies move into new regions—such as, for example, Africa, Asia, and South America. Washington, DC, on the other hand, is the capital of a country that is close to what we could call a corporate state. But both China and Russia on the one hand and the United States on the other hand are administered while taking into consideration a geofinancial rationale: that is, the financial and political leadership in all three countries are entirely aware that a national competitive edge can be obtained only through a wide range of financial freedoms conferred on private-sector actors.

The amount of state control and intervention differs from country to country, but there is an understanding in all nation-states that the state's representatives have a responsibility to govern in such a way that the country remains powerful and competitive (i.e., in a fashion similar to what companies do). However, power and competitiveness as objectives might be replaced in the future with resiliency and sustainability. Indeed, populations from advanced economies as well as large developing countries gradually become aware or (more likely) are compelled to realize that their material development is limited; therefore, they ought to be aware of the consequences of this need for power and competitiveness so that their world remains habitable. But this awareness has not yet fully taken hold.

For nation-states, geopolitics has been a much more straightforward paradigm to address. While geopolitics was in the ascendant, primarily in the late eighteenth, nineteenth, and twentieth centuries, a state reached a sovereign competitive advantage mainly through its own initiatives and decisions, chiefly and ultimately by going to war. At the turn of this new century, nation-states are coming to see that war is no longer the only viable plan for remaining in command. The best evidence of this is the set of wars conducted by the United States and the Soviet Union since WWII. These wars have mostly been failures, not just from a humanitarian perspective but financially, too.

Seeing this, the powerful and competitive nations of the future are reallocating their resources toward science, education, production, and trade (SEPT)—what we will refer to as the "golden process" in geofinance. The rationale is pretty straightforward: first, you make scientific progress; then, you teach those scientific advances to others and incorporate the newly acquired knowledge into new products and services that you bring to market, preferably also overseas. You then reinvest the newly gained earnings as a capital expenditure in science. And the cycle goes on.

Some governments get resources transferred back into science by inciting private organizations to donate to research faculties in the way that is common in the United States, the United Kingdom, Canada, New Zealand, and Australia. Others, including a majority of European and many Asian countries, use taxation as a way to fund these investments. The underlying reason that the Anglo-Saxon model seems to be working better in this respect (i.e., eighteen of the world's twenty leading research universities are American and private) is not because these academic centers of excellence are independent of the government but because they are based on a meritocratic system. But that is a different debate.

The history of geopolitics has been intimately connected with that of the nation-state. The nation-state rose with the Enlightenment and industrialization. Before that—for instance, during the Middle Ages and the Renaissance—ancient societies functioned more according to a geofinancial logic. City-states and local princelings administered their business affairs much like companies do today. This was the case at an early period for Venice, Florence, Milan, and Genova but later also for Antwerp, Amsterdam, Hamburg, and other cities in Europe. In Asia, there was the city-state in the Longshan Phase[4] as well as in Asia Minor[5] (e.g., Tripoli, Byblos, and Carthage). Traders were organized using guilds and put under strict meritocratic supervision.

Each society was, in principle, a harmonious organism governed by a concern for financial growth, at least until it was attacked by another government. The key thing was not only to build a strong army, but also never to use it unless you could be sure of victory. This strategy worked less well when the nation-state became more powerful, as evidenced mainly by the twentieth century with its two global wars. In the twenty-first century, with even more deadly weapons in existence, the disastrous consequences of conflicts between powerful states have become yet more apparent.

This may prevent superpowers in the future from getting involved in large-scale disputes with one another. Sadly, it seems that they will have more than enough to do deterring and intervening in military conflicts within smaller nations, if only because media now makes human suffering more transparent and hence creates immediate public concern. As television shifts to the Internet and 5G and 6G Internet technologies spread, political pressures to intervene are likely to increase.

---

[4] Robin D. S. Yates, *The City State in Ancient China* (New York: Columbia University, 1958), 71–89.
[5] W. Travis Hanes, "Kingdoms and City-States in Southwest Asia," in World History Now, 2009, accessed February 20, 2018, https://historyonlinenow.weebly.com/section-4-kingdoms-and-city-states-in-southwest-asia.html.

Both geofinance and geopolitics also explore how power is derived from the management of resources, be they natural or financial. Thus, the end result for nation-states is much the same in both cases. Through the rationale of these disciplines, countries become weaker or stronger politically and financially as a result of how these various resources are managed. In the English-language literature, we call this "the competitive advantage of nations." This was the premise for the study of finance and economics as advocated by Adam Smith in his 1776 book, *The Wealth of Nations*.[6] Countries are each seeking a competitive advantage.

At the same time, no one nation or culture has managed to stay ahead consistently in this race. Instead, we repeatedly see one government taking over from another as leader of the competitive pack. The duration during which given cultures or countries have managed to maintain their leadership has varied significantly—from a thousand years or more in some past cases (such as Egypt, India, the Roman Empire, and ancient China) to a hundred years or less in others (the United Kingdom, France, and the United States). The tendency is for it to become ever more challenging to retain the leading position because of a combination of more intense competition and greater individual freedom.

How can we understand what makes some countries more competitive and powerful than others? This is the fundamental question that we are concerned with in this book, and it forms the starting point for the study of geofinance. Consequently, we will seek the answer in an approach that diverges from the assumptions of "classical" and "neoclassical" finance. This means that we will find ourselves questioning the value of the discipline of finance as currently practiced.

---

[6] Adam Smith, *The Wealth of Nations* (London: William Strahan and Thomas Cadell, 1776).

The Genesis of Geofinance as a Concept

How it all started

Many of you are familiar with Tim Marshall's *Prisoners of Geography*[7] as well as Robert D. Kaplan's *The Revenge of Geography*.[8] These authors both convincingly explain world political events through the prism of geography. One can understand why geographers show interest in politics and international relations, but why would they, who are naturally interested in how mountains and rivers map the countries of the world, suddenly pay attention to capital markets, cash flows, financial institutions, and financial statements? The latter fields would typically belong to the schools of economists and finance experts, right?

Well, in this day and age of globalization, interconnectedness, and integration of markets, one can undoubtedly claim that the world of finance is the perfect illustration of how the liberalization of national financial and capital markets, coupled with rapid improvements in information technology and the globalization of national economies, have catalyzed financial innovation and spurred the growth of cross-border capital movements.

This globalization of finance shows that space and place no longer matter to financial markets and their stakeholders. Whereas an economy is attached to the development of a society, nowadays you can have a very active financial services industry in a particular country without it improving the development of that country. Quite the contrary—because of its open borders, it is global finance that has been blamed more than, let's say, the

[7] Tim Marshall, *Prisoners of Geography* (New York: Scribner, 2016).
[8] Robert Kaplan, *The Revenge of Geography* (New York: Random House, 2012).

manufacturing or agricultural industries for creating higher income inequalities.

Indeed, for at least two decades, we have known that for advanced economies to thrive, they need deep and broad financial systems.[9] But what is right for advanced market economies may not be right in the developing world. That is, global finance could very well be a double-edged sword; when access to credit is relatively low, higher levels of debt add to growth. But there is a threshold beyond which global finance and debt become a burden. There is now considerable evidence that productivity grows more slowly when a country's government, corporate, and household debt exceed 100 percent of its GDP.[10]

In essence, scholars should not study finance in a silo as economics does. Finance is at the nexus of many fields, and one of them is geofinance. Particularly in these times of complexity, one needs to avoid simple ideas whereby researchers view finance as a branch of economics. Also, with the recent events that have affected the international financial markets, such as Brexit, the global financial crisis, the euro-debt crisis, the role of "fintech" and big tech, and so on, it is time to take a more holistic approach that embraces an interdisciplinary method.

The map of the financial world is in a state of turmoil, with significant implications for development. Geofinance is well positioned to take advantage of this opportunity because of its open, mixed-method approach. Studying the significance of power, space, territory, and scale in finance is crucial for advancing knowledge and public policy.

[9] Ross Levine, "Financial Development and Economic Growth: Views and Agenda," *Journal of Economic Literature* 35(2) (1997), 688–726.
[10] Carmen M. Reinhart and Kenneth S. Rogoff, "Growth in a Time of Debt," *American Economic Review* 100(2) (2010), 573–8.

But geofinance is much more than the geography of finance (i.e., the space and location of finance), just like geopolitics is much more than the geography of politics (i.e., international politics). Geofinance is the study of the effects of power and geography (human and physical) on financial institutions and financial markets. In other words, geofinance is about the impact of power and geography on the management of money and investments. Geofinance focuses on financial power in relation to geographic space.

Research on finance and financial services has, over the past three decades, garnered growing attention outside economics departments and the financial community. Geographers' interest in finance grew in the 1970s following the end of the Bretton Woods system[11] coupled with the hegemony of neoliberal economic policies that helped spur contemporary globalization.

The specific deregulation of the financial services industry, the liberalization of capital controls, and improvements in telecommunications enabled financial institutions and investors alike to mobilize capital easily across space and time, leading some researchers to claim that free movement of capital has made geography irrelevant. Geographers responded to the "end of geography" thesis by showing that space, place, and location remain essential to financial practices and to the shifting geography of finance.[12]

Early study was conducted primarily from the political economy perspective and was shaped by the seminal work and the Marxist theory of David Harvey. These studies focused on issues such as

[11] International Monetary Fund, "The End of the Bretton Woods System," last modified on January 25, 2018, accessed January 25, 2018, https://www.imf.org/external/about/histend.htm.
[12] Jayson J. Funke, "Geography of Finance," Oxford Bibliographies, last modified September 30, 2013, accessed February 20, 2018, http://www.oxfordbibliographies.com/view/document/obo-9780199874002/obo-9780199874002-0024.xml.

the global and local connectivity of financial flows and networks (tacit knowledge and relational proximity), financial globalization and state sovereignty, and unequal growth and financial exclusion. Other research emphasized the creation of new financial spaces (world cities and financial centers, both offshore and onshore) shaped by the de- and re-territorialization of global economic space wrought by the growing power of finance, not to mention the spatial patterns of financial services.

More recently, research has turned to the field of financialization as a theoretical attempt to characterize the emerging global capitalist and the post-Fordist system of capital accumulation. Research tends to focus on how the financial system affects economic, cultural, and political life across a series of scales from the global to the individual and shows how uncertainty, risk, and volatility are part of the geography of finance.

This field of financialization has been enriched by sociological economics, cultural studies, and feminist theory that place emphasis on social relations. This type of study advances the understanding of how financial firms and institutions are made up of a combination of individuals, institutions, knowledge, and technologies that, on an ongoing basis, create and build financial markets and practices through extensive, interconnected social networks.

Geographers' perspectives on the never-ending vitality of place and location in the geography of finance have been further confirmed and impacted by the theoretical development in the 1990s of the 'varieties of capitalism' school heralding the comparative political economy approach. This body of research stresses the institutional differences among financial institutions and infrastructure in advanced capitalist economies. Research centers on institutional-path dependencies and institutional convergence, divergence, and the emergence of new and hybrid configurations.

Debt, finance, and crises have become, alas, defining features of the contemporary global economy. Geographic scholarship on crises, finance, and debt is typically incorporated within the geography of finance and economic geography. Geographers have helped increase the comprehension of the spatial dynamics of debt, finance, and crises by illustrating their network connections and uneven geographies and by highlighting the importance of scale in understanding financial crises, debt, and systems. Again, much geographic research on debt and crises has been influenced by the Marxist political economy framework of David Harvey. Harvey's spatialization of Marxist crisis theories was particularly significant, especially his elaborations on the contradictions of capitalism (uneven development, overaccumulation, etc.) and the resulting tendency toward crises of capital buildup that manifest geographically (for example, in imperialism) and socially (such as social conflict due to fiscal austerity).

Capitalist crises of accumulation manifest in "spatial-temporal fixes," Harvey's term for different forms of sociospatial reorganization that serve to temporarily manage crisis via the geographic dispersal of capital (capital switching) and crisis impacts such as devaluation. Harvey's work has enabled the development and sustainability of a body of critical geographic scholarship on the political economy of indebtedness and crises, which has been augmented more recently by cultural political-economy approaches, frequently inspired by the work of Michel Foucault, that tend to center on the financialization of global capitalism.

Geographic research on debt and crises can be categorized into three broad and interrelated themes. The first idea is concerned with theoretically contextualizing indebtedness and financial crises, particularly within the current nexus of capital-driven power relations and governance and the broader need to manage global economic development and crises under financialization. The second theme tends to emphasize the sociospatial effects of uneven growth under financialization and globalization (e.g., the spatial allocation of credit and debt). The third theme studies the connections among financial flows, crises, and the built environment, especially urban systems, mortgage markets, et cetera.

This work illustrates the significance of geographic scale (like local real estate markets but global mortgage markets—so-called globalization), social networks, and institutional practices and financialized technologies of risk management. Researchers typically use case studies to evidence how various groups of people (e.g., women, communities, regions, and institutions) and identities are affected.

Geographic studies on credit-risk provision and risk-management practices situate spaces of financial exclusion and inclusion particularly in urban environments, where case studies reveal spatial patterns of racial, gendered, and class-based redlining (credit exclusion) and predatory lending (exploitative inclusion).

Some of the most challenging issues greeting the year 2017 were not so local. Would cross-border reinsurance contracts operate correctly in the wake of a hurricane or an earthquake? How might an adverse outcome in Ukraine, on the Korean peninsula, or in the South China Sea affect international banks and their financial markets? Regulators of the world's leading international financial centers have always had to handle domestic and global risks.

In between them, however, is a dynamic that is paramount to consumer and commercial finance in the modern economy. It is a force at play in the precarious risks from Brexit and the differences of view between countries over Basel IV finalization. What about the impact of borders, distance, and location on the shape of insurers, asset-management companies, banks, and financial regulation? Put simply: there is an effect of geography on the geometry of finance—a dynamic we might call geofinance. With the never-ending need for more prudential regulation following the financial crisis combined with the ongoing changes to the geopolitical landscape looming large, geofinance is likely to be the critical challenge of the next few decades.

The saga of the concept

There is actually no official definition for *geofinance*. If you search on Google or look it up in the *Oxford Encyclopedia*, you will find none. Why? Because it is a brand-new field.

As far as I can trace it back, the term was first coined by Charles Goldfinger in his 1986 book about geofinance.[13] The author explores the world of financial centers, new forms of money, the different actors in the system (i.e., banks and nonbanks), and their contrasted evolution. He talks about the then-latest developments in financial matters, emphasizing the role of the euro currency markets and the changes brought about by information technology and deregulation.

I personally used the word *geofinance* when establishing my company Value4Risk Geofinancial Risk Consulting in 2012 in Australia, where I provided research and training about the interplay between finance and geopolitics and the use of the geography of finance as a power-projection and risk tool.

In June 2017, Sami Hammana[14] talked about geofinance and the social dynamics of finance (financialities of the Anthropocene era), where he postulates that finance must always be read in a reciprocal relationship to the earth. To test this hypothesis, we need to elaborate an understanding of an anthropocentric finance power—a finance power surpassing the correlationist

---

[13] Charles Goldfinger, *La Géofinance: Pour Comprendre la Mutation Financière* (Paris: Collection Odyssée, 1986).

[14] Sama Hammana, "Geofinance: Financialities of the Anthropocene," PhD thesis, Goldsmiths University of London, 2017, accessed January 29, 2017, https://schizoaesthetic.org/images/geofinance.pdf.

understanding of political power exertion by the *anthropos*. For such comprehension to be achieved, finance as a social practice needs to be thought of as a reordering of social relations not only among humans (traders, socioeconomic classes, etc.) but also beyond the human.

Then in October 2017, Sam Woods, deputy governor of the Bank of England and chief executive officer of the Prudential Regulation Authority, made a public speech about geofinance.[15] His statement discussed the impact of location, distance, and borders on the shapes of insurers, banks, and financial regulation. Again, this is the effect of geography on the geometry of finance, a dynamic he called *geofinance*.

In January 2018, Fabio M. Parenti and Umberto Rosati published *Geofinance and Geopolitics*,[16] offering a concise insight into the complex financial dynamics on the global scale and their broad geopolitical implications. The book's aim is to provide a study tool not only to university students but also to those who wish to gain a deeper understanding of the actual phenomena (financial globalization, financial capitalism, and new alternatives) at the base of the definitions and redefinition of international power relationships. In essence, Parenti and Rosati study the main geopolitical implications of the financial processes, bringing out the apparent relationship among financial, geopolitical, and military instability and between financial globalization and international politics.

[15] Sam Woods, "Geofinance," speech given at the Mansion House City Banquet, London, October 4, 2017, accessed January 29, 2017, https://www.bankofengland.co.uk/-/media/boe/files/speech/2017/geofinance-speech-by-sam-woods.pdf?la=en&hash=1B7B8C099846ED4D305128BBB265F7BB71A354BA.
[16] Fabio M. Parenti and Umberto Rosati, *Geofinanza e Geopolitica Copertina Flessibile* (Milan: EGEA, 2016).

The nondeterministic nature of geofinance

Geofinance is defined by the belief that the life of financial markets, being similar to those of human beings and animals, is not shaped by scientific determinism but instead by laws of chaos and randomness. Determinism is, in essence, the philosophical theory that all events, including moral choices, are ultimately determined by previously existing causes.

However, the world in which markets operate is not rational or deterministic. The phenomenon of black swans is the perfect illustration of such randomness. Indeed, just as the black swan reappeared out of the blue on the surface of this earth, many calamities affecting financial markets also surface without perceived warning, seemingly out of nowhere. And this lack of perception happens exactly when people have completely forgotten and are complacent about the fact that such an event could ever take place.

Financial markets have become a random, fractal system in which there are patterns but not repetitions. Financial markets operate like systems whose behavior is very sensitive to small variations in initial conditions.

This is what chaos theory studies. Chaos theory is hardly a perfect metaphor for geofinance, but it is of a higher caliber than the usual overly simplified methods that have dominated the theories of finance for previous decades (e.g., capital budgeting, diversification and portfolio selection, equilibrium pricing of risky assets, and the theory of efficient markets).

Interestingly, biologists and mathematicians are much more at ease with the reality of indeterminate complexity than social scientists. Indeed, they have accepted that we live in a system of complex systems (political, economic, geophysical) that regularly intersect, modify, disrupt, and amplify one another.[17] Instead of treating complexity as an exception to rigid rules, quantum physics is now providing an approach into which everything fits sensibly.

Being a social science, finance is, by definition, not an exact science—but neither is it pure chaos. While you cannot really predict the likelihood and timing of a (geo)financial event in the way that you could forecast the outcome of, for example, a storm brewing over the Atlantic Ocean, you can still pick out the signal from the noise and from that derive the likely path, if not the sequence, of upcoming events.

In fields that revolve around human interaction and behavior, such as geofinancial behaviors, predictors must also contend with the caprices of markets, societies, and mankind.

There are so many factors affecting geofinancial events and decisions, including ego and a sense of humiliation, that one can never predict with absolute certainty the ultimate scenario that will drive a future geofinancial event. However, one can set up scenario cases that suggest the likely paths that such an event would follow.

[17] Parag Khanna, "Want to Understand How Trump Happened? Study Quantum Physics," *Quartz*, November 11, 2016, accessed January 27, 2017, https://qz.com/834735/want-to-understand-how-trump-happened-study-quantum physics/?lipi=urn%3Ali%3Apage%3Ad_flagship3_pulse_read%3BTk2d2dnyTY6jiek0AGOmjg%3D %3D.

Geopolitics as a guide for defining geofinance

All of us are familiar with the definition of *geopolitics*. According to the *Encyclopedia Britannica*, it is the "analysis of the geographic influences on power relationships in international relations" and also "the study of how geography and economics have an influence on politics and the relations between nations." The *Oxford Dictionaries* indicate that geopolitics "relates to politics, especially international relations, as influenced by geographical factors."

In other words, geopolitics can be seen as a branch of political geography in which the power of the politics (the state) is determined or influenced by geography (e.g., a territorial space, such as the borders of a country, a chain of mountains, or a river). Thus, to extrapolate a similar definition for *geofinance*, we could say it is the study of how state politics are influenced by the spatial (geographic) phenomenon of global finance and big multinational companies. Indeed, geofinance, from Greek γῆ gê ("earth, land") and χρηματοδότηση ("finance"), in the strictest literal sense would be the study of how financial globalization impacts the state politics of a nation or the relations between nations and global companies.

In geopolitics, the main actors are states, while in geofinance, the main actors are governments, global financial companies, and multinational companies. And, in the case of geopolitics, it is the need for borders that influences the power relations of the state, while for geofinance it is the absence of borders that determines the power relations of the state. But that power can be political (in the case of geopolitics) or financial (in the case of geofinance).

In essence, geofinance combines two branches: namely, of the spatial nature of global finance (or financial economics) and state politics. But, in this day and age of neoliberalism and globalization, state politics goes much further than merely the management of the political power of a state. Indeed, given the international financialization of the global economy, state politics also embrace the need for the state to keep the country at a competitive advantage over other nations, and one way to get to that competitive advantage is through the power of finance that the state wields.

As already alluded to, by geography we mean not only physical geography (mountains, deserts, oceans, rivers, etc.), but also spatial geography (across borders) and human geography (i.e., the importance of networks). The latest book from Niall Ferguson[18] highlights the fact that social networks have always played a key role in history, even before Facebook, LinkedIn, and so on. Again, geofinance is a relatively new concept that marries, word for word, the geography of the world of finance, being the cross-border operating activities of financial institutions and financial markets, and the financial policies of a state or organization.

But we should go one step further and look at geofinance in a broader sense: namely, as delineating an intellectual terrain concerned with and influenced by the interaction of geography, knowledge, power, and financial institutions and markets. Geofinance would be, then, a discourse concerned with the relationship between power, knowledge and financial relations. In other words, geofinance focuses on financial power in relation to geographic space.

Geofinance is the use of financial power to promote and defend national interests and to produce beneficial results, and it includes the effects of other nations' financial actions on a country's goals. With geofinance, we also study the geographic influences on power relationships in international financial markets, such as the phenomenon of financial concentration in

---

[18] Niall Ferguson, *The Square and the Tower* (New York: Penguin, 2018).

so-called international financial centers or sovereign wealth funds. At the level of international financial markets, geofinance is a method of studying global financial markets to understand, explain, and predict general financial behavior through geographical variables such as demography, topography, natural resources, and so on.

A financial-risk analysis can no longer focus solely on financial and monetary phenomena as it did during the Cold War era for the following reasons: first, geofinance encompasses all factors related to the geography and resources of nation-states, from river grids, impassable mountains, minerals, gas, and oil to labor forces, populations, and their religions and political systems; and second, these factors are undergoing dramatic changes. Failing to recognize these facts, an analysis will continue to produce unacceptably inaccurate financial outlooks. Postmodern international financial markets are becoming increasingly geofinancially influenced; thus, we live in the era of geofinance.

Geofinance is primarily about financial analysis and reasoning that takes into account financial forces and factors that influence international activities. Geography and the control over all types of commodities shape not only foreign policy and the political process but also, increasingly, global finance and financial markets. Nevertheless, this is not an exclusive one-way causality but with causality in both directions. Geofinancial interests are increasingly driving financial and monetary policy, but financial stakes are also shaping military, foreign, and energy policy. This illustrates the complexity of fast-evolving globalized financial markets with their feedback loops.

The rise of geofinance research is in part a response to the fact that over the past twenty years, global bond, stock, and derivatives markets have been dramatically affected by so-called external shocks and forces. Some of the most prominent moves in financial markets were not driven by financial variables but rather by powerful forces such as policy makers, trade flows, energy supply and demand, and geopolitics.

For example, the recovery of equity prices from 2009 to 2016 was mainly achieved by a massive intervention by US policy makers. They drove the prices of sovereign bonds higher to lower bond yields in financial markets, single-handedly shifting risk and inflation expectations out of a liquidity trap. The rise of India, Brazil, Turkey, China (the United States' biggest creditor), and other powers as key trade partners but also contenders for global supremacy played a role in the magnitude and timing of policy making.

The difference between geopolitics and geofinance

Studies of intelligence and geopolitics have a long history of concurrence with mutual influence and inventiveness. Members of the world's intelligence organizations, politicians, civil servants, and officers of the armed forces have always been keen readers of geopolitical publications. Recently, senior executives and managers of private-sector organizations have also become more interested in geopolitical ideas as international commerce and global finance have expanded, and managers' perspectives on the world have become truly global.

Concomitantly, it has become clear that this is not geopolitics in the old sense but a new version. Hence, we need to explore the differences as well as the similarities between geofinance and geopolitics. The power dimension is common to both fields. However, their forms, the emphases, and the variables they choose to study and analyze are often dissimilar, as indicated in the table below:[19]

[19] Jesper Strandskov, "Sources of Competitive Advantages and Business Performance," *Journal of Business Economics and Management*, 7(3) (2006), 119–29, accessed January 20, 2017, http://www.tandfonline.com/doi/pdf/10.1080/16111699.2006.9636132.

Variables	Geopolitics	Geofinance
Beliefs	Values	Financial targets
Position	Geographical location and size	Spatial and across borders
Resources	Natural resources	Financial strength and networks
Weight	Population size	Cash flow and global networks
Structure	Political stability, laws, and organization	Financial stability, regulations, and network
Base	Infrastructure	Markets, balance sheets, and network
Security	Military	Financial knowledge and connections
Communication	Languages	Numbers

Notwithstanding the somewhat distinct perspective from the doctrine of realpolitik, these two subjects ultimately operate in a sort of symbiosis. There will always be an active political component in geofinance and a robust financial component in geopolitics. How we approach the real political doctrine very much depends on our perspective, whether we are a private-sector organization or a nation-state. A responsible company also tends to view problems from the perspective of the nation-state and vice versa.

Some pundits will claim that there is no real distinction between geofinance and geopolitics—that in the end, politics is all about finance, as it all comes down to resources expressed in some monetary form. But even if this is true, it might come off as simplistic. The fundamental distinctions have to do with the users—managers versus public administrators—but also the circumstances of the respective studies regarding their different working environments.

Decision makers in private-sector organizations differ in many ways from their public-sector colleagues. They focus more on financial goals, and they pay less attention to public opinion and political agendas. The circumstances differ, first of all, concerning regulations, competition, and internationalization. There is also a distinction in the academic homes associated with these studies: political science for geopolitics and global finance and financial management for geofinance.

Pundits on political affairs are seldom experts on global finance, if for no other reason than that such persons move in a different social context and in different circles, and they have distinct tactics and goals—but also because they have had different training and education. This has also led to opposing organizational cultures. A diplomat typically knows little of managerial accounting, and likewise, a businessman lacks knowledge of the ways (legal, administrative, social) in which a nation-state operates.

When the ideas of geography and power were new, only strategy was in play, with no separation among government, economic, or military intelligence. We find an illustration of this in Sun Tzu's *Art of War*.[20] Lack of separation between the financial, economic, and political spheres remained until much later, as in Machiavelli's *The Prince*.[21] (These two books are still used as primary literature in many courses on geopolitics.) The first attempt to separate finance, economics, and political science in

[20] Lionel Giles, *Sun Tzu on the Art of War* (London: Luzac & Co., 1910).
[21] Niccolò Machiavelli, *The Prince* (Rome: Antonio Blado d'Asola, 1532), accessed July 2017, https://www.gutenberg.org/files/1232/1232-h/1232-h.htm.

connection with the study of geography was made in Germany, under the term *Wirtschaftsgeographie*.[22]

This process of divergence has continued to the point at which there is no longer much politics left in the academic discipline of finance. As a result, that subject has reached a higher level of theorization, abstraction, and specialization, but it has concomitantly become less relevant as a body of literature to assist us in understanding more complex and broader sociopolitical issues. Another weakness in the modern discipline, from the perspective of financial reality, is that it systematically leaves out the power dimension. Current studies of finance and business administration reveal a lack of interest in who has the most resources, where they live, how they think, and how they use their resources. These are vital data that have a significant effect on organizational development in general.

Such information, in fact, is often looked upon as meaningless and left to popular magazines such as *Stern*, *Forbes*, or *Focus*. Scholars view themselves and their work as something more important, conducted at a higher level; they deal in theory and the abstract. So we should not be amazed when their findings turn out to have little relevance to today's complex world of financial and business reality.

There are tens of thousands of academic articles out there, but they rarely seem to provide practical answers. Consequently, there is a disjunction nowadays between financial theory and financial reality. *The Economist*, though, has pitched upon a right mix of politics, geography, history, and real-life descriptions of economic and financial phenomena, probably in large part because it was shaped by successful practical businessmen and financiers.

[22] Karl Haushofer, "Geopolitik des Pazifischen Ozeans," *The Canadian Historical Review* 5(3) (1925), 268–9.

The situation in political science is even more troublesome. Politics is impossible to explore without the proper assistance of political realism. The acutest problem with political science lies in its overspecialization and in the fact that it has forsaken most understanding of financial realities, treating these as the domain of international business and global finance. Political science has forgotten so much about basic financial mechanisms that it no longer seems to be capable of explaining what makes a state or an organization strong or weak. Instead, it occupies itself with piecemeal social engineering:[23] descriptions of organizational structures, party politics, and legal questions. As a result, both subjects—finance and political science—have become weaker as fields of study, less able to understand and describe the realm we observe.

Geofinance and geopolitics acknowledge an obligation to keep these two dimensions in mutual contact, and that is very much appreciated by scholars and by practical businessmen. An interdisciplinary perspective lies at the heart of both subjects. Thus, it is no revelation that courses in geopolitics have become highly favored not only in military circles and naval academies but also at schools of political science, public administration, and business. But also, vice versa: more and more students in political sciences feel the need to explore even business- and finance-related fields.

Harold Wilensky[24] says that the most significant threats to the intelligence function are specialization, centralization, and hierarchy, in that order. What kind of questions, then, are raised in the discipline of geofinance? On the one hand, there are financial and political issues as discussed above. On the other side, there are the geo-questions, so often neglected. The real

[23] Karl Popper, *The Poverty of Historicism* (Oxford, UK: Routledge & Kegan Paul, 1957).
[24] Harold L. Wilensky, "The Professionalization of Everyone?" *American Journal of Sociology* 70(2) (1964), 137–58, accessed January 2, 2017, http://www.journals.uchicago.edu/doi/abs/10.1086/223790.

strength of geofinance first becomes apparent when we combine the two. For example, the location of critical financial markets, such as Moscow, London, Paris, and Frankfurt, can be explained by the fact that many rivers lead to these places, providing a safe haven—but even more important, a site—for trade. New York, Shanghai, and Hong Kong are located along coastlines, near the naturally sheltered outlets of major bays. Ultimately, these patterns are so prevalent that it is hard to find exceptions; most of the more significant human settlements on this planet result from considerations relating to natural resources and financial interests, which boil down to the quest for competitive benefit or merely the trial of survival.

The value of social-science competence has been overstated in the Western world over the past thirty years or so. Other than the financial services sector, which we find concentrated in places such as London and New York, there are not many financially successful centers that were not founded on a local concentration of people with natural-science backgrounds. What is essential is to export and to create export surpluses, preferably in high-value products. This is a lesson we used to understand in Europe but that much of Europe has primarily forgotten (though countries such as Germany, Switzerland, the Netherlands, and Sweden are exceptions).

Geopolitics is traditionally linked to variables of ethnicity, country, religion, and language—in other words, slow-changing variables. Geofinance is linked to more rapidly changing variables, particularly technological change and developments in finance. These distinct relationships to the notion of change can result in the two fields of study coming to opposing conclusions. As an illustration, let us look at some of the arguments used in the current debate about the EU membership of Turkey.

Geopoliticians often suggest that the Turks cannot belong to the EU because they are a Seljuk tribe of Mongol origin and thus very unlike us Europeans in many respects. They are Muslims and have been at war with Europe and European interests for most of the time since they first invaded Anatolia and the Algarve some thousand years ago, until the violent conquest of Constantinople and the fall of the Byzantine empire in May 1453.

And then later on, during the decline of the Ottoman Empire, the Turks massacred hundreds of thousands of Christians and violently occupied parts of Central Europe as well as the Balkans. Therefore, Turkey cannot possibly join the EU. Furthermore, Roman Catholics and Orthodox Christians (in both Western and Central Europe) and Greeks would not accept its joining. Nor would the French, the Dutch, or the Italians. Leftist groups would not allow it either, since they argue that Turkey systematically violates human rights and suppresses its Kurdish minority—to say nothing of the rights of other minorities.

The logic of geofinance, however, tends to follow a different line of reasoning by incorporating a financial aspect along with the political ideology. From a geofinancial perspective, what matters is, first of all, financial performance. With a population of seventy-one million, Turkey would constitute the second-largest market in the EU after Germany. With a GDP of about $858 billion in 2016,[25] the Turkish economy is already stronger than that of the Netherlands ($771 billion).[26]

But despite these seemingly good numbers, the public finances are in shambles, as evidenced by lingering deficits and high indebtedness, not to mention a volatile currency. Also, Turkey has a young population, which might potentially help improve Europe's demographics, but the level of education is low. Additionally, Turkey has gone backward on the political level,

---

[25] Trading Economics, "Turkey GDP," accessed February 20, 2018, https://tradingeconomics.com/turkey/gdp.
[26] Trading Economics, "Netherlands GDP," accessed February 20, 2018, https://tradingeconomics.com/netherlands/gdp.

with Erdogan embracing radical Islamism, restraining freedom of the press, and fomenting a fake coup to justify an even more prominent overtaking of the Turkish state apparatus.

Consequently, Turkey cannot comply with the social and political criteria set by the EU, and it seems unlikely ever to become an EU member. The controversy over Cyprus is not solvable due to Greek veto power. Besides, Turkey has made some aggressive moves in the region and is now siding with Moscow. So in the case of Turkey, even by considering a geofinancial component to the study, and while the prospect could be exciting and add value, the overall geofinancial opinion about its membership to the EU remains negative.

Given that the world is always changing, we need to understand what is happening. We need a more pragmatic framework for the social sciences, allowing them to better explain to us what is happening. We need a broader understanding of human behavior, which can incorporate finance as an explanatory variable and can reintroduce the power dimension to the equation.

Geofinance as a mirror of the geography of finance

Just like a mirror reverses images, geofinance shows an opposite reflection of the geography of finance. Indeed, just like geopolitics points in the opposite direction of political geography, geofinance is the mirror image of the geography of finance. Both are obviously intimately related, but they are still different.

To continue the analogy with geopolitics, consider the following: political geography is busy with the interrelationships between people, state, and territory, whereas geopolitics looks at the sequence of events that shape the interrelationships between people, state, and territory.

- Geopolitics belongs to political science. It examines the impact of space and place on state policy. The research tools of geopolitics are based on political science, geography, history, the military, and the economy. It focuses on the future. It is interested in the relationship between the centers of power. The object of research is the real balance of forces. It is used as a handbook of power, so to speak. In other words, geopolitics focuses on political power in relation to geographic space—in particular, territorial waters and land territory in correlation with diplomatic history.

Whereas:

- Political geography belongs to geographical science. It examines the impact of the state on a space. Its research tools are based on socioeconomic geography, and it focuses on the present. It is interested in a description of the geographical space. It is used as a handy atlas, so to speak, of the official political division of the globe.

We could extrapolate the same kind of distinction as it relates to geofinance:

- Geofinance belongs to the field of finance. It examines the impact of the space (that is, location, distance, and borders) on the configuration of finance (i.e., markets, financial institutions, and government financial policies). Its research tools are based on finance, geography, history, the military, and markets. Geofinance focuses on the future. It is interested in the relationship between the centers of power. The object of research is the real balance of forces. It is used as a handbook of power, so to speak. In other words, geofinance focuses on financial power in relation to spatial geography—in particular, the importance of international and borderless activities in correlation with financial history. Geofinance studies the effects of finance (financial markets, financial institutions, and financial policies) that affect the nation's sovereignty and culture, and the various kinds of spatial barriers from the perspective of globalization, such as the importance of global networks.

- The geography of finance belongs to geographical science. It examines the impact of finance on a space. Its research tools are based on geography, and it focuses on the present. It is interested in a description of geographical space. It is used as a handy atlas, so to speak, of the official financial division of the globe. The geography of finance is a field of economic geography that studies issues of financial globalization and the geographic patterns of finance. It also researches the establishment of new financial centers around the globe, both onshore and offshore. The geography of finance studies the effects of state sovereignty, culture, and the different kinds of barriers that affect the spatial distribution of finance.

Geofinance versus geo-economics

The term *geo-economics* is too broad, particularly in light of the vital and distinct role of financial markets in a country—not just for the economy but for the society as a whole. The impact of financial markets on the economy (that is, financialization) is becoming more significant. (Look at the percentage of GDP contributed by financial services.) In other words, the relevance of global finance to economics is gaining steam and thus deserves an increasing focus. This is underlined by the fact that the value of financial transactions is often multiple times larger than the real economy.[27]

The term *geo-economics* is popular today but almost always without a specific working definition. Some scholars tend to focus on the use of geopolitical or military power for economic ends. Other pundits tend to define geo-economics more broadly as "the entanglement of international economics, geopolitics, and strategy," a kind of catchall definition that obscures more than it clarifies.

These and other earlier interpretations of geo-economics are useful, but they are also incomplete. Strikingly, none of the existing written understandings of geo-economics succeeds in comprehensively capturing the phenomenon that, as an everyday empirical matter, seems most responsible for the term's recent renaissance: the utilization of economic instruments to yield geopolitical benefits. With this latter definition in mind, here is

---

[27] Robert Z. Aliber and Charles P. Kindleberger, *Manias, Panics, and Crashes: A History of Financial Crises* (Hoboken, NJ: Wiley, 2001).

the Blackwill/Harris definition of geo-economics (page 20): "The use of economic instruments to promote and defend national interests, and to produce beneficial geopolitical results; and the effects of other nations' economic actions on a country's geopolitical goals."[28]

China is often correctly described as the world's leading practitioner of geo-economics. It is also the principal reason that the capability of projecting regional and global power has become such a trade (as opposed to a military) exercise. Beijing curtails the import of Japanese cars to indicate its objection to Tokyo's security policies. It lets Filipino fruits rot on China's shipping docks because Manila opposes Beijing's politics in the South China Sea. It provides rewards to Taiwanese companies that march to Beijing's cadence and punishes those that do not. It promises business and trade with South Korea in exchange for Seoul rejecting a US bid to deploy missile-defense systems there. It reduces economic benefits to European governments that welcome and engage with the Dalai Lama.

It initiated the establishment of the BRICS group, purposely excluding the United States. It promotes the Chinese-led Asian Infrastructure Investment Bank as a rival to the Washington-based World Bank. In its economic assistance to Africa, it privileges nations that vote with China at the United Nations. It provides more loans to Latin American countries than the International Monetary Fund and the World Bank combined. Its economic assistance props up the economy of Venezuela, the most anti-American regime in Latin America. Washington has no coherent policies to deal with these Chinese geo-economic actions, many of which are aimed squarely at America's allies and friends in Asia and beyond.

---

[28] Robert D. Blackwill and Jennifer M. Harris, *War by Other Means: Geoeconomics and Statecraft* (Cambridge, MA: Harvard University Press, 2017).

As for geofinance, it is the United States (along with some other Western countries) that is the leader in practicing this instrument of power against other countries. This is mostly due to the fact that financial services are much more important to the US economy than to the Chinese economy. Also, Wall Street is a vital financial center in the world, and Wall Street banks have a genuinely global outreach whereby their activities influence overseas markets. Last but not least, the impact of the US dollar also plays a critical role in privileging the use of geofinancial tools instead of geo-economical tools by the United States.

The US financial services industry represented only 10 percent of total nonfarm business profits in 1947, but it increased to more than 50 percent by 2016.[29] Over the same period, finance industry income as a proportion of GDP rose from 2.5 percent to 7.5 percent, and the financial services industry's portion of all corporate income rose from 10 percent to 20 percent. The average earnings per employee-hour in finance compared to all other industries has closely mirrored the portion of total US income earned by the top 1 percent of income earners since 1930.

The mean salary in New York City's financial services industry increased from $80,000 in 1981 to $365,000 in 2016, while average New York City salaries rose from $40,000 to $75,000.[30] In 1988, there were about 12,500 American banks with less than $300 million in customer deposits and about 900 with more, but by 2016, there were only around 4,100 banks with less than $300 million in customer deposits in the United States and more than 1,800 with more.[31]

---

[29] US Department of Labor, "Current Employment Statistics—CES (National)," accessed March 23, 2017, https://www.bls.gov/ces/.
[30] Payscale, "Average Salary in New York, New York," accessed February 20, 2018, https://www.payscale.com/research/US/Location=New-York-NY/Salary.
[31] US Federal Reserve, "Large Commercial Banks," federal statistical release, accessed February 20, 2018, https://www.federalreserve.gov/releases/lbr/current/.

The New York Stock Exchange, measured by the value of its listed companies' securities, is more than three times bigger than any other stock exchange in the world. As of mid-2017, the combined capitalization of all domestic NYSE-listed companies was $21.3 trillion in US dollars.[32]

NASDAQ is another American stock exchange and the world's third-largest exchange after the NYSE and Japan's Tokyo Stock Exchange. However, NASDAQ's trade value is larger than Japan's TSE. NASDAQ is the most prominent electronic, screen-based equity-securities trading market in the United States with approximately 3,300 companies and corporations;[33] it has more trading volume per hour than any other stock exchange.

Due to the influential role that the US stock market plays in global finance, a New York University study in late 2014 interpreted that in the short run, shocks that affect the willingness to bear risk independently of macroeconomic fundamentals explain most of the variation in the US stock market.

In the long term, the US stock market is significantly affected by shocks that redistribute the benefits of a given level of production between shareholders and workers. Productivity shocks, however, play a small role in historical stock market fluctuations at all horizons in the US stock market.

[32] NYSE, "Shares Outstanding and Market Capitalization of Companies Listed," accessed February 20, 2018,
http://www.nyxdata.com/nysedata/asp/factbook/viewer_edition.asp?mode=tables&key=333&category=5.
[33] ADVFN, "NASDAQ Company Listings," accessed February 20, 2018,
http://www.advfn.com/nasdaq/nasdaq.asp.

The failure of geo-economics as a geopolitical tool for sanctioning

Geo-economics is a trendy term, but geo-economics has proved insufficient when it relates to sanctioning the policies or behavior of a foreign government. A sanction is essentially a penalty imposed on another country or on private citizens of another country. It is an instrument of economic coercion and foreign policy that can be described as a kind of carrot-and-stick method for coping with international trade and politics.

Russia's March 2014 annexation of Crimea, for example, continues to be the gift that keeps on giving, unleashing sanctions and countersanctions that only seem to escalate. In September 2015, Ukraine's prime minister, Arseny Yatseniuk, announced that his country would ban Russian planes from Ukrainian soil. Just days after Ukraine's announcement, Moscow's Ministry of Transport responded by threatening a retaliatory prohibition against Ukraine, according to TASS, Moscow's official government-run news firm.

These announced aircraft bans came twelve months after Washington and Brussels froze the American and European assets of members of Vladimir Putin's inner circle, which comprised business leaders, politicians, and one bank. At the time, Russia responded by sanctioning several American politicians as well as European leaders. The impact of Russian sanctions on Western politicians was seemingly limited.

While the targeted Russians did not all have overseas assets, they faced financial issues. They were not able to settle transactions denominated in the US dollar; banks were less willing to assist them out of fear of angering Western governments, and American businesses were not able to work with them. In the long run, though, these sanctions were likely to have less impact than the range of broader sanctions on Russian energy exports to Europe. Indeed, roughly 55 percent of Russia's gas exports goes to the EU, worth an estimated $26 billion a year.

A sovereign nation has various types of sanctions at its disposal. While some are more widely utilized than others, the general objective of each is to impose a change in behavior. There are several types of sanctions:

- Tariffs—taxes imposed on goods imported from another country;

- Quotas—restrictions on how many products can be either imported from a country or exported to it;

- Asset seizures or freezes—preventing assets owned by a nation or individual from being sold or moved;

- Embargoes—restrictions that prohibit nations from trading. For instance, a government can prevent its citizens or businesses from supplying products or services to a particular country; and

- Nontariff barriers (NTBs)—limits that are typically not levied on imported products. These can include packaging and licensing requirements, product standards, and other requirements.

Sanctions are labeled in different ways. One possible way to describe them is by the number of parties ordering the sanction. A unilateral sanction means that a single country is enacting the sanction, while a bilateral ban means that a group of nations is supporting its utilization. Since bilateral penalties are enforced by groups of countries, they can be considered less hazardous because no one state is on the line for the sanction's result. Unilateral sanctions are more dangerous but can be very useful if enacted by an economically powerful nation.

Another way of labeling sanctions is by the types of trade they restrict. Export sanctions prevent goods flowing into a country, while import sanctions prohibit products leaving the country. The two options are not the same and result in different economic ramifications. Preventing goods and services from entering a nation via an export sanction generally has a lighter impact than prohibiting the import of products or services from that country.

Export sanctions can create an incentive to exchange the blocked products for another product. An example in which an export sanction could work is the restriction on sensitive technological know-how going to a target country. (Think advanced weapons.) This is meant to make it more difficult for the target country to create this sort of product domestically.

Restricting a country's exports through an import sanction increases the possibility that the target country will suffer a substantial economic burden. For example, on July 31, 2013, the US Congress passed H.R. 850, a bill that basically prevented Tehran from selling any oil overseas because of its nuclear program. This followed a year in which Iran's oil exports had already been cut in half by international sanctions. If countries do not import the target nation's products, the target economy can face an industry collapse and significant unemployment, which can put strong sociopolitical pressure on its government.

While the objective of sanctions is to compel a country to change its behavior, there is much variation in how the penalties are leveled and whom they target. Sanctions can target a nation as a whole, as in the case of an embargo on a country's exports (e.g., US sanctions on Cuba). They can focus on specific economic sectors, such as an embargo on the sale of weapons or energy products. From 1979 until 2016, Washington and Brussels prevented the export and import of products and services to and from Iran.

Sanctions can also target individuals, such as business and political leaders, as in the aforementioned European and American sanctions on Putin's allies in the spring of 2014. Enforcing this type of ban is meant to cause financial headaches for a small set of private individuals rather than affecting a country's entire population. This kind of penal strategy is most common where economic and political power is concentrated among a few individuals who have vital international financial interests.

While governments have utilized sanctions to coerce or influence the merchant policies of others for hundreds of years, trade policy is rarely the only strategy available in foreign policy. It can be accompanied by both military and diplomatic actions. A sanction, however, might be a more attractive tool because it imposes an economic cost on a nation's activities rather than a military one. Military conflicts are expensive, resource intensive, and costly in terms of lives and can elicit the ire of other countries due to the human suffering caused by violence.

Also, it is not feasible for a country to react to every political problem with military force; armies are often not large enough. Some issues are just not well suited to armed intervention. Countries generally use sanctions when diplomatic efforts have failed.

Sanctions may be enforced for several reasons (e.g., as a retaliatory measure for another country's trade activities). For example, a steel-producing nation might use a restriction if another country tries to shield its own nascent steel industry by implementing an import quota on foreign steel. Sanctions may also be utilized as a soft-power tool, primarily as a deterrent to human rights abuses, as in the US sanctions against apartheid-era South Africa. The United Nations might condone the utilization of bilateral sanctions against a government if it perpetrates human rights violations or if it breaks resolutions regarding atomic weapons.

Sometimes the threat of a penalty is enough to modify the target country's policies. A threat implies that the state issuing the warning is willing to punish the target country with economic hardship if a change does not take place. The cost of the threat is not as significant as that of military action, but it still bears economic weight. For instance, in 2013, Zimbabwe's former president Robert Mugabe and his inner clique were sanctioned by the United States due to alleged human rights violations.

At times, a government may consider imposing a sanction for domestic reasons rather than international ones. Indeed, sometimes nationalism comes into play, and one country's government can utilize a sanction as a way to reveal resolve or to create a distraction from domestic woes. Because of this issue, multilateral organizations such as the World Trade Organization (WTO) seek to relieve some of the pressure and establish panels to neutrally review disputes among nations. This is especially helpful in staving off more significant problems down the road because sanctions can trigger economically damaging trade wars that can spill over into countries not involved in the original conflict.

The extent of economic hardship caused by a sanction is usually not immediately known. Research has established that the economic impact on the target country becomes more severe as the level of international coordination and cooperation in its inception increases. The economic hardship is also more pronounced if the governments involved in the sanctioning previously had good relations, since commerce ties are more likely to be significant if the states had a rapport.

The direct impact of an import ban on the target country is that the country's exports are not bought overseas. Depending on the target country's economic dependence on the exported products or services, this could have a crippling effect. The sanction might cause the sort of economic and political instability that results in a more authoritarian regime, or it can create a failed state due to a sudden absence of power. The target country's suffering is ultimately on its citizens, who in times of crisis may unite with the regime in charge rather than overthrow it. A crippled nation can be a fertile ground for terrorism and extremism, which is a scenario that the initiating country would most likely choose not to deal with.

Restrictions may follow the law of unintended consequences. For instance, the Arab members of the Organization of Petroleum-Exporting Countries (OPEC) voted for an embargo on oil products meant for the United States in 1973 as a punishment for resupplying Israel with weapons. OPEC was using the embargo as a tool of diplomatic policy, but the consequences spilled over and made the worldwide stock market crash of 1973 to 1974 worse. The inflow of capital from higher oil prices resulted in an arms race in Middle Eastern countries—a destabilizing problem—and did not result in the policy change envisioned by the Arab members of OPEC. Also, many embargoed countries cut back on oil consumption and required a more efficient use of petroleum products, further reducing demand.

Sanctions can cause increased costs to consumers and businesses in the countries that issue them because the target country is not able to buy goods, resulting in a socioeconomic loss through unemployment as well as production loss. Also, the issuing nation reduces domestic consumers' choice of products and services, and this may cause the cost of doing business to increase, as companies suddenly have to look elsewhere for supplies. If a sanction is made unilaterally, the target country can use a third-party government to circumvent the effect of blocked imports or exports.

The rate of success of sanctions varies by how many parties are part of the process. Bilateral sanctions are typically more efficient than unilateral penalties, but the success rate in general is relatively low. In many cases, the sanctions trigger economic harm without modifying the target country's policies. Sanctions are essentially blunt tools of foreign policy because their deployment is rarely surgical enough to impact only the target economy and because they presuppose that economic hardship will lead to the sort of sociopolitical pressure that will benefit the instigating country.

When sanctions have modest objectives and are imposed on countries that are not terribly powerful but have tasted a little flavor of democracy and have close economic connections to the sanctioning coalition, they succeed in modifying countries' behavior in about 50 percent of cases. But when the objective is ambitious, the economic relations are not overwhelmingly strong, the target country is powerful, and the target government autocratic—think Russia, Ukraine, and hacking—the track record for sanctioning is not particularly good. A very small fraction of these sanctions leads to success.

Bashar al-Assad is still in power in Syria, as are Kim Jong-un in North Korea, Vladimir Putin in Russia, Nicolas Maduro in Venezuela, and Omar Al-Bashir in Sudan, notwithstanding more than ten years' worth of economic sanctions by Washington and Brussels. Then there is the tale of Havana, in which fifty years of embargo failed to bring down the regime in this tiny, economically fragile country only a hundred miles off the US coast of Florida. Sanctions have proved powerless to push Turkey out of Cyprus; to move Colombia, Venezuela, or Nigeria to comply with Washington's war on drugs; or to persuade India or Pakistan to abandon their nuclear arsenals.

Economic sanctions and restrictions are the primary tool of geo-economics and can oscillate between stricter sanitary controls and full-blown economic blockades. What matters is the capacity and size of the country being sanctioned, not to mention the power of the sanctioning state or international coalition. These tools are used alongside economic incentives such as export credits, trade regimes, tied aid, and other forms of sovereign-backed trade finance.

Trade sanctions are typically a double-edged sword. The government imposing the sanctions hurts its own businesses that trade with or invest in the target country. US companies have had to stay away from Iran, French navy shipyards have suffered through the abrogation of the sale of the Mistral naval vessels to Russia, and German equipment builders have had to cut their exports to Russia. Sanctions can also provoke countersanctions. In 2014, Russia retaliated against Western measures by banning food imports from the countries that had joined sanctions against Moscow.

The result of these geo-economic campaigns is not a zero sum. The stronger economy backed by other forms of power can inflict more damage on the target country than it sustains in return, but it does not always alter the political behavior of the government being punished. Sometimes sanctions can make its attitude even more problematic. Ironically, the real winner may be the third party that jumps into this window of opportunity. A couple of examples are Beijing as it relates to Western sanctions against Russia, European countries in the initial phases of US-Iran sanctions, Istanbul when Brussels's pressure made Moscow abandon its South Stream gas pipeline project, and Russia in the case of the post-Tiananmen Western weapons ban on China.

Politically and counterintuitively, sanctions are most lethal against allies and friends; in the case of adversaries, they can stiffen their resolve—at least in the first year. The sanctions imposed on Russia in 2014 during the crisis over Ukraine have resulted not just in a surge in Vladimir Putin's popularity but, more important, in the growth of Russian nationalism and patriotism. In moments of bravado, the Kremlin even hopes that an extended period of sanctions can warrant political regime stability in the country for many years to come. (Although the economic downturn in the Russian economy could have had the opposite effect, the economy is again doing well.)

And, in the case of Russia, Western sanctions increased Russia's internal reliance on domestic products and services, which in turn spurred research and development in the domestic economic sectors, making the country less vulnerable to future external shocks.

The reemergence of state capitalism in the aftermath of the financial crisis is turbocharging the rivalry among states for power and influence. Although Washington still dominates financial markets, increasingly, countries that do not share the US belief in limited state intervention play a lead role in the origin, destination, and intermediation of capital via markets and real economic sectors. In their models, the government tries to play a leveling role in markets to ensure that booms and busts are limited in time and that unrestrained capitalism is moderated by the interests of the state and other interested parties. In some ways, this is not new—for many years, governments have used their ownership of financial institutions and companies to strengthen their strategic goals—but today, they are extending their influence in powerful new ways.

In a global world of free movement of capital but also dependence on capital flows, where creating jobs and expanding trade is as critical as free access to mature consumer markets, it is probable that over the course of this twenty-first century, a more pragmatic modernization of diplomacy will revolve around a substantially more significant focus on geofinancial statecraft—rather than on geo-economic sanctions—to address political conflicts and promote national interests.

A shift from geopolitics and geo-economics to geofinance

Until recently, many pundits claimed that geo-economics would gradually replace geopolitics in importance and that the transition would be marked by the start of the process called globalization.

The latter is about twenty years old now but was still in its infancy when government and state institutions discovered that they no longer were self-evident vital actors and watchmen of world events.

It was said that the process would end the Cold War and mark a strategic shift from political ideologies to economic realities.

However, what those so-called scholars forgot to take into account was the financialization of economies, whereby a country's financial sector increases in size and importance relative to its overall economy.

Financialization has occurred as advanced countries have shifted away from industrial capitalism. The term *financialization* is not valid for emerging and underdeveloped countries whose economic bases are still conditioned by industrial and agricultural production cycles.

Figure 1: Percentage Contributed to GDP

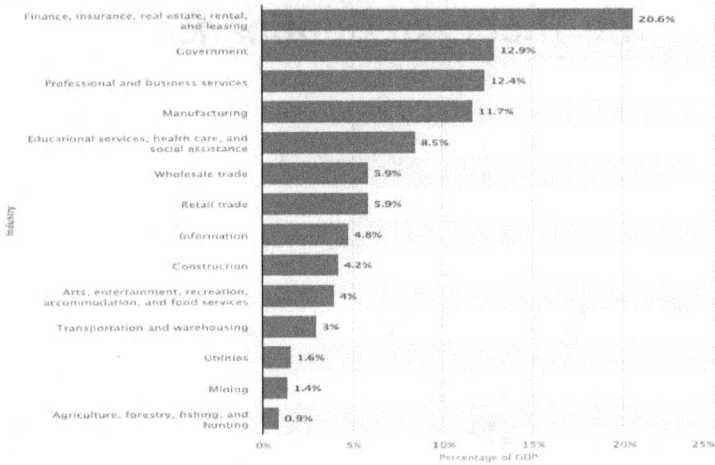

Source: Statista[34]

For decades, fellow economists have praised the value of public and private investments and the production of services at the expense of the production of goods, but they have underestimated the importance of financial flows that affect the economy of not only individual countries but also regions (groups of countries).

They have done so because they have failed to see what makes an advanced developed nation, a region, or a city wealthy in the long run.

---

[34] Statista, "Percentage Added to the Gross Domestic Product (GDP) of the United States of America in 2016, by Industry (as a Percentage of GDP)," accessed February 20, 2018, https://www.statista.com/statistics/248004/percentage-added-to-the-us-gdp-by-industry/.

The Theory of Geofinance

In this section, we define a place and scope for the study of geofinance. As indicated previously, there is currently no official definition for *geofinance* and thus no theory built around that definition. Some of you might wonder why there is a need to construct an approach. Well, a method guides research and organizes its ideas. Like bricks lying around randomly in a brickyard, facts of different sizes and shapes have no meaning unless they are drawn together into a theoretical or conceptual framework.

In other words, the benefit of building a theory of geofinance is that a method is a model or architecture for understanding and observation, and that then shapes both what we see and how we see it. Theory allows the scholar to make links between the abstract and reality, the theoretical and the empirical, thought statements and observational statements, and so on. A theory is a generalized statement that asserts a connection between two or more types of phenomena.[35] Theory is a system of interconnected thoughts or ideas that compacts and organizes knowledge about the world. Theory assists with explaining and predicting the relationship between variables.

Elements of geofinance

The historical method has been stigmatized since WWII; part of the reason is that people have been showing less interest in history since then, so the phenomenon has become a self-fulfilling prophecy, a downward spiral. The disciplines of history and geography have been systematically neglected in the United

---

[35] Christopher E. Sunday, "The Role of Theory in Research," University of the Western Cape, 2015, accessed February 20, 2018, https://www.uwc.ac.za/Students/Postgraduate/Documents/The%20role%20of%20theory%20in%20research.pdf.

States and, indeed, in the West more generally, right up to the university level.

If we knew more about the past, this would reinforce our ability to learn from history and thus to make more robust predictions about future events. Instead, it is often mistakenly assumed that we know as much as there is to know about history. The field of finance suffers significantly as a consequence as we fail to learn from, for example, past financial crises.

This abandonment of history has resulted in another dangerous but frequent hypothesis: namely, that a scholar or an analyst can know what is going to happen by merely studying the appropriate parallel among current events—that to understand the past well is not meaningful because the world has changed. A further dangerous premise is that knowledge of geography has become less important because of human conquest of the environment via advances in technology, such as Google Earth and GPS.

We may think we know where to find something, but that does not mean we know what to look for or even when to look for it. It just means that if we are given the proper question, then we can usually find the right answer and get to it much more swiftly than before. Often, the tricky thing is to know the right questions to ask and then to detect possibilities and similarities when essential topics come to the surface.

Yet another dangerous postulation is that if the facts are apparent, then decision makers will know how to deal with them. Thus, the whole intelligence function is conceived of as a question of subscribing to the right sources—such as magazines, journals, or Internet services—and merely knowing where to look. This is also what is most comfortable to do technically, which helps explain why so many companies come to think this way. Furthermore, it is what is most natural to sell. But what we find will only make sense if we know what context to place our intelligence in and how to analyze it.

When interests meet head on, there is a problem of convincing. When one interest triumphs over another, we have a power relationship. Studies of power without the moral aspect are what is understood by realpolitik, which lies at the nucleus of geopolitics. Geopolitics, then, is the blended study of geography, history, and realpolitik.

The methodological strength of such an analysis is that its components are built from the things that are most certainly found within human behavior and the human environment. That kind of study is probably what will eventually give us the best forecasts. But our current social science model is defined very much in contrast to this method.

For political scientists and economists alike, this often has a disastrous impact, as when they are asked for their views on current events. Either they alter a few economic elements, or they choose the safe path of commonsense concepts. Most economists usually just reiterate what they have read (i.e., what people they rely on have said). Critical, independent thinking is often missing. All the knowledge may be there, but no one seems able to connect the dots because no one has mastered how to do it; pundits, by definition, have restricted frames of reference and are casualties of their own narrow reading. We are all "specialists," which often becomes a pretext for failing to take responsibility for the larger picture.

A definition of geofinance

Geofinance is at play when actors such as political leaders, countries, organizations, and corporations assess how their actions may affect other political leaders, nations, organizations, and companies. Geofinance isn't a new phenomenon in finance by any means. Trying to anticipate the reaction of others in different parts of the world (a.k.a. *behavioral finance*) has been part of global finance for thousands of years, but it's expanded since 1945 with the growing preeminence of finance above economics.

So what exactly is geofinance? It's kind of complex in its straightforwardness, actually. A fitting way to explain it is by detailing what's needed for geofinance. Geofinance requires at least two actors to be separated geographically, usually in different markets, countries, or continents. All participants must be aware of one another. Geofinance depends on this kind of geographical location and knowledge.

Knowledge of one another is essential because this assumes that all actors will act strategically. For instance, if two people are interested in making a finance deal for an acquisition, we can assume that each is interested in how the other approaches the valuation of the underlying asset because the price affects everyone. Someone is accountable. If no one knew of the other's intention, the deal would never take place.

But here's the thing: these actors have to be able to interact through markets and networks. If the actors keep to themselves and don't disturb the world around them, then geofinance is not present. So how can actors interact? There are too many ways to name, but some examples of interaction that you may be familiar with are commerce, investment, lending, making deposits, imposing financial sanctions, and so on.

The first two interactions are more comfortable to comprehend. If your company buys goods that my company makes, then my company has a reason to be interested in the financial situation of your business to see whether you can financially afford to buy my goods. On top of that, my company may pass a risk policy to ensure that our companies can make the trade through a system of compliance. Consider this question about fraud: What would happen if your company committed a fraudulent activity? It could quickly become a serious financial issue. This is the reason that geofinance is simple in its complexity; there is no easy answer to this question.

Geofinance is primarily an analysis that takes into account the mutual interaction between geopolitical factors and financial forces—how geography controls all sorts of resources defines not only foreign policy and the political process but, increasingly, financial markets and institutions. The inverse is also true; financial interests can also define the geopolitics[36] of a country.

Because geofinance encompasses all factors related to the geography and resources of nation-states—from river grids, impassable mountains, minerals, gas, and oil to the absence of borders, to labor forces, networks, populations, and their religions and political systems—and those factors are undergoing dramatic changes, a risk study can no longer focus merely on either financial phenomena or geopolitical ones, as it could between 1945 and 1991. If it does so, it will continue to produce unacceptably inaccurate outlooks. The postmodern global finance world is becoming increasingly geopolitically influenced, and vice versa. Thus, we live in the era of geofinance.

The above definition springs from my more than twenty-five years of exposure to academic theory, empirical research and practice as a risk manager in commercial banking, and passion for geopolitics. It is the result of a real-life career as a professional decision maker. Also, risk studies can no longer be conducted in a silo, away from external influences. This type of approach is too cloistered and results in an isolated "bubble" mentality and thus is no longer practically relevant for nations or organizations.

How will a geopolitical risk affect the world of finance, trade, and currencies? Which types of financial markets will benefit or

---

[36] Note that geostrategy, itself a subfield of geopolitics, is a foreign policy guided principally by geographical factors and therefore is mostly nationalist, while geopolitics is a method of foreign-policy analysis.

suffer? Organizations cannot allow themselves to worry about every crisis somewhere on the globe. That said, organizations need to adopt the new realities of a world in which political and geopolitical factors affect financial market activities as well as financial policy decisions.

Geofinance traditionally studies the links between financial power and geographic space, and it examines strategic prescriptions based on the relative importance of the balance of power between financial markets and nations as well as, more generally speaking, the balance of power among government-sponsored and private organizations across world history. The geofinancial tradition has consistent concerns with geofinancial correlations of power in world politics, the identification of global core areas, and the relationships among financial markets and governments.

Academically, the study of geofinance analyzes geography, history, and social science concerning spatial finance and patterns at various scales, with a particular viewpoint on how the combination of these factors affects the financial risk profile of a business or financial institution. Geofinance also includes the study of the ensemble of relationships among the interests of international financial actors—interests focused on an area, space, and geographical element. These relationships create a geofinancial system. Geofinance is multidisciplinary in scope and incorporates all facets of the social sciences with a particular focus on financial geography, international relations, the territorial aspects of financial science, and international finance and business law.

Geofinance delineates an intellectual terrain concerned with and influenced by the interaction of geography, knowledge, power, and financial institutions and markets. Geofinance is a discourse concerned with the relationship between power knowledge and global finance.

Building a theory of geofinance

Once a definition of geofinance has been agreed on, one needs to build a theory of geofinance around it. It is generally accepted that the strength of a theory is related to the diversity of phenomena it can explain as well as its simplicity. The paleontologist Stephen Jay Gould wrote that "facts and theories are different things, not rungs in a hierarchy of increasing certainty. Facts are the world's data. Theories are structures of ideas that explain and interpret facts."[37] And typically, for any model to be embraced within most academic circles, it must be repeatable and observable. This requirement is critical to prevent fraud and perpetuate science itself.

A rendition of descriptions of knowledge can be called a theory if it fulfills the following criteria:

- It makes falsifiable forecasts with consistent precision across a broad area of scientific inquiry;

- It is well supported by many independent strands of evidence rather than just a single foundation; and

- It is compatible with preexisting experimental results and is at least as accurate in its predictions as are any preexisting theories.

So let's develop this theory of geofinance.

As a preliminary remark, however, theories are essentially never-ending works in progress. At any point in time, portions of a theory can be subjected to internal or external tests of validation, resulting in potentially new research questions being asked and thus a search for new relationships. This means that researchers

---

[37] Stephen Jay Gould, "Theory, Fact, and the Origin of Life," *Nature: Structural & Molecular Biology* 12 (2005): 101, accessed February 20, 2018, https://www.nature.com/articles/nsmb0205-101.

can enter at any stage of the theory-building process and challenge existing building blocks.

In his or her analysis, a researcher is influenced by academic training, skills, and professional and personal background. Consequently, working at the early stages of theory building exposes a scholar to future critiques, as he or she may not have forecast the new developments and future correlations. The approach I have sought to follow is multidisciplinary and dynamic, inspired by the evolutionary theories around mutation and selection.

But in practice, how are scientific theories developed? Scholars have observed over the years that there is no common series of events that reveals itself in the scientific process. However, several leading philosophy-of-science scholars have identified a number of common themes within the scientific process.[38]

The most common of these was stated by Bergmann[39] and reiterated over the years by others (Popper,[40] Bohm,[41] Kaplan,[42] Stinchcombe,[43] Blalock,[44] and Greer[45]): "The three pillars on which science is built are observation, induction, and deduction." This school of thought was later summarized into a series of elements and first mapped by Wallace.[46]

[38] Robert Beaudoin Handfield and Steve A. Melnyk, "The Scientific Theory-Building Process: A Primer Using the Case of TQM," *Journal of Operations Management*," accessed February 20, 2018, https://www.researchgate.net/publication/222225902_The_Scientific_Theory-Building_Process_A_Primer_Using_the_Case_of_TQM. July 1998.
[39] Gustav Bergmann, *Philosophy of Science* (Madison: University of Wisconsin Press, 1957).
[40] Karl Popper, *The Logic of Scientific Discovery* (New York: Science Editions, 1961).
[41] David Bohm, *Causality and Chance in Modern Physics* (London: Routledge & Kegan Paul, 1957).
[42] Abraham Kaplan, *The Conduct of Inquiry: Methodology for Behavioral Science* (San Francisco: Chandler, 1964).
[43] Arthur L. Stinchcombe, *Constructing Social Theories* (New York: Harcourt, Brace & World, 1968).
[44] Hubert M. Blalock Jr., *Theory Construction* (Englewood Cliffs, NJ: Prentice Hall, 1969).
[45] Scott A. Greer, *The Logic of Social Inquiry* (Chicago: Aldine Atherton, 1969).
[46] Walter L. Wallace, *The Logic of Science in Sociology* (Chicago: Aldine Atherton, 1971).

The key criteria are being observable, empirical, and repeatable, and thus, the theory of geofinance should stay clear of any mention of moral values. Instead, the theory of geofinance should concern itself with what observable conditions cause wars or a sovereign default, financial negotiations, what causes financial sanctions to be successful, and so on. I will bring to the foreground two aspects of geofinance that can be observed and that are empirical and repeatable. First, I will look at geofinance as a relationship between nature and finance. Second, I will consider geofinance as a tool of financial power.

From the classical theories of finance to geofinance

I have offered a number of definitions so far. In this section, I will show how the study of geofinance builds on a dynamic approach to the social sciences that can be tracked back to Darwin's theory of mutation and adaptation.

Classical finance is a static method in the social sciences inspired by the study of physics using the theories of equilibrium and algebra. It was an attempt to build a purely scientific research of the individual and his or her environment, avoiding moral issues and values as explanatory reasons for any finding. Instead, the approach privileged by geofinance is different from that of classical finance.

It is based on multidisciplinarity, global strategic thinking, and the tradition of critical theory. As I have noted, in this day and age, one can no longer study a problem in a silo or ivory tower. The researcher needs to go down onto the field and look from different perspectives when trying to find answers. Unlike classical thinking, this field of study is based not on physics but on biology.

One of the foundations of classical finance theory has been the efficient-market hypothesis. The efficient market can be described as "a market where there are large numbers of rational profit-maximizers actively competing, with each trying to predict future market values of individual securities, and where important current information is almost freely available to all participants."[47]

Under this hypothesis, there is no speculation in the markets as long as everyone is rational. The only difference among investors is the information at their disposal. There will be no trade if there is no data—that is, in a rational trade. In other words, agents maximize discounted sums of expected utilities based on their beliefs or forecasts.

All agree on all future prices and events: perfect foresight and market rationality, right? And to broaden the scope of the criticism even more, current belief is that theories based on irrational exuberance, loss aversion, excess volatility, and market risk will soon swap the building blocks of classical finance along with arbitrage pricing and mean-variance analysis.[48]

However, the theory of classical finance is based on a misconception—namely that the laws of social life can be analyzed from the safety of a bubble by exposing narrowly defined correlations in much the same fashion as advances are made in physics.[49] But the issue is more complicated than that. As both finance and political science have been required to operate value neutrally—for instance, by shutting out the aspect of power so paramount in any research on geopolitics—each of these

[47] John H. Cochrane, "Eugene F. Fama, Efficient Markets, and the Nobel Prize," *Chicago Booth Review*, May 20, 2014, accessed February 20, 2018, http://review.chicagobooth.edu/magazine/winter-2013/eugene-fama-efficient-markets-and-the-nobel-prize. May 20, 2014.

[48] Klaus Reiner Schenk-Hoppé, "Survival of the Fittest on Wall Street," *Evolutionary Finance*, last modified February 2, 2004, http://www.evolutionaryfinance.ch/papers/surv_of_the_fittest.pdf.

[49] Thorsten Hens, Klaus Reiner Schenk-Hoppé, and Martin Stalder, "An Application of Evolutionary Finance to Firms Listed in the Swiss Market Index," *Zeitschrift für Volkswirtschaft und Statistik* 138(4) (2002), 465–8, http://citeseerx.ist.psu.edu/viewdoc/download?doi=10.1.1.312.1290&rep=rep1&type=pdf.

research fields has become less significant. The field of finance has lost the notion of power and abandoned its feeling for Adam Smith's notion of the competitive advantage of nations.

But it has not always been that way. Between 1850 and 1900, for example, it looked as though finance was destined to be grounded in biology and evolutionary theory rather than physics. It was then called evolutionary finance. Indeed, in the latter part of the nineteenth century, economists and other social scientists began looking for similarities among people and organizations in society and organisms in an environment.[50] These scholars were known as Darwinists; Herbert Spencer, William Graham Sumner, and Simon Nelson Patten were among them. This led other economists to become excited by the theoretical possibilities of swapping the mechanical equilibrium analogy, borrowed from physics, which had underpinned virtually all contemporary economics, for an evolutionary analogy borrowed from biology that focused on adaptation, survival, and mutation.

During the period of the World Wars (1914–1945), this approach was abandoned, only to be picked up again later by, among others, Milton Friedman. In 1953 Friedman stated that corporations would be compelled to adapt to profit-maximizing routines by evolutionary pressure. But Friedman's contribution notwithstanding, the evolutionary approach in finance has remained elusive.

And then there is the historical method that was adopted by Karl Marx, who attempted to plot history. Alas, though Marx elaborated a theory of history, it was not rooted in biological analogy either. For him, history was a merely the continuation of developmental phases punctuated by sudden, dramatic changes.

---

[50] Goncalo L. Fonseca, "Evolutionary Economics," The History of Economic Thought, March 1, 2014, accessed February 20, 2018, http://www.hetwebsite.net/het/schools/evol.htm.

These were not exogenous, of course, but fabricated by the internal contradictions of the previous stage.

But still, if evolutionary finance was a reliable method, how could this field be put on the sidelines? If we cannot learn from the past, then history should not play such an important role in the future study of politics or finance. When finance developed as an independent field of study, it was defined as the study of market equilibrium—not as seen from a societal perspective but merely from the narrow point of view of the markets.

The hypothesis was erroneous when taken to the extreme: namely, that what is best for the markets is deemed best for society, too. What we call theory in the study of finance today is, most of the time, a long list of empirical research that only rarely applies directly to the underlying issue at hand and from which scholars tend to draw unduly broad conclusions.

Geofinance and Darwinian theory

Here we will evaluate some of the critical issues and notions relevant to the study of geofinance as a theory: the power dimension, its systems of connections (networks), its inter- and transdisciplinary nature, its relationship with evolutionary theory, and the differences from both relativism (the doctrine that truth and morality exist only in relation to a society and are not absolute) and neoclassical empiricism (the study of human knowledge, a.k.a. epistemology). The primary purpose of this section is to show how geofinance can be founded in an evolutionary method by offering research on the development of the study of finance.

There cannot be any politics without political realism, and financial issues lie at the core of politics—especially nowadays, given the financialization of the global economy. The organization or nation that possesses financial wealth has resources, and money is power where power is determined by the capability to exert control over the actions of others, thus increasing one's own opportunities for creation of further and future wealth. We find this concept in Michael Klare's analysis of geopolitics as the study of "the contention between great powers and aspiring great powers for control over territory, resources, and important geographical positions, such as ports and harbors, canals, river systems (fresh water supply), oases, and other sources of wealth and influence."[51]

The study of geopolitics accounts for some of the more valuable contributions to political realism. Geofinance shares the same belief but differs in its perspective, as it argues that development is driven not so much by the nation-state as by global corporations seeking control over strategic global commodities and financial resources. It is a perpetuation of the dogma of national competitive advantage[52] but by other means. It is the gradual substitution of competitive knowledge and finance to the detriment of arms and diplomacy.

While studies of geopolitics represent the single most substantial body of literature under the intelligence umbrella, close to nothing has been published under the heading of geofinance. Current contributions are most numerous in Europe, mainly in France and, recently, Italy. (See the section on the saga of geofinance as a concept.)

The reason for European dominance in this field is partly historical; geopolitics never really disappeared from European colleges even when it became a taboo subject after 1945. But it is probably also due to the admiration for and interest in the art of synthesis, which is so apparent in European intellectual and

[51] Michael Klare, "The New Geopolitics," *Monthly Review* 55(3) (2003), accessed January 29, 2018, https://monthlyreview.org/2003/07/01/the-new-geopolitics/.
[52] Michael E. Porter, "The Competitive Advantage of Nations," *Harvard Business Review*, March-April 1990, accessed January 29, 2018, https://hbr.org/1990/03/the-competitive-advantage-of-nations.

academic life. The topic of *géopolitique* has always been appreciated in political and military circles.

The revival of geopolitics in the form of first geo-economics and now geofinance is an excellent fit for growing French skepticism about what has increasingly been seen as American political and economic financial aggression in the 1980s and 1990s. Concomitantly, it is too simple to label geofinance as merely a European phenomenon and wrong to think of it as mere fashion. It is both universal and permanent, following the tradition of real political thinking. Its home is not just in Europe but in the world; its oldest written traces are actually Chinese[53] and Indian.[54]

In the French literature and tradition, there has been a tendency to understand geofinance as financial warfare. This is a potentially dangerous metaphor. *Warfare* means armed conflict that involves killing. It is true that keen financial competition can lead to use of less acceptable techniques, such as bribery or even forms of extortion, but very rarely do private-sector organizations or the agencies of state that support them use actual violence. The utilization of violence for business purposes is still almost exclusively restricted to organized crime and pariah states.

The Mafia is, by definition, an organization that has established a niche relating to products and services that the government has outlawed. In other words, the Mafia must embrace violence to survive and thrive. Government authorities have not been entirely innocent of this. Some nation-states have been known to resort to force to acquire new markets. We have witnessed such violent behavior more than once since WWII, primarily from the United States but also from the former Soviet Union and recently from

[53] Hailong Ju, *China's Maritime Power and Strategy: History, National Security and Geopolitics* (Singapore: World Scientific, 2015).
[54] Leonid Savin, "India and Its Strategic Culture," Katehon, accessed February 20, 2018, http://katehon.com/article/india-and-its-strategic-culture.

Russia and also from France, China, the United Kingdom, Serbia, Iran, and Iraq, just to mention the most notorious examples.

These states have utilized their armed forces to safeguard their financial interests overseas. The danger in using the term *war* concerning finance is that it implies something about what tools are acceptable in a financial rivalry. It is one thing to anticipate and plan for the likelihood of foul play and another thing to incite its utilization by failing to distinguish clearly between acceptable and unacceptable behavior from inception.

Violence and threats of violence in a world of global finance tend to result in companies getting trapped in a spiral of strikes and counterstrikes that is rarely good for business in the long run. These practices have a propensity to catch up with their offenders. For instance, oil corporations with a presence in Nigeria anticipate and prepare for violent attacks, but they do not use similar methods to defend themselves. For one thing, violence and dirty tricks often have unforeseen repercussions.

Corporate practices in emerging countries can be rough. Because most developed countries have well-established economies, their financial markets are relatively mature and saturated, making them more difficult for outsiders or newcomers to penetrate and conquer. For this reason, new financial markets in emerging countries are often more enticing, even though they can be very risky. Newly founded nations, as well as states that have gone through a period of violent turbulence, constitute an extraordinary occasion. These markets are up for grabs, so to speak.

This is still the condition of most markets adjoining the former Soviet Union. In Europe, the conflict in Bosnia-Herzegovina has evolved from a political fight into an economic struggle or rivalry. Companies from significant nations such as the United States, the United Kingdom, Germany, France, Austria, Italy, and Japan are fighting for market share in a whole range of consumer-product-related markets. The chief direct investors in Bosnia-Herzegovina over the past decade have been Croatia, Lithuania, Austria, Slovenia, Germany, the Netherlands, Kuwait (a fellow Muslim country), Serbia, and Montenegro.

Access to these markets typically goes through "foreign aid" programs, which, as Russia under Putin has guessed, are often concealed forms of government support for exports, an easy way of opening up a new market. For the United States, it has been the US Agency for International Development (USAID), investing primarily in agriculture, timber, and tourism. It is a four-step plan: first, you send in the nurses and the doctors, then the businesspeople; then you involve the locals to start an insurrection, and then you send in the combat troops.

It looked as though that was how things were going to go in Ukraine and especially in Georgia. Both popular revolutions, the Orange and the Rose, started very much like so-called philanthropic projects, supported by the American businessman George Soros. By showing force in Georgia, Moscow wanted to send a clear warning that it would not accept foreign interference within its sphere of interest. Thus, mastering markets that border Russia is a delicate balance between political and financial considerations.

Elsewhere, governments are cooperative and feel safe enough to deal with the multinationals directly. This is not the case for a number of states adjoining Russia. Here, multinationals risk encountering various mafia groups, some of which may or may not represent their governments. Belarus, Uzbekistan, Turkmenistan, and Kyrgyzstan are probably the most explicit examples. But the same holds true to some extent for Kazakhstan and Ukraine.

Ever since the Cold War ended in 1991 with the collapse of the Soviet Union, geofinance as a national strategy has gradually become more relevant than geopolitics. The former is a strategy based on financial activities rather than on military and diplomatic interventions. Power has steadily shifted from nation-states to private-sector banks and corporations to the point where we can now expect that the twenty-first century will be a century of geofinance.[55] In the next part, we will ask how we are to understand this new phenomenon, this shift in paradigms. How do we account for it from a scientific methodological perspective? We will suggest an answer based on an organic view of the social sciences and thus of social behavior.

The link to evolutionary theory

The affiliation with Darwin's evolutionary theory is more productive. The idea is as follows: all living organisms are studied with the help of the evolutionary theory and biology around concepts such as mutation and selection.[56] Why should human life be so much different? We expect it to be more complicated, given that humans can reflect on their own actions, but not fundamentally different. Evolutionary theory and the notion of change (i.e., cycles, development, and progress) provide the discipline of finance with stronger predictive power than it has had through equilibrium theories.

This should lead us to be wary about the use of algebra for solving financial economic problems. Even history and logic are far better foundations for the social sciences than most of mathematics, which should be seen mainly as just a more efficient language. For example, if savants in finance had acknowledged the timeline of what took place among the chairmen of the Western world's central banks at the beginning of the twentieth century rather than wasting their time developing mathematical formulae such

[55] Sam Woods, "Geofinance," 2017.
[56] Klaus Reiner Schenk-Hoppé, "Evolutionary Finance: A Tutorial," University of Leeds, July 13, 2008, accessed February 20, 2018, http://www.optirisk-systems.com/papers/KlausReinerSchenkHoppe.pdf.

as value at risk and the Black-Scholes formula for option pricing, then perhaps the demise of the banking system might have been prevented. In such a case, maybe someone would have looked at similarities in previous financial crises and asked the right questions. But we had already abandoned the historical method, and with it, we left the critique of economic history. It might seem bizarre to take a step back and prescribe more history, but the issue is whether there is more to be achieved by keeping it behind the curtains.

Consider the discipline of marketing as an illustration. Notwithstanding scientific papers (amounting to hundreds of thousands), there are very few self-critical historical articles in this field, and few observers even seem to find that strange. Likewise, I argue, too, for a return to syllogisms (i.e., deductive reasoning), notwithstanding the fact that the tradition of standard logic is *démodé*, to say the least. But straight thinking demands no less.

From one perspective, we are all part of the same zealous system: nation-states, organizations, and individuals. These entities are only different elements of the same biological machine whereby nature determines who is fit to survive and multiply. Apparently, in a modern welfare state, the consequences are never as dramatic as that due to the fact that we can select to live a different life and rescue those who stagger, even though this just means that we are moving responsibilities between citizens.

The paramount mechanism is similar—always present, always reminding us of what is necessary to survive and thrive. From the individual's perspective, this struggle takes the form of rivalry, expressed in modern times primarily in economic competition. In other words, whether we work in the private or the public sector, we learn to compete today mainly through some sort of financial performance rather than by fighting.

Ultimately, it is the sum of the activities of all individuals in a society that determines the competitiveness of a nation. In just the same way, and as much as we may dislike it, it follows that in every country, there are those who contribute to the competitiveness of the state and those who live off it. And there are nations that systematically perform better than others. This we know from measures such as GDP, unemployment rates, fiscal deficits, borrowing levels, credit ratings, and the like. In the short run, measured in years and sometimes decades, we see this from the rise and fall of firms. In the long term, measured in generations and centuries, we know it from the rise and fall of great nations and empires.

The world of finance is shaped by geography

One of our above definitions of geofinance stated that it is merely the influence of human and spatial geography on financial activities. Plato, Aristotle, and other ancients clearly understood that finance, just like politics, is shaped and constrained by nature or space.

To prove this postulate, one can compare the biosphere with the "financiosphere." Indeed, both spheres are dazzling in their complexity, with striking similarities. Both are dynamic systems in which the selfish actions of countless individuals—whether they be cells or investors—lead to unpredictable consequences at the system level. In turn, these collective efforts and outcomes influence individual actions in endless cycles of adaptation and evolution.

This adaptive period is the essence of a complex system. It's also what makes complex systems challenging to understand, hard to predict, and tricky to manage. Not surprisingly, in both the biosphere and financial markets, resulting system-level emergent phenomena include unexpected crises and collapses—from population crashes to stock devaluations, from the desertification of lush landscapes to market failures, from the disappearance of species to the demise of industries.

But biological systems also exhibit remarkable resilience. By studying how evolution has made them more robust, might we develop new and wiser approaches to financial regulation? I believe so[57].

Finance as a tool of power

And then there is another definition, stating that geofinance focuses on financial power in relation to geographic space. In other words, geofinance is "the use of financial power to promote and defend national interests, and to produce beneficial results; and the effects of other nations' financial actions on a country's goals."[58] We will show a series of observable and empirical examples of how finance exerts power on human and physical geography—first, as a tool of influence, and second, as a tool for sanctioning.

57 Simon Levin, "What Can Mother Nature Teach Us about Managing Financial Systems?" Christian Science Monitor, August 22, 2016, https://www.csmonitor.com/Science/Complexity/2016/0822/What-can-Mother-Nature-teach-us-about-managing-financial-systems.

58 Robert D. Blackwill, "America Must Play the Geoeconomics Game," The National Interest, June 26, 2016, accessed January 29, 2018, http://nationalinterest.org/feature/america-must-play-the-geoeconomics-game-16658.

Finance as a vector for influence

As alluded to earlier, during the three decades following WWII, the financial services sector performed a secondary role in advanced countries. During these postwar years in the economies of Western Europe and the United States, people manufactured goods and provided services, transport moved them, wholesale and retail trade distributed them, and the financial sector supplied short- and medium-term funding when required.

That type of an economy—manufacture and then distribute, with finance facilitating production—ended with the Reagan-Thatcher financial deregulation, which was then broadened under Clinton and Blair. This policy change, not globalization, liberated financial capital to break free of the production-distribution cycle that had severely restricted its capacity for profit taking. Instantaneously, financial capital had a new and powerful engine to accumulate profit: speculation.

Below is a list of examples of how finance exerts power and influence.

- On most issues, governments worry mainly about the views of voters and key constituents. On financial matters, however, policy makers are often far more concerned with the judgment of financial markets, which is delivered instantly and quantitatively. When prime ministers and presidents explain their plans to tax and spend and create jobs, they are often talking straight to the bond investors who lend them the money for these plans.

- While most countries commit to cooperating on global economic policy, not all motives are pure, and suspicions often run rampant. Currency policy and trade are often the most contentious conversations among economic officials, since exchange rates and commercial regulations can have immediate consequences on the profits of firms, the outlook for jobs, and the mood of voters.

- Global media organizations supply much of the context and interpretation of international financial policy, whether through instant analysis of central-bank statements or more large-scale reporting on economic and financial developments. The political parley is often extreme and emotional, while even the most sophisticated investors must take into account the fear, greed, and "animal spirits"[59] that often drive markets.

- After WWII, global political leaders tried to bring order to the global economy using the Bretton Woods framework of pegged exchange rates, and after that, they congregated in groupings like the G7 to coordinate economic and financial policies. In 2008, with the global economy subsiding, US officials struggled to include a more representative group of countries in the discussions, including China, India, and Brazil.

- More often than not, politics drive conversations about financial policies out of the traditional fringes of economics and deep into the realm of philosophy. Who is wealthy and who is poor becomes a judgment of who "merits" being rich and who "deserves" to be penniless. In a financial crisis, some concentrate on reinstating stability while others focus first on disciplining those who were responsible. For example, the response to the 2008 global financial crisis, with a specific focus on the forces that led to the Dodd-Frank Act, is perhaps

---

[59] "Animal spirits" is a notion that the economist John Maynard Keynes refers to in his book *The General Theory of Employment, Interest and Money* to describe the emotions and instincts that apparently affect and drive human behavior.

the most significant redesign of US financial policy making since the Great Depression.

- The global reach of the US dollar means that the United States' ability to freeze assets or hinder transactions has become an enormously powerful tool, gravely undermining the activities of significant criminal and drug organizations. Over time and with allied support, Washington has put enough pressure on Tehran and the Iranian economy to negotiate a disruption to its atomic enrichment program, while sanctions against Moscow have so far delivered more mixed results.

- No single country occupies the attention of international financial and economic policy makers more than China. Although China is barely smaller than the United States, its dynamism, reach, and unpredictability ensure that it enters into virtually every conversation about the future of the global economy—for instance, the financial discussion between Washington and Beijing, which ranges across such topics as global growth, trade barriers, currency manipulation, patent protection, investment reviews, cybersecurity, banking rules, climate targets, and more.

- The crisis that nearly destroyed the postwar European-integration project provides another dramatic demonstration of economic policy cooperation as a morality play. While European leaders kept insisting that markets should trust their ability to resolve the crisis, it was also clear that they didn't really believe one another. The financial policy was subsumed in the rancorous domestic politics of very different countries bound together by the same currency.

- Financial diplomacy is important beyond standard issues of global growth and trade. A partial list of the issues might include negotiations of limits on carbon emissions, formulating economic assistance packages for Egypt and Pakistan, reviewing national security concerns around Chinese investments, protecting transatlantic data-sharing regimes, reforming the International Monetary Fund, and boosting electricity investment in Africa.

The use of finance as a tool to sanction

Economic sanctions have a long history, dating back to the Greek city-states more than two thousand years ago. Their utilization has become more prevalent since WWII, often being employed by the United Nations, regional entities, and individual countries, including the United States. Although these entities and nations continue to use a range of sanctions, financial penalties have become essential. This stems in part from the rapid increase in international financial transactions. Also, the terrorist attacks of September 11, 2001, provided great impetus to the United States to improve significantly the tools and techniques for tracing and identifying financial transactions by terrorists and others.

Financial sanctions focus on the flow of funds and other forms of value to and from a target country, corporation, individual, or other entity. These penalties can have an extensive impact because they not only freeze financial assets and prohibit or limit financial transactions but also impede trade by making it difficult to pay for the export or import of products and services. Financial sanctions are often used in tandem with business and other penalties to maximize their impact.

In the United States, financial sanctions are imposed by statutes and executive orders and are generally implemented through regulations. The Office of Foreign Assets Control (OFAC) of the Department of the Treasury, in consultation with the State Department and sometimes other federal agencies, generally has primary responsibility for implementing these financial sanctions.

Financial sanctions can prescribe rules for a wide range of activities by financial institutions and other persons and entities around the world. Enforcement can be by a variety of measures over which the United States has jurisdiction—for example, when the sanctioned body might seek to undertake activities within the United States because the entity or its assets are within the United States or because US persons are involved in the activities.[60]

Financial sanctions as a geopolitical tool are more efficient than broad, comprehensive commercial sanctions. In general, economic sanctions might work at the threat stage, work only after being imposed (at the implementation stage), or fail at both stages. A significant problem with comprehensive economic sanctions is the collateral damage to the civilian population in the target country and to countries beyond the two directly involved. Such collateral damage often weakens the support for sanctions.

Economic sanctions are increasingly being utilized to sponsor the full range of US foreign-policy objectives. Yet all too often, sanctions turn out to be little more than utterances about US leanings that affect American economic interests without modifying the target's behavior for the better. As a rule, sanctions need to be less unilateral and more focused on the issue at hand.

A parliament or an executive branch needs to institute far more rigorous oversight of penalties, both before adopting them and regularly after that, to ensure that the expected benefits outweigh likely costs and that sanctions accomplish more than alternative foreign-policy tools. Where economic sanctions are too comprehensive, financial penalties are more efficient. For example, in the case of Russia, Russian companies were unable to conduct dollar-denominated transactions, financial institutions were less willing to assist them out of fear of angering Western

---

[60] Barry E. Carter and Ryan Farha, "Overview and Operation of U.S. Financial Sanctions, Including the Example of Iran," Georgetown University Law Center, 2013, accessed February 20, 2018, http://scholarship.law.georgetown.edu/cgi/viewcontent.cgi?article=2267&context=facpub.

governments, and American businesses were not able to work with them.

Also, financial sanctions are often simple to circumvent because they take a long time to implement, and therefore it is possible for targeted decision makers to plan preemptive action or find new ways to launder money, for example. Targets might fashion protective safeguards by studying previous cases of sanctions against other countries. Therefore, to be effective, even "smarter" targeted sanctions might have to be designed.

Furthermore, selective financial sanctions arguably work best against targets with unique characteristics such as limited resources and scarce opportunities for the accumulation of wealth. And if targeted sanctions harm civilians less than comprehensive sanctions do, a dictatorship could tax or extract other resources from its citizens more harshly to compensate for frozen assets and other penalties. Finally, the UN has limited experience in administrating targeted sanctions.

Another way to exert power is not through influence but through the capability to hurt and inflict damage. Financial and trade penalties have long been used as foreign-policy tools and are sometimes perceived as the preferred tools for states where diplomacy has not yielded the desired results. Yet as widely used as they are, and notwithstanding the fact that some penalties may remain in place for years, they generally fail to achieve their targets.

One of the most comprehensive studies on the effectiveness of sanctions, covering the period from 1915 to 2006, has shown that extensive sanctions are adequate at best in 30 percent of cases and that the more comprehensive the sanctions, the lower their level of success. Despite this, sanctions remain one of the few internationally accepted means, short of military conflict, of trying to alter the behavior of political leaders.

So sanctions actually have a mixed track record. While they worked well in countries such as South Africa, for example, they have failed to stop North Korea from pursuing its atomic weapons program. In Russia, sanctions have probably affected the local economy but not nearly as much as the fall in global oil prices, and they have not resulted in a change in Russia's behavior vis-à-vis Ukraine. The ruble has primarily risen in tandem with the rise in global oil prices in spite of sanctions. While sanctions are often intended to affect a country's leadership or elite, sometimes they have the opposite effect.

For instance, in Russia, Mr. Putin's popularity has rarely been as high as it is today, and in Iran, it is the country's elite who have benefitted most from the implementation of sanctions due to their ability to engage in widespread illicit commerce below the international radar.

Sanctions rarely succeed in restricting goods from a state; they merely support black-market trade and push the price of those products significantly higher. Currency speculators are often the most significant beneficiaries of penalties.

In contrast, it is nearly always the case that a state whose economy is already weak and most vulnerable suffers the most when sanctions are imposed. One line of research shows that financial penalties have a lot more impact on the target country than do trade sanctions.

When GNP declines more than 2.5 percent as a result of sanctions, it has some effect, but after GNP drops more than 5 percent, it has a substantially negative impact on the targeted country 90 percent of the time.[61] In Moscow's case, the price of oil is likelier

---

[61] Gary Clyde Hufbauer, Kimberly Ann Elliott, Tess Cyrus, and Elizabeth Winston, "US Economic Sanctions: Their Impact on Trade, Jobs, and Wages," Peterson Institute for International Economics, Working Paper Special, April 1997, accessed February 20, 2018, https://piie.com/publications/working-papers/us-economic-sanctions-their-impact-trade-jobs-

to be the most critical determinant of whether penalties will profoundly affect the economy of the country.

If Washington wanted to really hit at Moscow, it would cut Russia out of the SWIFT banking-clearance architecture. But doing so would risk Moscow's launching an alternative method to SWIFT with China and contenders to Washington, which could end up damaging the United States. Perhaps that is why Washington has rarely taken this tack in the past. It did so against Iran, but one of the results was that Iran became one of the most self-sufficient countries in the world. Also in the case of Iran, the financial sanctions still had a more powerful impact than the trade sanctions.

Four drivers of geofinance

The financialization of the economy

By *financialization* we mean an increase in the size and importance of a country's financial sector relative to its overall economy. This is also known as development of financial capitalism, whereby economic exchange is facilitated through the intermediation of financial instruments. In other words, financialization refers to a "pattern of accumulation in which profit making occurs increasingly through financial channels rather than through trade and commodity production."[62]

More popularly, however, financialization is understood to mean the vastly expanded role of financial markets, financial motives, financial institutions, and financial actors in the operation of domestic and international economies. Or, in a nutshell, a world

and-wages.
[62] Greta R. Krippner, "The Financialization of the American Economy," *Socio-Economic Review* 3 (2008):173–208, https://papers.ssrn.com/sol3/papers.cfm?abstract_id=811461.

where the economy no longer rules finance but where finance rules the marketplace.

Roots of financialization

The origins of the term *financialization* are obscure, although it began to appear with increasing frequency in the early 1990s.[63] The fundamental gravitational shift toward finance in capitalism as a whole, however, has been around since the late 1960s. The first figures on the left (or perhaps anywhere) to explore this question systematically were Harry Magdoff and Paul Sweezy, writing for *Monthly Review*.[64] There are three underlying trends[65] that shape the recent history of capitalism, the period beginning with the recession of 1974 through 1975: 1) the slowing down of the overall rate of growth, 2) the worldwide proliferation of monopolistic (or oligopolistic) multinational corporations, and 3) what may be called the financialization of the capital-accumulation process.

One of the central elements[66] of the 1970s economic crisis was "stagflation"—namely, the simultaneous occurrence of slow or no economic growth and high price inflation. Slow growth led to fewer outlets for domestic investment. Price inflation undermined the traditional banking business model of borrowing money from

---

[63] The current usage of the term *financialization* owes much to the work of Kevin Phillips, who employed it in his *Boiling Point* (New York: Random House, 1993) and a year later devoted a key chapter of his *Arrogant Capital* to the "financialization of America," defining *financialization* as "a prolonged split between the divergent real and financial economies" (New York: Little, Brown & Company, 1994, 82). In the same year, Giovanni Arrighi used the concept in an analysis of international hegemonic transition in *The Long Twentieth Century* (New York: Verso, 1994).

[64] Harry Magdoff first raised the issue of a growing reliance on debt in the US economy in an article originally published in the *Socialist Register* in 1965. See Harry Magdoff and Paul M. Sweezy, *The Dynamics of U.S. Capitalism* (New York: Monthly Review Press, 1972), 13–6.

[65] John Bellamy Foster, "The Financialization of Capitalism," *Monthly Review* 58(11) (2007), accessed February 18, 2018, https://monthlyreview.org/2007/04/01/the-financialization-of-capitalism/.

[66] Donald Tomaskovic-Devey and Ken-Hou Lin, "Financialization: Causes, Inequality Consequences, and Policy Implications," UNC School of Law, *North Carolina Banking Institute Journal* 18 (2014): 166–94, accessed February 20, 2018, http://scholarship.law.unc.edu/cgi/viewcontent.cgi?article=1365&context=ncbi.

depositors and lending it to borrowers, and this led to a sharp drop in bank profitability.

These three trends were intricately interrelated. Monopolization tends to swell profits for the major corporations while also reducing the demand for additional investment in increasingly controlled markets. The logic is one of more and more profits and fewer and fewer profitable investment opportunities—a recipe for slowing down capital accumulation and therefore economic growth, which is powered by capital accumulation.

The financialization of the nonfinancial sectors

Again, in the United States, the deregulation of financial activity, especially the ending of organizational limitations on financial activities, allowed nonfinancial firms to expand their financial investment strategies as well. Manufacturing and retail firms have long been known to offer consumer debt to increase sales of their main products. A good example is the case of General Motors Acceptance Corporation (GMAC, now Ally Financial), which was established in 1919. GE Capital was founded in 1943. Ford launched its financial services provider, Ford Motor Credit, in 1959.

During the 1980s, these companies and many others modified their behavior. In the 1980s, both GM and Ford went into the mortgage market, and in the 1990s, they expanded their financial activities to include banking, insurance, and commercial finance. In the 1980s, GE Capital broadened into real estate, small-business loans, mortgage lending, insurance, and credit cards. After running a close second for many, many years, it surpassed GMAC as the largest nonbank lender in the United States. These are not isolated examples.

Since the late 1970s, financial income has become a significant stream of revenue for US corporations. Among nonfinance firms, the ratio was relatively stable and hovered around 20 percent through the late 1970s. The proportion of financial revenue to profits increased to more than 35 percent by 1990, rising again to 40 percent around the year 2000. The scheme is more extreme among manufacturing firms; reliance on financial income increased by a factor of three over the past thirty years. In this century, earnings generated through financial channels are more than half the total profits earned by manufacturing firms.

The change in firms' investment behavior was not only due to changes in regulation. During the 1980s, the finance conception of companies replaced managerial commitments to investment and innovation in production.[67] The managerial goal of increasing stock prices in the short term displaced increased market share.

The emphasis on stock prices was reinforced by the linking of top-management pay to stock options rather than long-term sales, market share, or production-based profit. The increased financial engagement of nonfinancial business, the development of a market for corporate control, and the rise of shareholder activism shifted managerial orientation from the long-term goals of corporate growth to short-term goals of profitability.[68] To summarize, there are two faces to this financialization of the economy. First, we have the growing centrality of the financial services sector to the US economy. This was caused by modifications in the prudential environment for financial markets and resulted in the transfer of large chunks of national income to the financial services sector, as well as the more colloquial "too big to fail" (or jail) and systemic risk issues associated with the resulting market concentration of finance. The second face is the movement of the nonfinance parts of the economy into the world of financial investment rather than investment in production. This

---

[67] Neil Fligstein, *The Architecture of Markets: An Economic Sociology of Twenty-First-Century Capitalist Societies* (Princeton, NJ: Princeton University Press, 2002).
[68] Engelbert Stockhammer, "Financialisation and the Slowdown of Accumulation," *Cambridge Journal of Economics* 28(5) (2004), 719–41; Michael Useem, *Investor Capitalism: How Money Managers Are Changing the Face of Corporate America* (New York: Basic Books, 1996).

expression was also the product of new financial-market institutions, exacerbated by finance-sector pressures for short-term profit orientations in the management of nonfinance firms and the agency-theory-based linkage of CEO pay to equity options.

The collateral damage of financialization

The financialization of the advanced economies is one of the principal vectors of the increase of income inequality in these developed countries. It is not only the fact that financial income is concentrated within the top 1 percent of the population through equity ownership but also that it disrupts the remainder of the economy. This has brought down employment and socioeconomic well-being for many citizens and increased inequality while also increasing the portion of national income channeled toward capital and corporate executives to the detriment of employees and their families.

Financialization disrupts capital investment and decreases the mutual dependence of labor and capital, eroding the social contract in which a capitalistic system supplies profits to the owners of wealth and a growing standard of living to citizens.

Much of the debate around prudential regulation of the financial services industry focuses on the issue of financial institutions being too big to fail and a banking system that is said to be too vulnerable to survive even more regulation. The problem is worse than that. The Occupy Wall Street movement in the United States forced the tremendous growth in US income inequality into the public's consciousness.

At this point, the trends are well known. Among earners, the United States is now one of the most unequal countries in the world, with its inequality level rising since the late 1970s and now comparable to that of China. Disturbingly, the share of national income that goes to employees, in contrast to capital, is at an all-time low. Finally, an incommensurate portion of all growth in national income since the late 1970s has been hoarded by the top 1 percent of households.

Financialization goes beyond the financial system and distorts income distributions, job creation, and investment throughout the economy. High inequality reduces economic growth and leads to the concentration of political power in the hands of a narrow elite.

Almost all social problems and public-health indicators, from homicide to teenage pregnancy, are worse in more unequal societies. Rising inequality damages the social fabric and has been the trend in the United States and Europe for the past three decades. In policy discussions, growing inequality is usually described as the result of market forces.

Technological change in the skills required in manufacturing and globalization are the two most common explanations. Prior research shows that the financialization of the US economy has been a significant vector for the rise of income inequality in the United States and Europe as well as for the destruction of well-paying jobs. One feature of this evolution has been the concentration of economic, political, and market power in the hands of a few global financial corporations, allowing them to absorb an increasing proportion of the economic value yielded in the United States and Europe.

Another dimension of this trend is, as noted, that companies in nonfinance industries have increasingly shifted their investment strategies from manufacturing and employment in the real economy to financial speculation and, as they have done so, reduced employment and increased inequality.

Financialization as a percentage of GDP

Financialization has taken place as countries have moved away from industrial capitalism. This shift affects both the

macroeconomy and the microeconomy by modifying how
financial markets are structured and operated and by influencing
corporate behavior and economic policy.

Just as major economies shifted from agricultural to industrial
economies, they now have transformed from industrial to
postindustrial economies to which the financial services industry
is vital. For example, in the United States, the finance, insurance,
and real estate (FIRE) sector now accounts for 20 percent of GDP,
compared to only 10 percent back in 1947.[69]

At the same time, the manufacturing industry fell from 30 percent
of GDP in 1950 to 10 percent in 2010. The finance industry
swelled as the rest of the economy weakened. The excessive
growth of finance diverted income from labor to capital.[70] The
defining feature of financialization in developed countries has
been an increase in the volume of debt. According to a recent
study by McKinsey, global debt has increased by $57 trillion,
outpacing world GDP growth.[71]

[69] Christopher Witko, "How Wall Street Became a Big Chunk of the U.S. Economy—And When the
Democrats Signed On," *Washington Post*, March 29, 2016, accessed January 28, 2018,
https://www.washingtonpost.com/news/monkey-cage/wp/2016/03/29/how-wall-street-
became-a-big-chunk-of-the-u-s-economy-and-when-the-democrats-signed-
on/?utm_term=.2f2079d05dea.
[70] Mike Collins, "Wall Street and the Financialization of the Economy," *Forbes*, February 4, 2015,
https://www.forbes.com/sites/mikecollins/2015/02/04/wall-street-and-the-financialization-of-
the-economy/#5d5620857834.
[71] Richard Dobbs et al., "Debt and (Not Much) Deleveraging," McKinsey & Company, February 2015,
accessed February 20, 2018, https://www.mckinsey.com/global-themes/employment-and-
growth/debt-and-not-much-deleveraging.

Figure 2: Change in Debt-to-GDP Ratio, 2007–2014

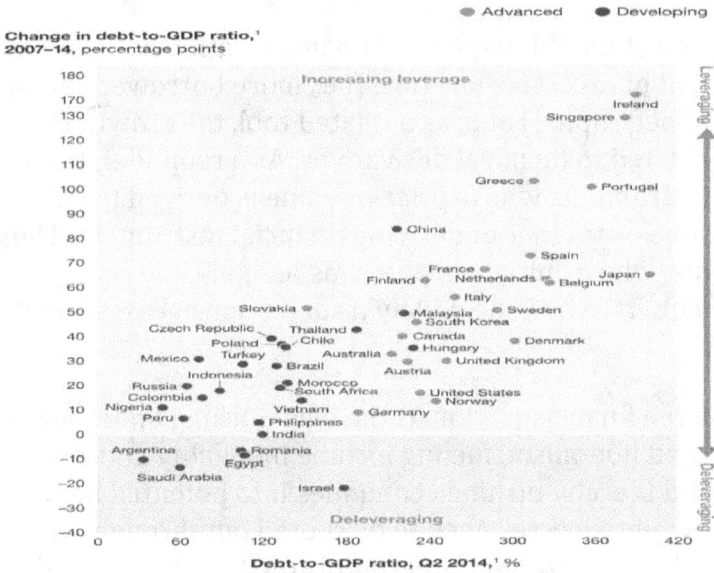

Source: McKinsey Global Institute and Haver Analytics, 2015

The financial services (banking, insurance, investment, etc.) have become a critical sector in developed economies, contributing to a sizeable share of the GDP, and a vital source of jobs. These activities have also played a crucial role in facilitating the globalization of the economy. As a result, since the 1980s, the financial industry has pursued short-term financial returns over long-term goals such as technology and product-development investments. The financial sector, consequently, has played a significant role in the decline of manufacturing in the advanced economies for a variety of reasons. The banks followed their capitalist instincts and saw that there was more profit in making money from money than in engineered products. They wanted the quick returns of financial instruments and software rather than investing in the brick and mortar of expensive factories.

They were also supportive of products that could be sold at the big retailers and manufactured overseas.

One of the most notable aspects of financialization has been the development of excessive leverage (i.e., more borrowed capital and less owned capital) and, as a related tool, the growth in activities related to financial derivatives. As a reminder, these are financial instruments whose price or value is derived from the price or value of another underlying financial instrument. Those instruments, whose initial purpose was hedging and risk management, have become widely traded financial assets in their own right.

Many now see financialization as the devil lurking underneath globalism and liberalism, fueling income inequality and excessive leverage and thereby turning economies into potential houses of cards. But while excesses need to be rooted out through regulation, financialization foregrounds the fact that many more businesses have access to financial instruments now than ever before. In the old days, many corporations were held by families or private individuals, while nowadays, capital markets and financial intermediation allow those same businesses—and a whole string of new ones—to tap into new sources of funding.

Many of the instruments that accompany the financialization of an economy, such as derivatives and structured products, are hard to measure or value, given their complexity. In other words, the structuration of vast amounts of debt has introduced a higher risk into global finance, but at the same time, these same structured finance products have allowed for the allocation of enormous quantities of capital toward buyouts and other power schemes.

Interestingly, the development of these instruments of financialization has allowed for the emergence of technocapitalism, such as the Facebooks, Googles, Apples, Alibabas, and so on of the world, as well as others in the nanotechnology and biotech sectors. Given that the majority of these businesses fail to make any profit in their first years while being highly capital intensive, had it not been for the excess capital generated through the financialization of the economy, these sectors would have remained at an incubation level for a very long time.

Everyone remembers the Internet bubble of the early 2000s, when vast sums of money went into Internet-related technology companies notwithstanding the fact that many of them had no realistic business plans or prospects for profit. This bubble led to a significant number of market adjustments wherein investors lost some funds into those assets. This phenomenon was the hallmark of what is called fast capital accumulation.

Apparently, one reason that capital was being rushed into nonrealistic investments was that investors were hungry for yields. Indeed, the Federal Reserve Bank and other central banks had a zero interest-rate policy, which made classical investments yield low returns in comparison to the cost of capital, thereby pushing investors into the arms of structured finance products. In other words, government authorities, using the central banks, had created an environment that was propitious to higher speculation as accommodative monetary policies kept yields too low for too long a time.

Financialization increases vulnerability

Financialization is, at its root, a mechanism of income redistribution that privileges the financial services sector over nonfinance industry, financial investments over investments in production, and shareholders and top executives over workers and middle-class citizens.

Financialization is the result of regulatory decisions made by politicians that have led to the deregulation of financial activities, encouraged the concentration of financial power in a few large corporations, and ultimately led to the failure to regulate new financial instruments and strategies. As a consequence, income increasingly becomes diverted away from investment, employment, and production toward the owners of financial instruments and financial service firms. The hyperconcentration in the financial services sector increases the vulnerability of any advanced economy.

The consensual solution to reduce the systemic risk posed by concentrated finance is either to deleverage the large banks or, better yet, to break up these banks altogether. The amalgamated market power of these large banks creates a systemic risk and also generates economic rent (i.e., the never-ending transfer of income from the productive sector to the finance sector).

Breaking up the large financial institutions would reduce the likelihood of future financial catastrophes as well as fraud, antitrust violations, and conflicts of interest, all of which are all-too-standard practices in today's financial services sector. Furthermore, if markets are dominated by less-sizeable firms, the incentive to preserve reputation may become higher than the incentive to accumulate short-term profits.

Another approach is to create one or more government-owned corporations to provide affordable credit to households, local authorities, and small businesses directly. A public option would force the financial services sector as a whole to become more competitive and more efficient, provide prudent loans, and protect households and small business from predatory lending and fee-based financial services.

Financialization is the epitome of geofinance

Geofinance ignores the laws of geography and national borders. Geofinance can be synthesized as an amalgamation of global money, information technology, political power, and deregulation. To that effect, the globalization of financial markets plays a critical role, and this phenomenon has been driven by the financialization of the economy. Globalization and financialization should be analyzed as interrelated tendencies.[72]

One can identify a wave of internationalization that started in the mid-1990s and then a wave of financialization that reached a peak in 2004. These two waves had transformed the industry into a highly globalized and financialized one by the eve of the 2008 crisis. However, international expansion slowed down dramatically at the beginning of the 2000s.

Figure 3: A Stylized View of Capital Mobility in Modern History

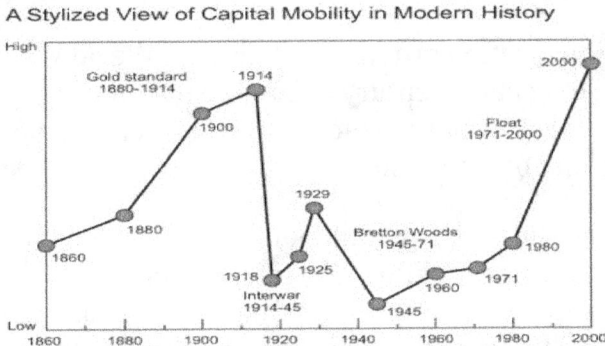

A Stylized View of Capital Mobility in Modern History

Source: Maurice Obstfeld and Alan M. Taylor. *Global Capital Markets: Integration, Crisis, and Growth* (Cambridge University Press, 2005).

As indicated earlier, financialization goes hand in hand with financial globalization, which in turn leads to a rise in international, cross-border flows. Indeed, financialization goes far beyond a mere increase in financial operations. It entails necessary changes in the way finance operates and how agents relate to it.

[72] Celine Baud and Cedric Durand, "Financialization, Globalization and the Making of Profits by Leading Retailers." *Socio-Economic Review* 10 (2011): 2–26, accessed February 20, 2018, http://cemi.ehess.fr/docannexe/file/2483/3._baud.durand.pdf.

A few studies explicitly use the term *global financialization*.[73]

Contrary to popular belief, globalization did not start thirty or forty years ago but about a century and a half ago, in the period from 1800 to 1914. This period is also known as the First Age of

Globalization and incorporates the latter portion of the Industrial Revolution, the growth of large-scale capital investments such as railways and highways, the increasing importance of global finance, and more prosperity. In this same period, cross-border lending and borrowing by financial institutions helped fund large-scale investment projects.

This First Age of Globalization ground to a halt with World War I. After a break of roughly half a century due to the two world wars, the Second Age of Globalization started, spanning a period from the 1960s until the end of the twentieth century.

The era marked fierce financial assimilation. One of the most popular metrics of international financial integration demonstrates this point. Constructed using data on global assets and liabilities relative to GDP, the indicator illustrates the number of periods of accelerating financial integration (concentration).

[73] Bruno Bonizzi, "Financialization in Developing and Emerging Countries," *International Journal of Political Economy* 42(4) (2013), 83–107, accessed February 20, 2018, https://www.researchgate.net/publication/269488087_Financialization_in_Developing_and_Emerging_Countries.

Figure 4: International Financial Integration

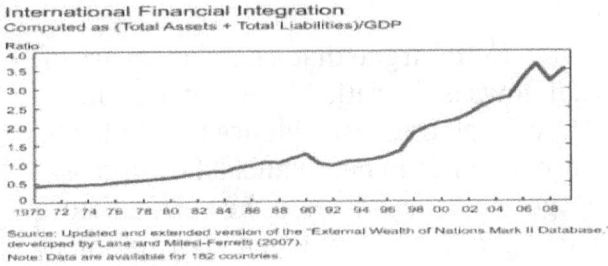

International Financial Integration
Computed as (Total Assets + Total Liabilities)/GDP

Source: Updated and extended version of the "External Wealth of Nations Mark II Database," developed by Lane and Milesi-Ferretti (2007).
Note: Data are available for 182 countries.

A few other broad remarks describe that last half century of financial integration. One is that the format of international lending activity changed; another is that the counterparties to these activities also changed during that period. Initially, the primary format of global banking activity was cross-border lending; activity in the form of local lending was minimal. Flows from investors in large developed countries were intermediated through banks and often were utilized to finance the fiscal imbalances of emerging market sovereigns.

Concomitantly, international banking activity among industrialized countries grew. From less than $5 trillion around 2000, the amount soared to more than $15 trillion over the next decade. The use of derivatives, the extension of guarantees, and the use of credit commitments also rose after the turn of the century.

The internationalization of financial markets can be tracked using cross-border financial flows. An analysis of the evidence[74] on financial flows seems to indicate that the degree of internationalization of financial markets has increased over the years to reach levels broadly similar to those observed in the

[74] Otmar Issing, "The Globalisation of Financial Markets," European Central Bank, September 12, 2000, accessed February 20, 2018, https://www.ecb.europa.eu/press/key/date/2000/html/sp000912_2.en.html.

period of intense financial market integration that preceded World War I.

Bordo, Eichengreen, and Kim[75] argue that a good measure of international financial flows is the ratio of current account balance over GDP. They noted there is evidence that indicates that, in contrast to recent trends in net financial flows, gross financial flows are larger nowadays than in the period before World War I. In particular, although not much information is available from before WWI, it would seem that turnover in the foreign-exchange markets was lower than it is now, in line with the study conducted by Bloomfield.[76]

In the past thirty years, while more progress was made in the internationalization of financial markets, there have been a number of financial crises as well. Some of them exerted protracted and disruptive effects on economies both locally and globally. As a result, economic policy makers, together with market participants, have given considerable attention to the problem of how best to avoid financial crises. Specifically, in April 1999, a multilateral organization called the Financial Stability Forum (FSF) was established with the objective of sponsoring international financial stability through data exchange and global cooperation in financial supervision and surveillance.[77]

In financial terms,[78] the risks to financial stability come primarily from inefficiencies in the market. As pointed out earlier,

[75] Michael D. Bordo, Barry Eichengreen, and Jongwoo Kim, "Was There Really an Earlier Period of International Financial Integration Comparable to Today?" NBER Working Paper 6738, National Bureau of Economic Research, September 1998, accessed February 20, 2018, http://www.nber.org/papers/w6738.
[76] Arthur A. Bloomfield, *Short-Term Capital Movements under the Pre-1914 Gold Standard*, Princeton Studies in International Finance 11 (Princeton, NJ: International Finance Section, Department of Economics, Princeton University, 1963).
[77] The Financial Stability Forum (http://www.fsforum.org) was created in accordance with the conclusions of a report prepared by then-president of the Deutsche Bundesbank, Hans Tietmeyer, at the request of the finance ministers and central-bank governors of the G7 countries.
[78] Issing, "The Globalisation of Financial Markets," 2000.

inefficiencies remain significant in global financial markets, presumably because of transaction costs and data asymmetries. In broad terms, these inefficiencies declare themselves in various ways, including coordination problems and externalities.

These externalities seem to occur in particular with the setting up of market architectures such as settlement and payment systems. Coordination issues seem to happen mainly in the form of principal-agent problems affecting the relationship between lenders and borrowers due to the existence of information asymmetries or data-validation issues.

As a remedy for financial crises, some observers have proposed to reinstate some limitations on capital flows in certain specific cases. An example often mentioned is the case of Chile, where short-term capital inflows were restricted in the 1990s through the imposition of minimum-reserve requirements. Certain commentators, considering the performance of the Chilean economy and its resilience to the financial crises of recent years, have said that this penalization system may have been successful in avoiding crises and sponsoring economic growth in Chile, but Edwards has shown that a careful analysis of the evidence does not validate any positive impact.[79]

Another suggested remedy is James Tobin's idea to tax foreign-exchange transactions or, more generally, all short-term financial flows. Advocates of the Tobin tax argue that it would help decrease financial market volatility while costing next to nothing for financial market participants, especially for long-term transactions.

A convincing argument against the suggested Tobin tax is that it would be hard to put in place. Other arguments opposing the

---

[79] Sebastian Edwards, "Crisis Prevention: Lessons from Mexico and East Asia," NBER Working Paper 7233, July 1999, doi:10.3386/w7233.

Tobin tax are more closely in line with economic theory. The
Tobin tax would lead to a rise in transaction costs.
Notwithstanding the fact that the increase might be small relative
to the transacted amounts, it could nevertheless amplify the
market inefficiencies already observed within the current
framework, which seem to arise partly from even low transaction
costs and are apparent in particular in the home-bias and
Feldstein-Horioka puzzles.[80] Hence, it would seem hard, given the
present condition of economic research, to provide a clear-cut
case in favor of the Tobin tax.

Let's return to the two manifestations of financial market
inefficiencies mentioned above that may result in financial crises:
information problems and externalities. Externalities are
especially consequential in the development of the infrastructure
of financial markets—particularly payment and settlement
systems.

In many cases, economic agents are not able to endogenize the
benefits associated with well-functioning payment and settlement
systems, such as the ability to process transactions with a large
number of potential counterparties and in conditions of high
safety. As a result, economic agents may content themselves with
suboptimal payment and settlement systems unless further
incentives are provided to upgrade existing systems. It has
become widely accepted that the most secure systems for
processing large-value payments are real-time gross-settlement
systems.

For the euro, the payment system operated by the European
System of Central Banks, TARGET, falls into the category of real-
time gross-settlement systems. Over recent years, the setting up
of a more secure infrastructure for the settlement of foreign-

---

[80] For example, James Tobin, "Prologue," in *The Tobin Tax: Coping with Financial Volatility*, Mahbub
ul Haq, Inga Kaul, and Isabelle Grunberg, eds. (New York: Oxford University Press, 1996), x–xviii.

exchange transactions has become a more prevalent issue to minimize the risk of payment-system gridlock of the type occasioned by the failure of the Bankhaus Herstatt in 1974. Building on the recommendations published by the Committee on Payment and Settlement Systems of the Group of Ten central banks, promotors launched several private initiatives over recent years to set up a new, more secure foreign-exchange settlement system. As of 1997, some of the promoters of these endeavors joined their efforts in the so-called Continuous-Time Linked Settlement Bank (CLS Bank). According to Kahn and Roberds, the system designed by the CLS Bank permits a substantial reduction in foreign-exchange settlement risk with limited costs and in a sufficiently safe and secure manner.[81]

Over recent months, concerns of a nature similar to those posed by foreign-exchange settlement risk have arisen following the electronification of trading systems, which has proceeded at a remarkable pace, in particular in the foreign-exchange markets. Persaud notes that on certain days in 1998 and 1999, there were some unusually sharp moves in foreign-exchange rates over very short periods.[82] He suggests that this so-called gapping behavior may be attributed to the adaptation of the market to the new infrastructure. As the electronification of financial markets progresses further, it is obviously important that the providers of electronic trading platforms adopt sufficiently safe procedures to limit the risk of system failures, including the risk of gridlock in trading activity in case of market turbulence.

Turning to the second occurrence of financial market inefficiencies, data—or coordination—problems happen when

---

[81] Charles M. Kahn and William Roberds, "The CLS Bank: A Solution to the Risks of International Payment Settlement?" *Carnegie-Rochester Conference Series on Public Policy* 54(1) (2001), 191–226.

[82] Avinash Persaud, "The Liquidity Puzzle," Risk.net, June 1, 2000. For foreign-exchange markets, an indicator of the global volatility level was proposed in Vincent Brousseau and Fabio Scacciavillani, "A Global Hazard Index for the World Foreign Exchange Markets," European Central Bank Working Paper, Series 1, 1999.

lenders and borrowers are not capable of exchanging all the information needed to transact efficiently. Consider, for example, the so-called adverse-selection problem. To prevent potential credit losses, lenders with limited information on the creditworthiness of borrowers can only offer relatively high-interest rates on loans. This tends to attract the less creditworthy borrowers, which may result in credit rationing for the best borrowers.

More generally, when the financial soundness of borrowers is low and information asymmetry is high, there may be sizeable inefficiencies in financial markets. In such cases, the release of information revealing the actual creditworthiness of borrowers may result in a disorderly withdrawal of funds when lenders realize that they do not have sufficient capital to buffer possible credit losses. The risk of such a scenario materializing is obviously unusually high when the modalities of corporate governance are such that the executives of companies do not comply with minimum standards of transparency and honesty.

These problems can explain why, when financial markets are poorly managed, their liberalization can increase the risk of financial crises. As discussed in a recent economic issues publication of the IMF, financial institutions may react to more competition with laxist lending, or they may be unable to handle the information problems that are magnified in the transition period.[83] Bernard and Bisignano show that information problems play an essential role in the international interbank market.[84] They state that the issues can be so intense as to make it necessary to introduce a grant to market agents in the form of implicit guarantees of support in case of default. However,

[83] Giovanni Dell'Ariccia et al., "Liberalizing Capital Movements: Some Analytical Issues," *IMF Economic Issues* 17 (1999), 1–21.
[84] Henri J. Bernard and Joseph Bisignano, "Information, Liquidity, and Risk in the International Interbank Market: Implicit Guarantees and Private Credit Market Failure," BIS Working Paper 86, March 2000.

Bernard and Bisignano show that this appears to have resulted in moral hazard, leading to the excessive risk taking that may have amplified the financial market chaos of autumn 1998.

These information issues can be addressed if financial market participants commit themselves to measuring risk exposures as well as possible and constituting capital cushions adequate to handle potential losses. Apparently, risk exposures should be defined according to several possible degrees of severity of circumstances. For normal conditions outside periods of market stress, the so-called value-at-risk indicator can provide reliable measures of risk exposure.[85]

However, caution requires that financial market agents also evaluate their risks of loss in periods of intense market stress in order to measure the extent to which their capital buffers would be wiped out in such conditions. The recommendations proposed by the Basel Committee on Banking Supervision indicate how market-risk exposures should best be measured. The Basel Committee is in the process of establishing a new range of recommendations dealing with more varied and accurate measurement tools for credit-risk exposure.

In the capital-adequacy architecture that the committee has elaborated, the necessity for large financial institutions to reveal data about their risk exposures and their equity buffers plays a vital role. When such a condition is in force, financial institutions with low equity will find themselves being monitored, as they will be seen as potentially more dangerous, giving the incentive for a vertical adjustment of their equity buffers. Additionally, the publication of data on the evaluation of risks by large financial institutions will contribute to the formation of a consensus among financial market participants about the real creditworthiness of

---

[85] The value-at-risk indicator can be contrived as a measure of bundled risks, covering the various classes of risks, including foreign-exchange, interest-rate, equity, and credit risk. Some authors have suggested using value at risk as an indicator of aggregate risk exposures.

borrowers in the economy. Hence, the disclosure of data about risk exposures and equity buffers can assist in both reducing information asymmetry among borrowers and lenders and enforcing discipline among financial market participants.

To fend off financial crises, then, it seems crucial to have both a robust financial infrastructure and sound financial institutions that publish information about their risk exposures and capital buffers. As Grenville suggests, the existence of these features in financial markets, such as those of Australia and Hong Kong, may help to explain why these economies were able to successfully weather the episodes of financial turbulence in East Asia in 1997 and 1998, despite close trade links with the economies in crisis.[86]

Further shielding against the impacts of financial turbulence, as Alan Greenspan has suggested, would be a "spare tire" in the form of healthy banks for when capital markets cough and in the form of deep and liquid capital markets if banks seize up.[87]

Liberalization or deregulation?

Many confuse deregulation with liberalization. The latter relates to the government removing barriers and restrictions on the whole economy, while the former means that the government eliminates obstacles and constraints on specific sectors of the

---

[86] Stephen Grenville, "Financial Crises and Globalisation from an Australian Perspective," paper delivered to the Reinventing the Bretton Woods Committee Conference on International Capital Mobility and Domestic Economic Stability, Canberra, July 15, 1999.

[87] Allan Greenspan, "Do efficient financial markets mitigate financial crises?" Speech delivered to the Financial Markets Conference of the Federal Reserve Bank of Atlanta, Sea Island, Georgia, October 19, 1999, accessed March 4, 2018, https://www.federalreserve.gov/boarddocs/speeches/1999/19991019.htm.
Some commentators have observed that many financial crises follow a common pattern that involves contagion effects leading to a panic. In an illuminating analysis of how panics unfold, Dupuy argues that financial markets can make it possible to achieve efficient outcomes in the vast majority of cases, although the pattern of behavior of economic agents is permanently characterized by a strong tendency toward herding in the presence of uncertainty. See Jean-Pierre Dupuy, *Le Sacrifice et L'envie: Le Libéralisme aux Prises avec la Justice Sociale* (Paris: Calmann-Lévy, 1992), 318–29.

economy. (And then there is privatization, which involves the transfer of ownership from the state to the private sector.)

Before 1980, the financial services industry was regulated to shield both consumers and the economy more generally from the concentration of speculative investment and financial power that had occurred before and led to the Great Depression. The low-growth, high-inflation macroeconomy of the 1970s led the large-firm corporate sector to push for economic deregulation, lower taxes, and a smaller state. One of the central developments of the 1970s crisis was stagflation, defined as the joint occurrence of slow or no economic growth and high inflation. Slow growth led to fewer outlets for domestic investment. Price inflation undermined the traditional banking practice of borrowing money from depositors and lending it to borrowers and led to a sharp drop in bank profitability. The Federal Reserve Bank fought inflation by rapidly increasing interest rates between 1979 and 1981.

This tight monetary policy slowed down price inflation in the early 1980s and lured foreign capital to invest in US interest-bearing bonds. In 1984, the Reagan administration removed the 30 percent tax on foreign interest income, intensifying the influx of foreign investment into the United States.

Inflation, of course, is suitable for people with debt but bad for debt holders. In this way, price inflation transferred income from banks to households and firms with fixed-interest debt. While tight monetary policy stabilized the income of the finance sector by taming price inflation, it was deregulation that fundamentally shifted the basic structure of the economy to favor the financial industry.

As a result, in 1985, the Federal Reserve began to allow holding companies to own banks in multiple states.[88] The 1994 Riegle-

Neal Interstate Banking and Branching Efficiency Act repealed the final prohibitions on interstate banking. The outcome was a surge in bank mergers, resulting in a growing concentration of finance activity in fewer, larger banks.

Eventually, the US Congress, in the Gramm-Leach-Bliley Act of 1999, repealed parts of the 1933 Glass-Steagall Act, making it legal for investment banks, commercial banks, and insurance companies to become affiliates through ordinary holding companies.[89]

This legitimized the already-ongoing expansion of bank-holding companies, which conducted business simultaneously in all financial markets; created a new, consolidated financial services industry in which commercial and retail banking, insurance, and investment services could all be delivered by a single firm; and eventually generated the systemic (i.e., concentrated, densely networked) risk associated with the financial collapse of the later 2000s.[90]

---

[88] *Northeast Bancorp, Inc. v. Governors, FRS*, 472 U.S. 159 (1985), finding state statutes that allowed interstate bank acquisitions by bank holding companies to be authorized by the Bank Holding Company Act and not to violate the Constitution.
[89] Gramm-Leach-Bliley Act, Pub. L. No. 106-102, 113 Stat. 1338 (1999).
[90] Mauro F. Guillén and Sandra L. Suárez, "The Global Crisis of 2007–2009: Markets, Politics, and Organizations," in *Markets on Trial: The Economic Sociology of the U.S. Financial Crisis*, ed. Michael Lounsbury and Paul M. Hirsch (Bingley, UK: Emerald Group Publishing Limited, 2010), 257–79.

Figure 5: Growing Financial Assets and Concentration of Finance

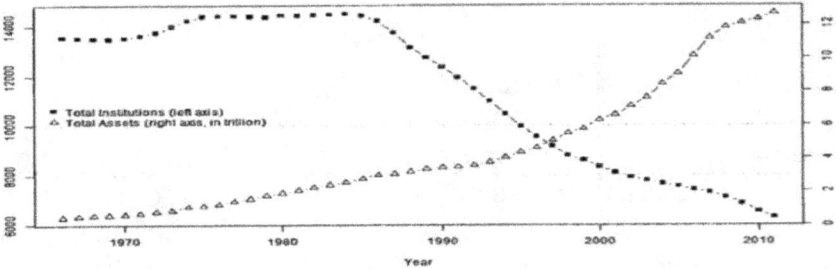

Source: Historical Statistics on Banking (HSOB),
http://www2.fdic.gov/hsob/index.asp.

Figure 6: The Concentration of Assets in the Banking Industry

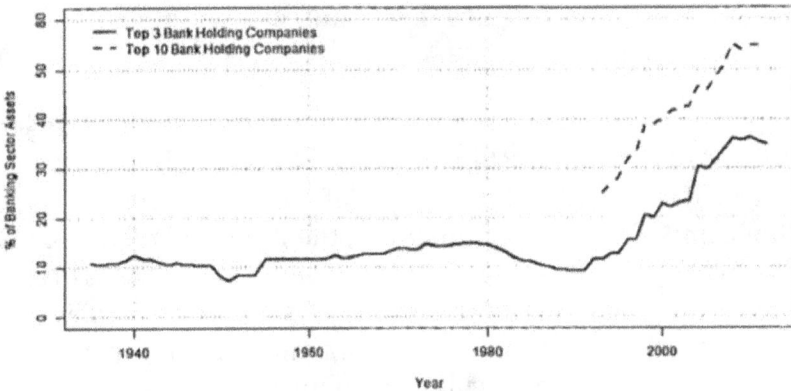

Source: Historical Statistics on Banking[91]

The resulting double process of faltering real investment and
burgeoning financialization as capital sought to find a way to
utilize its economic surplus first appeared with the waning of the

---

[91] "Historical Statistics on Banking," FDIC Bank, accessed February 20, 2018,
https://www5.fdic.gov/hsob/SelectRpt.asp?EntryTyp=10&Header=1.

golden age of the post-WWII decades and has persisted, with increasing intensity, into the present.[92]

The globalization of the economy

Several definitions for *globalization* exist. One, from Martin and King, is "the increasing interaction of people, states, or countries through the growth of the international flow of money, ideas, and culture."[93] Investopedia refers to the tendency of international trade, investments, information technology, and outsourced manufacturing to weave the economies of diverse countries together.[94] The *Oxford Dictionaries* state that globalization is the process by which businesses or other organizations establish international influence or start operating on a global scale.[95] In other words, globalization is fundamentally an economic process of integration that has cultural and social aspects. It involves products and services and also the resources of capital, technology, and data.[96]

The spinning-jenny wheel, the steam train, the steamship, the jet engine, and the container ship are some of the developments in the means of transport, while the rise of the telegraph and telephone and their modern offspring, the Internet and mobile phones, highlight advances in telecommunications infrastructure. All these improvements that society enjoys in the modern era have been significant aspects of globalization and have generated further interdependence of cultural, financial, political, and economic activities.

[92] Paul M. Sweezy, "More (or Less) on Globalization," *Monthly Review* 49(4) (1997), 3–4.
[93] Martin Albrow and Elizabeth King, eds., *Globalization, Knowledge, and Society* (London: Sage, 1990).
[94] Investopedia, "Globalization," April 1, 2015, accessed February 20, 2018, https://www.investopedia.com/terms/g/globalization.asp.
[95] *English Oxford Living Dictionaries*, s.v. "Globalization," accessed February 20, 2018, https://en.oxforddictionaries.com/definition/globalization.
[96] International Monetary Fund, "Globalization: A Brief Overview," May 1, 2008, accessed February 20, 2018, https://www.imf.org/external/np/exr/ib/2008/053008.htm.

Origins of globalization

Though many pundits place the origins of globalization in modern times, others trace its history to long before the European Age of Discovery and voyages to the New World, some even to the third millennium BC. Large-scale globalization began in the 1820s. Indeed, modern globalization as we know it today erupted in the nineteenth century, shaped by Western imperialism and industrialism.

The second half of the nineteenth century witnessed the advent of globalization approaching its modern form. Industrialization enabled cheap manufacturing of household items using economies of scale, while fast population growth resulted in a sustained demand for commodities. Globalization during this period was defined by nineteenth-century colonialism and imperialism.

After the First and Second Opium Wars in China, which opened up the Middle Kingdom to foreign commerce, and the finalization of the British conquest of India, the vast populations of these Asian regions became ready consumers of European exports, and Europeans likewise became consumers of Asian imports.

It was during this period that regions of sub-Saharan Africa and the Pacific islands were integrated into the global system. In the meantime, the conquest of new parts of the globe, notably sub-Saharan Africa, by Europeans generated valuable natural resources such as rubber, coal, and diamonds and fostered trade and investment among the European imperial powers, their colonies, and the United States.

There are noteworthy differences, however, between globalization in the nineteenth and twentieth centuries. There are two major areas in which distinctions can be observed. One is global trade in these centuries as it relates to capital, investment, and the economy. The first phase of modern globalization started at the beginning of the twentieth century, with WWI. Globalization since WWII has partly been the result of planning by politicians to abolish any borders hindering commerce. Their planning resulted in the organization of the Bretton Woods Conference, a compromise by the world's leading Western politicians to lay down the framework for global commerce and finance and the creation of several multilateral agencies meant to monitor the processes of globalization.

Globalization was also fueled by the international expansion of multinational corporations based in Europe and the United States, as well as the global exchange of new advancements in technology, science, and products, with the most significant inventions of that period taking place in the Western world.

Growth and development of international telecommunication and transport has played a decisive role in contemporary globalization. In 2000, the IMF identified four essential features of globalization: capital and investment movements, migration and movement of people, commerce and transactions, and the dissemination of knowledge and education.[97]

Furthermore, environmental challenges such as air pollution, overfishing of the oceans, global warming, and cross-boundary water are connected with globalization. Globalizing processes affect and are affected by work and business organization, the natural environment, politics, finance, economics, and sociocultural resources. Academic research commonly categorizes globalization into three major areas: political globalization, economic and financial globalization, and cultural globalization.

[97] International Monetary Fund, "Globalization: Threat or Opportunity?" last modified April 12, 2000, accessed January 2, 2018, https://www.imf.org/external/np/exr/ib/2000/041200to.htm.

Four dimensions of globalization

Scholars usually discuss the following four dimensions of globalization, and these are all straightforward. First, there is the economic aspect, whereby economic globalization is the increasing economic reliance of national economies across the world through a fast increase in cross-border movement of finance, technology, products, and services.

While the globalization of business is emphasized by the reduction of international commerce regulations as well as taxes, tariffs, and other hindrances that suppress global commerce, economic globalization is the process of increasing economic integration among nations, leading to the eruption of a global marketplace or a single world market for global trade. Depending on the underlying theory, economic globalization can be looked upon as either a negative or positive experience.

Economic globalization consists of a number of factors. There is the globalization of manufacturing, which refers to the acquisition of products and services from a particular source from several locations around the world to benefit from differences in quality and cost. It also comprises the globalization of trade markets, which is defined as the union of different and separate trade markets into a massive global marketplace. Economic globalization also includes competition, technology, and corporations and industries.

The second dimension of globalization is the political dimension, through which globalization may eventually lead to the decrease in the importance of nation-states. Supranational institutions such as the World Trade Organization (WTO), the European Union (EU), the G8 (the eight largest economies in the world in terms of GDP), and the International Criminal Court in The Hague (ICC) replace or extend sovereign functions to ease international agreement.

These forms of multilateral global governance express the notion that there are many interacting authority frameworks at work in the emerging global political system. They highlight the intimate entanglement between the national and global levels of authority. And, increasingly, nongovernmental organizations (NGOs) affect public policy across national borders, including development and humanitarian-aid efforts.

Third, there is the financial dimension of globalization that is illustrated by the global financial framework of institutions, legal agreements, and both formal and informal financial actors that together facilitate international flows of finance for purposes of investment and trade financing.

Fourth, there is the cultural aspect of globalization—the conveyance of meanings, values, and ideas around the globe in a way that intensifies and extends cultural and social relations. This process is characterized by the collective "consumption" that spreads through popular culture and social media, the Internet, and foremost through international travel.

The circulation of cultures allows individuals to join in extended social and cultural relations that cross both regional and national borders. Cultural globalization also involves the establishment of shared knowledge and norms with which people align their individual and collective cultural identities. Consequently, it brings increasing interconnectedness among different cultures and populations.

There is also a set of other equally important but less discussed dimensions of globalization, such as environmental globalization. The latter aspect involves internationally coordinated practices and regulations, often in the form of international treaties, regarding environmental protection. There is also military globalization—the growth in the global extent and scope of security relationships. The North Atlantic Treaty Organization (NATO) is a perfect example of this.

The current global financial system

Global cross-border capital influxes, including stock and bond trading, lending, and foreign direct investment (FDI), have decreased by 65 percent since 2007, from $12.4 trillion to $4.3 trillion in 2016. Half that decrease reflects a steep reduction in cross-border banking activities. But it would be erroneous to believe that financial globalization is over. New research from the McKinsey Global Institute, "The New Dynamics of Financial Globalization,"[98] observes that what is emerging from the ashes is a more rational, risk-sensitive, and ultimately a more resilient version of global financial integration.

Figure 7: Global Cross-Border Capital Flows

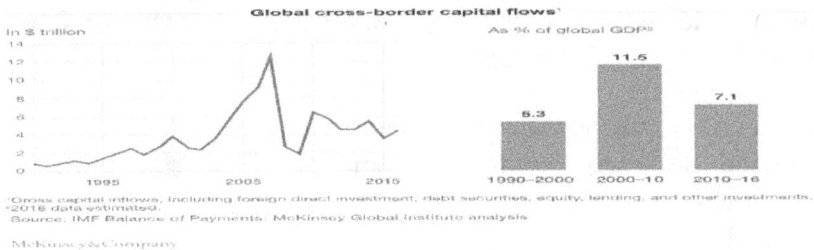

Global cross-border capital flows have declined 65 percent since the 2007 peak.

Source: McKinsey & Company

Notwithstanding the diminishment in global banking, the story of financial globalization continues. The global volume of foreign investment relative to GDP has changed little over the past eight years, standing today at roughly 180 percent of world GDP. In absolute terms, total foreign investments increased to $132 trillion in 2016, up from $103 trillion eight years earlier.[99] More

---

[98] Susan Lund et al., "The New Dynamics of Financial Globalization," McKinsey & Company, August 2017, accessed February 20, 2018,
https://www.mckinsey.com/~/media/McKinsey/Industries/Financial%20Services/Our%20Insights/The%20new%20dynamics%20of%20financial%20globalization/MGI-Financial-globalization-Executive-summary-Aug-2017.ashx.

than 25 percent of equities around the globe are owned by foreign investors, up from 17 percent in 2000.

In global bond markets, 31 percent of bonds were owned by foreign investors in 2016, up from 18 percent in 2000. International lending is the only aspect of foreign investment that has decreased since the global financial crisis in 2007 and 2008. While the volume of foreign investments remains highly concentrated among a couple of developed economies, more states are participating in this process of foreign investment.

MGI's Financial Connectedness Ranking[100] illustrates the total volume of foreign investment for a hundred countries, as well as their growth and composition. Developed economies and global financial centers are the most highly integrated into this globalized system. The United States, Luxembourg, the United Kingdom, the Netherlands, and Germany represent the top five countries in this MGI ranking.

But emerging countries are also becoming increasingly more connected to the world of global finance. Their portion of total foreign investment has increased from 8 percent to 14 percent in the past decade.[101]

Most notable is China's rise in global finance; the country rose from sixteenth place in 2005 to eighth in 2016. China's total volume of foreign bank lending, foreign direct investment, and portfolio equity and bond investments reached $3.4 trillion in 2016, exceeding its $3.2 trillion of central-bank foreign-reserve assets—a remarkable change.

---

[99] Ibid.
[100] Ibid.
[101] Gabriel Wildau, "Foreign Bank Lending to China Hits Record High," *Financial Times*, November 8, 2017, accessed March 4, 2018, https://www.ft.com/content/64e14e70-c510-11e7-a1d2-6786f39ef675.

The most significant difference in the postcrisis global financial system has been in cross-border lending activities. Indeed, as a result of the GFC, several large European banks, particularly those in the eurozone, are leading the retreat from overseas markets.[102]

Foreign claims of eurozone banks, including loans, lending by foreign subsidiaries, and other international assets have fallen by $7.3 trillion, or 45 percent, since 2007.[103] Nearly half has taken place within intra-eurozone borrowing, with interbank lending falling the most.

The international claims of UK, Swiss, and other noneurozone European banks have dropped by $2.1 trillion. Several of the most significant US banks are shifting their portfolios away from international activities, too.

[102] Dirk Schoenmaker, "What Happened to Global Banking after the Crisis?" Brueghel, March 14, 2017, accessed February 20, 2018, http://bruegel.org/2017/03/what-happened-to-global-banking-after-the-crisis/.
[103] Susan Lund and Hans-Helmut Kotz, "Financial Globalization 2.0," McKinsey & Company, September 5, 2017, accessed January 21, 2018, https://www.mckinsey.com/mgi/overview/in-the-news/financial-globalization-2.

Figure 8: Foreign Claims of W-European Banks & Other Advanced Economies

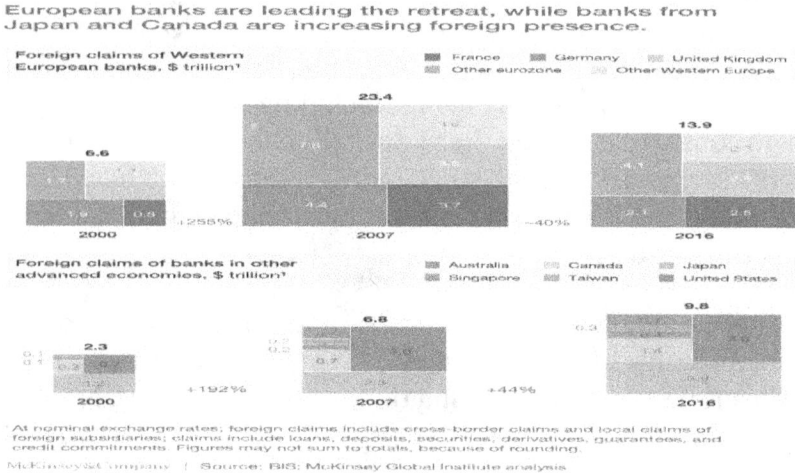

European banks are leading the retreat, while banks from Japan and Canada are increasing foreign presence.

The international financial markets

The global financial market is the place where financial wealth is exchanged among individuals, organizations, and countries. In other words, the global financial market connects investors to depositors across national boundaries by providing investors with a vast choice of investment products across a myriad of financial markets. It can be analyzed as a comprehensive set of rules and institutions where assets are exchanged between agents in a surplus and agents in a deficit and where organizations lay down the rules.

Global financial markets consist of mainly international banking and money-market activities. The banking services include activities such as foreign exchange, trade financing, project finance, hedging instruments like forwards and options, and so on. All these banking activities are provided by global banks. The international money market includes euro credits, euro notes, the euro-currency markets, euro commercial paper, and so on.

International markets primarily service multinational corporations. Businesses or traders with export and import activities are also frequent users of these markets.

Types of international markets

The global financial markets can be segmented as follows: 1) the foreign-exchange (FX) market; 2) the international money market (MM); 3) global capital markets consisting of the bond markets, stock markets, mutual funds, and exchange-traded funds; 4) the interbank market; 5) the commodities markets; and 6) the derivatives market. Every nation in the world has or is connected to a financial market.

Figure 9: Types of International Markets

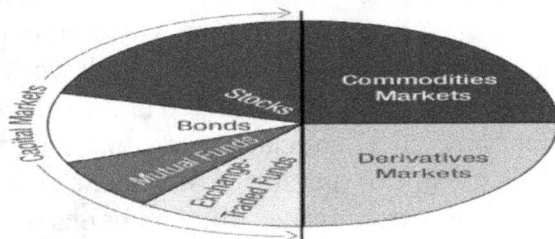

Source: Center for Capital Markets Competitiveness[104]

Some financial markets are tiny, with only a few participants, while others—such as the New York Stock Exchange (NYSE), Euronext, and the Forex markets—trade trillions of dollars daily. Investors utilize a vast array of financial markets representing a large number of lending and investment products.

Some of these financial markets have always been accessible to private investors; others remained the privileged domain of

[104] Anjan Thakor, "International Financial Markets: A Diverse System Is the Key to Commerce," Center for Capital Markets Competitiveness, February 10, 2015, accessed February 18, 2018, http://keytocommerce.com/assets/pdfs/international-financial-markets-report.pdf.

major global banks and financial agents until the very end of the twentieth century. In addition to these types of product markets, there are also markets segmented depending on the sort of sellers and buyers. At this moment, for example, we refer to the primary and secondary markets, the over-the-counter (OTC) markets, and the third and fourth markets. (A search on the Internet will provide an exact definition for each of these types of markets.)

Global financial system architecture

While global financial markets help companies tap liquid pools of capital to grow, these markets are just one component of a worldwide financial ecosystem. A global financial system includes financial institutions as well as financial markets. A long-standing question in finance has to do with the framework of the financial system: that is, the relative roles played by banking institutions and financial markets in the allocation of capital to individuals and organizations.[105] The question is which framework works better for economic growth: a market-dominated architecture or a bank-dominated structure? In a financial system dominated by capital markets, such as the one in the United States, the economy relies more on the bond and stock markets than on banks to allocate capital and finance projects.

However, in a bank-dominated financial system, such as the one in continental Europe, banks are more important than capital markets in allocating capital and credit to businesses and households. It is by now widely acknowledged that better-functioning financial systems (i.e., those that are more open and competitive) improve resource and capital allocations, irrespective of whether the financial system is market or bank dominated. Moreover, financing provided through external

---

[105] One of the earliest theoretical analyses of financial-system architecture appears in Arnoud Boot and Matej Marinc, "Financial Innovations, Marketability, and Stability in Banking," Research Handbook on International Banking and Governance, 2011, doi: 10.4337/9781849802932.00035.

sources has a more significant impact on different industries in more financially developed countries.[106]

Studies indicate that markets and financial intermediaries both affect economic growth, and that reverse causality alone (meaning that there is a higher demand for the financial services in more well-developed economies) does not fuel the findings of these studies.[107] The underlying reason for that is the fact that better-developed financial systems facilitate firms' financing restrictions, making it easier and less expensive to raise capital. However, specific features of development may be affected in various ways by whether a financial system is bank or market dominated. For instance, we may wish to know whether financial innovation is likely to be more significant in a given system or if technological advances are more likely in one system than the other.

One theoretical contribution has shown that market-dominated financial systems, in which commercial and investment banks are functionally separated, tend to produce more financial innovation than bank-based financial systems.[108] We can see this in the financial developments that have occurred in the United States and the United Kingdom compared with the European mainland, for instance. Financial institutions and other financial market participants in the United States and the United Kingdom have produced an impressive array of financial innovations that have assisted households and organizations in better managing risk, making investments they would otherwise not have made, lowering their capital costs, and so on. Excellent illustrations of these innovations are derivatives (futures, options, and swap contracts), securitization, mutual funds, and exchange-traded

[106] Ross Levine and Sara Zervos, "Stock Markets, Banks, and Economic Growth," *The American Economic Review* 88(3) (1998), 537–58.
[107] Ross Levine, "Finance and Growth: Theory and Evidence," NBER Working Paper 10766, September 2004, doi: 10.3386/w10766.
[108] Boot and Marinc, "Financial Innovations, Marketability, and Stability in Banking," 2011.

funds (ETFs), just to name a few. All these financial innovations are attributable to the United States and the United Kingdom but are now utilized globally in huge volumes, a testimony to the added value that these financial advances provide to the global economy.

Similarly, recent empirical research has examined whether a country's type of financial system (bank or market dominated) affects its rate of technological change, with a positive impact on long-run economic growth.[109] The dependent variable in this empirical study is technological change, and the critical independent variable is the country's financial framework.[110]

Other independent variables include the importance of banking accounted for by global banks as well as measures of banking concentration, such as the percentage of banking assets in the hands of the top three banks. The study's primary finding is that a more market-oriented financial system results in higher technological progress.

Additionally, technological advances are also positively affected by a more significant presence of international banking institutions and a more competitive banking system (i.e., one that exhibits lower concentration among a few large banks and has a lower lending-deposit interest-rate spread).

A stronger propensity on the part of companies to go public, not to mention a lower stock market volatility, also points to the importance of a financial system that is well developed and in which stock, bond, and derivatives markets flourish. In essence, this means having the appropriate amount of capital market

---

[109] The discussion below is based on Luca Giordano and Claudia Guagliano, "Financial Architecture and the Source of Growth: International Evidence on Technological Change," *Quaderni di Finanza*, 2014, doi:10.2139/ssrn.2474991.

[110] Financial architecture is measured by how total stock-market capitalization relative to GDP compares with bank credit relative to GDP, measures of market efficiency (total value of shares traded divided by average market capitalization), and so on.

regulation, but not so much that it inhibits growth, stifles innovation, and creates such excessive costs of compliance that companies ultimately choose to go to another regulatory jurisdiction.[111]

Another point to keep in mind is that one cannot conclude from research, such as the item highlighted here, that capital markets should be developed to the detriment of well-functioning and robust banking systems.

Anecdotally, a study of the Romanian financial system, for example, highlights that if attention in reforming a formerly centrally planned economy is focused primarily on establishing a stock market when the local banking system itself remains in its infancy, then the domestic economy will not reap the benefits of market development that would otherwise be found in marketplaces with stable banking systems.[112]

The underlying reason is that banks play essential roles in a market's function. One of these tasks is lending to opaque borrowers and enabling them to develop as creditworthy firms before going public. Other functions that banks can fulfill are, for instance, providing loan commitments to state enterprises, providing lines of credit to back up commercial-paper issues in the capital market, and expanding access to liquidity.[113]

Thus, if the financial system doesn't have a robust banking system, it is difficult for the bond and equity markets to function efficiently.[114]

---

[111] See Boot and Marinc, "Financial Innovations, Marketability, and Stability in Banking," 2011, for a discussion of this issue.
[112] Anjan Thakor, "International Financial Markets: A Diverse System is the Key to Commerce," Center for Capital Markets Competitiveness, February 10, 2015.
[113] See Boot and Marinc, "Financial Innovations, Marketability, and Stability in Banking," 2011, for a discussion of this issue.
[114] See Thakor, "International Financial Markets," 2015.

Agents of geofinance

As already alluded to, the globalization of capital markets goes hand in hand with the fall of national markets and the rise of international markets. The market in which residents of different countries exchange financial assets is called the international capital market. This market is not a single market; instead, it is a group of tightly interconnected markets in which asset exchanges with some international dimension take place.[115]

The main actors in the global finance realm are central banks, commercial banks, large corporations, nonbank financial institutions, treasury departments, regulators, and other government agencies. Global finance activities occur in a network of international financial centers connected by sophisticated communications systems. The professionalization of the markets amplifies the tendencies and dynamics of the market, meaning that there is an increase in the importance of professional investors who possess the same information and behave similarly. This results in their actions sometimes provoking brutal shocks, because all reactions often coincide (behavioral finance).

Aside from the typical financial actors active in the global financial markets, an array of nonfinancial institutions are also key in economic processes. I want to focus in particular on corporations, as they are counterintuitive actors in international finance—particularly those with multinational activities such as Toyota, Volkswagen, Procter and Gamble, British Petroleum, Coca-Cola, IBM, and Nike. These firms routinely finance their investments by drawing on foreign sources of funds. To obtain these funds, corporations may sell shares of stock, which give owners an equity claim to the corporation's assets, or they may

[115] Oana Mionel, "The Globalization of Financial Markets and the Main Actors," *Knowledge Horizons–Economics* 5(3) (2013), 66–8, accessed February 20, 2018, http://orizonturi.ucdc.ro/arhiva/2013_khe_3_pdf/khe_vol_5_iss_3_66to68.pdf.

use debt finance. Debt finance often takes the form of borrowing from and through international banks or other institutional lenders; when longer-term financing is desired, firms may sell corporate debt instruments in the global capital market.

Corporations frequently denominate their bonds in the currency of the financial center in which the securities are being issued for sale. Increasingly, however, companies have been pursuing novel denomination strategies that make their bonds attractive to a broader spectrum of potential buyers.

In addition to these financial and nonfinancial actors that are active in the international capital markets, there are also multilateral bodies (OCDE, G20, the European Union, etc.) as well as government agencies that have gained experience in global finance, such as foreign-affairs departments and their diplomats, intelligence agencies, ministries of finance, justice departments, and, of course, regulators and central-bank authorities.

While many may think that global finance has grown out of reach and beyond the control of national actors, it is the latter who have encouraged and permitted the process. States have indeed supported financial globalization by granting freedom to market actors through deregulation and liberalization initiatives and by choosing not to implement more efficient controls on financial movements. Contrary to common belief, states have enthusiastically embraced the financial globalization trend because of the growing domestic prominence of neoliberal advocates and internationally oriented corporate interests.

Last but not least, the intellectuals of geofinance also play a key role—the academics, consultants, and pundits who frequently participate in and make comments about the nexus between global finance and geopolitics. These professionals command the institutional and cultural resources necessary to project specific geofinancial arguments as authoritative and informed. Consequently, they cautiously uncover the ways in which global finance affects the realm of geopolitics and vice versa. However, to emphasize the intellectuals of geofinance is not to grant authentic or superior expertise to them or to unnecessarily embellish the high intellectual circles they rub elbows with.

What Is the Added Value of Geofinance?

Benefits of studying geofinance

Geofinance is the study of the spatial, cultural, and strategic aspects of resources with the aim of gaining sustainable financial benefit for government and corporate organizations alike. It is a continuation of the rationale of geopolitics, applied to the era of global finance. Consequently, the study is most relevant in the context of broader strategic entities such as nations, international banks, and multinational enterprises, all of which continuously face global competitive issues. Geofinance is an alternative multidisciplinary direction for the study of finance.

The discipline of geofinance is different from that of geopolitics in two fundamental ways. First, it is not primarily concerned with political and military activities but with financial operations. Second, geofinancial actions are not undertaken chiefly by individuals representing nation-states but by employees of private-sector organizations, whose loyalties are first and foremost to the owners of those organizations. However, geofinance, like geopolitics, is studied first of all with the interests of the nation-state in mind, or from the macro perspective. This makes it more complicated than the research of geopolitics, in which the state itself is the crucial actor.

Both geopolitics and geofinance are intimately connected to the study of strategy, in which we try to define an optimal plan for organizational or institutional objectives. As in the review of policy, right decisions are recognized as dependent on intelligence (i.e., valuable information). For the modern enterprise, it is not enough merely to conduct market research, which was traditionally carried out by a market-research department and is now frequently outsourced. It must become an intelligence organization in its own right, gathering information systematically not only about financial markets and customers but also about the other micro factors: venture capitalists, pension funds, banks, and the sector in general.

As if that is not enough, it also needs to collect information about the macro environment: financial, legal, cultural, sociopolitical, infrastructure, ecological, and technical factors. The underlying reason for this is that global markets and businesses have become more reliant on each other. What takes place in one company in one part of the globe today can have an immediate effect on another firm in another part of the world. The world's stock exchanges are a good illustration. With globalization comes greater mobility and much shorter business cycles, vulnerability, and interdependence.

The transition from major global corporation to failure can often be quite swift. The only way for firms to react quickly enough in this environment consistently is to develop an intelligence capability. This is one of the significant lessons of the information age—which, we should keep in mind, has existed for only twenty years. In the future, companies will rely on ever more advanced corporate intelligence systems.

The importance of a sound intelligence system has become increasingly visible during the past thirty to forty years, primarily for two underlying reasons: the abundance of information now available due to new technologies (mainly the Internet), and as a result, the need to distinguish between "nice to know" and "need to know." To deal with data overload and the requirement for assistance in analyzing it, organizations are developing a range of new software under the label of business intelligence.

Business intelligence solutions are fast becoming the nerve centers of large corporations whose very existence depends on their capability to mutate and adapt rapidly. Nation-states that want to attract multinational enterprises and remain competitive in the future need to understand this new situation and develop their systems for economic intelligence—the state's perspective and policies on these issues.

The great manipulation: Is geofinance destiny?

Can both the "Great Game" and the "invisible hand" be trusted? Repeats of historical events and financial crises are never exact mirrors of the past, but their repetitiveness does "rhyme," although they may differ in scale, magnitude, and reach. It is commonly said that geography is destiny, but geofinance is also destiny—since, to a considerable extent, geopolitics in combination with finance remains a strong indicator of future actions.

Timeless concepts such as balance of power (defined during the Napoleonic wars), divide and conquer (alluded to by Caesar and Napoleon), and, to a lesser extent, the invisible hand (coined in 1776 by Adam Smith in *The Wealth of Nations*) are indeed relatively as old as time, yet equally old is the intuition that the more distant the practitioners of such strategies or markets, the less likely they are to be directly affected by the negative consequences of their actions. This makes them potentially more damaging in the theaters they target.

Financial crises bear similarities. A significant one is the misuse of money supply by central banks. Regarding financial markets, memories are short—we seem to forget that central banks and regulators can bear massive liability for creating or perpetuating environments that foster financial crises or make them worse due to poor crisis-management skills. Though crises repeat over and over, each new cohort of investors believes that this time, it will be different, and so it dooms itself to repeat the mistakes of the previous generation.

Even when investors seek to learn the lessons of the past, they often try to fight previous wars. However, what drives one market cycle rarely hits the next, and so better analogies are sometimes found further back in time. Unfortunately, the current yield environment combined with Basel III will be a vector for the next crisis, as it is similar to the yield environment in the early 2000s in combination with Basel II.

Geostrategically speaking, it is no matter that a century has passed. One universal objective remains: namely, that the naval powers must utilize all methods (including intrigue and massive bloodletting) to prevent the Eurasian continental powers from conspiring against them. The continuum of history eerily highlights that the shadows of the past still hang over the heads of the future, and the thematic lessons leading up to and following global conflicts still ring dangerously true today.

The geopoliticians Alfred Mahan and Halford Mackinder understood this well at the turn of the nineteenth century. Alfred Mahan's 1890 *The Influence of Sea Power Upon History*[116] postulated that naval power is vital to controlling the mainland; Mackinder took this a step further in 1904 with *The Geopolitical Pivot of History*,[117] stating that sea power's obvious geographic limitations necessitate firm control over the heartland to dominate Eurasia. (This was initially understood as Central Asia in the Great Game, but its meaning has shifted over time.)

Interestingly, in relation to the creation of a continental Eurasian powerhouse, Brzezinski's *The Grand Chessboard*[118] cautioned US decision makers about the possibility (then distant, but today much closer) of a German-Russian alliance that would isolate

[116] Alfred T. Mahan, *The Influence of Sea Power Upon History* (New York: Little, Brown & Company, 1890).
[117] Halford J. Mackinder, "The Geographical Pivot of History," *The Geographical Journal* 23(4) (1904), 421–37.
[118] Zbigniew Brzezinski, *The Grand Chessboard: American Primacy and Its Geostrategic Imperatives* (New York: Basic Books, 1997).

America from Europe and thus collapse America's Eurasian strategy.

Allowing for this geopolitically, it makes sense that there is so much Western guilt mongering against Germany for supposedly starting WWI; the objective is to keep Germany and Russia divided and prevent their policy coordination. The spate of "color revolutions" is aimed solely at penetrating the former Soviet heartland and removing Russia from the great-power game. On the naval front, the United States continues trying to bait China into a disastrous collision course with its Asian neighbors over disputed maritime territories in the South and East China Seas.

The lesson should be that the combination of land and naval power, adequately applied and coordinated across Eurasia, is the primary formula for global control. A moment's glance at the geographical map of US overseas naval and military deployments easily evidences Mahan and Mackinder's theories without any additional words necessary. Because geography cannot be modified, these notions will continue to guide the United States and any other aspiring global hegemon. In today's world, the United States has merged Brzezinski's Eurasian Balkans concept with Gene Sharp's mass-agitation tactics (abetted by social media networks) to conceive the weapon of color revolutions to accomplish just that.

However, as an unintended consequence, Washington's recent policies regarding the Ukraine crisis have actually and unfortunately pushed Moscow into the hands of Beijing, which is feeling equally hindered by the United States in its South and East China Seas policies. This creates potentially the most significant Eurasian powerhouse history has ever witnessed, using the Shanghai Cooperation Organization (SCO).

Nations enter into military alliances with one another for some perceived benefit, which may vary depending on the actor. Russia needs China as a massive market, while Beijing needs Moscow for its energy and military know-how, and both face a common threat: the West (perhaps Washington and Europe, but also Japan and Australia, for instance).

But, as history shows, the larger alliance systems grow (SCO or NATO), the more convoluted they become, eventually ensnaring all who are weaved into the web. Large-scale wars can thus start based on miscalculation or peripheral events. Indeed, the larger the alliance is, the greater the chance for unintended outbreaks of major war and for middle players to manipulate the other members. Alliances can complicate the political situation just as much as they can clarify it. The unfortunate great manipulation is that history and power perception have not changed over time: Eurasia was and will remain a key battleground where the great powers will use the existing military alliances to manipulate history and to achieve their geostrategic objectives.

Maybe surprisingly, manipulative balancing powers paradoxically have both foresight and blindness. They have a specific vision of what global or regional order should look like, yet to bring this concept to fruition, they must make many difficult moves in advance. However, they also show a blindness to the fact that when risky gambits of colossal consequence are made, unintended consequences of varying nature usually follow (such as Moscow and Beijing becoming partners of convenience), and more than likely, these tend to have disastrous results for some or all the affected parties.

Concerning financial markets, the best analogies are sometimes found further back in time. For instance, following WWII, the Federal Reserve Bank engaged in a period of quantitative easing by manipulating the money supply. Indeed, between the mid-1940s and the early 1950s, the Fed scooped up pretty much all Treasury bonds in a bid to keep yields low. Despite periodic spikes in inflation, yields remained below 3 percent. So when people worry today what might happen to the capital markets when the US monetary stimulus is totally unwound, they don't have to guess. They can look at what happened on Wall Street seventy years ago.

The great manipulation of capital markets seems to be reaching its limits. Bubbles are significant, and so are threats. The central banks' money-printing engines, along with low interest rates, are working perfectly well. The yields on sovereign bonds are at historic lows in the United Kingdom, Germany, United States, and France. In fact, they are working too well; those securities do not even match the inflation rate—a visible sign of a bubble.

Indeed, the recent financial crisis was not about a lack of capital buffers but about excessive leverage in poorly underwritten financial products and an erosion of confidence leading to a fall of liquidity that triggered payment defaults. But then again, the reason that so much was invested into poorly underwritten financial products was an anesthetized environment where volatility had been eliminated and risk deemed inexistent, driving banks to operate outside their comfort zones in a quest for higher speculative yields.

Another industry where money could find safety was real estate. However, even if we witness bubbles and tensions here and there (in China, emerging countries, or specific areas in Australia and Europe), investors are not ready to plunge, not even ten years after the subprime crisis. So we observe that, within significant asset classes, limits have been reached. Central banks cannot lower their key rates, already at nearly zero; sovereign bonds cannot indefinitely yield less than price inflation; and the equity market cannot make believe that the economy is fundamentally better than it was in 2007. The real estate market is making a little progress and is still an alternative, but actors remain prudent.

The issue is that high indicators are bets on the economy's capability to bounce back and the countries' capacities to undo their substantial debt mountains, which is not happening at the moment. To the contrary, public debt in the United States, Europe, and Japan continues to climb. There is a blatant and growing disconnection between the real economy and the financial markets, and this cannot last for long. The little growth achieved is through the "wealth effect," whereas only an improvement in productivity followed by a rise in income may give birth to healthy growth. But tough luck—corporate investment remains depressed.

During the last significant period of growth, bought with credit (2000 to 2006), gold played its role of warning signal by clearly rising, showing that credit had exceeded the economy's capacity, and too much money was being created. This time, its price is more erratic, but it is under surveillance. After discreetly staying around $300 an ounce in the '80s and '90s, its rise, starting in 2000, put it in the spotlight. And when it got too close to $2,000 per ounce in August 2011, central banks and sovereign states did not appreciate their paper currencies being so utterly pushed aside. Since that time, as we know, the price has more or less been manipulated to the downside.

Geofinance as a risk-management tool

There is a new world of geofinancial risk management. Most of us, including entrepreneurs and financial professionals, are becoming increasingly aware of the global world in which we operate—a global society that is rife with volatility and uncertainty. And this volatility and change are mainly driven by political and financial events that shape all regions and markets throughout the world. These events were once viewed as highly infrequent and irregular and described by mathematicians as fat-tail events:[119] events with low probability but high severity.

---

[119] Fat-tail events are statistically unusual circumstances, also known by the buzzword *black swans*

In the current environment, understanding the interaction between financial markets and geopolitics is paramount for investors and entrepreneurs for predicting the outcome of an investment, be it financial or business related. And this is where geofinance steps in—by marrying geography, in its broadest sense, with financial markets and business activities. Put another way, it looks at the landscape of financial and business geography from a risk-management perspective. Therefore, spotting future financial market trends and political events can be difficult to quantify, mainly fat-tail events. But without a doubt, they count. Market participants and entrepreneurs today cannot afford to step into the world without exploring phenomena that might not express themselves in numbers.

In practical terms, money and finance are necessary to the form and operation of the economic landscape, yet traditionally, risk managers have accorded relatively little attention to the spatialities of financial systems. At Value4Risk, we were concerned with exploring this small area and constructing a new economic geography of finance from a risk-management perspective. Its crucial underlying objective was to show that the spatial structure of the global financial system is far from neutral in its consequences but instead influences the risk allocation of funds, capital, and credit across firms, institutions, regions, and localities.

In recent years, financial systems in many advanced countries have undergone rapid and transformative change as globalization, new technologies, and deregulation have combined to stimulate organizational change within and among financial institutions (such as concentration, centralization, rationalization, and outsourcing), the emergence of new avenues of finance (such as

---

that was popularized a few years ago by Nassim Taleb. In essence, a fat-tail event refers to an unexpectedly high occurrence of what we thought were or should have been statistically improbable events. For *fat tails*, just think "very unusual events."

venture capital), and increasing uncertainty and volatility in capital markets. Some have argued that globalization and further information and communications technologies are increasingly rendering geography and location irrelevant in financial risk management, but they are wrong. Location remains key to the conduct and risk management of financial markets and transactions and to how economic decision making and the allocation of capital remain concentrated in the major cash centers, with the implication that markets and regions lacking such centers and those remote from them could well be weak in accessing finance, at least on the same terms and conditions as regions and locations containing financial centers.

Associated work highlights how critical changes in the financial system, such as the privatization of public utilities and industries involving the sale of vast numbers of shares to the public and the operation of pension funds, have benefitted regions that contain the primary financial markets and institutions. So, from a risk-management perspective, financial geography really matters. It matters that we understand the geographic nature of the flows and stocks of finance and financial investment in a firm, region, and country and on a global basis. Where there are geographic needs, geofinancial risk management is a powerful weapon either to mitigate or reinforce them.

Disclosure of financial and banking flows therefore also really matter. They mean that we can map how financial investment and banking finance match up, or don't, with the areas of greatest need and, indeed, map the greatest economic opportunity. From this, we can see the gaps and opportunities in finance and banking—and whether finance and banking are part of the problem or part of the solution in making business investments, yielding earnings, and creating jobs, economic prosperity, and opportunity.

In determining the state of international financial markets, geofinancial risk managers seek to demonstrate the importance of considerations such as the acquisition of natural boundaries, access to vital sea routes, and the control of strategically important land areas. Geofinancial factors have become more significant in the global economy because of the growing importance of financial markets' improvements in communications and transportation.

Geofinance traditionally studies the links between financial power and geographic space and examines strategic prescriptions based on the relative importance of capital markets' power as well as, more generally speaking, the financial and capital strengths of businesses and companies in world history. The geofinancial tradition has had some consistent concerns with geofinancial correlations of power in world politics, the identification of general core areas, and the relationships between financial markets and business capabilities.

Academically, the study of geofinance analyzes geography, history, and social science concerning spatial finance and patterns at various scales. Geofinance also studies the relations between the interests of international financial actors, interests focused on an area, space, and geographical element,—relationships that create a geofinancial system. Geofinance is multidisciplinary and includes all features of the social sciences, with a particular focus on economic geography, international relations, and the territorial issues of economic science, international finance, and business law.

While finance and risk management are well-established research topics in economics, it is only relatively recently that the other social sciences have changed their focus on capital markets. Each of these disciplines has something to add to the overall academic picture. Financial economics starts from a perspective where real-life financial data are contrasted with model-based outcomes to explain the irrationalities of economic actors and the imperfections of existing markets. International and comparative political economy stress the importance of deregulatory measures and institutions to understanding the growing importance of capital.

This is where geography becomes essential. The very essence of today's geopolitics is exploring the spatial impacts of changing social practices and its reverse: analyzing how spatial and physical structures frame the dynamics of social practices. The money world is what geographers call a space of flows—partly real and partly virtual streams that directly and indirectly mold the areas of places. Money flows and their organization have strong links with the spatial structure of consumption and production. Like the way the Industrial Revolution modified the townscapes and landscapes of the nineteenth and twentieth centuries, the banking and money revolution of the 1980s and 1990s changed the physical aspects of capital cities and metropolitan regions all over the globe.

Geofinancial analysis

Geofinancial analysis is a research tool that analyzes the probability of an organization's expected profit or loss resulting from financial markets' movements due to political decisions, geographical conditions, or events occurring in the country or emerging market in which a business is operating or is affected by. A keen understanding of financial geography in combination with the behavior of financial markets has been proven vital to the success of business projects, especially those that are potentially controversial and involve, for instance, regional politics and border issues.

Geofinancial analysis can be defined as the study of the effects of geography (both human and physical) on international financial actors and markets as well as international trade, with a particular viewpoint on how the combination of these events affect the financial risk profile of a business or financial institution. Geofinance is a method of financial risk analysis that seeks to understand, explain, and predict international financial behavior primarily regarding geographical variables. Typical geographical variables are the physical location, size, climate, topography, demography, natural resources, and technological advances that potentially affect financial actors. Back in the day, the concept was utilized with regard to the impact of geography on finance, but its use has changed over the past hundred years to encompass broader connotations.

A geofinancial analysis consists of the following:

- evaluation of the international financial market that an organization relies on

- study of the capital markets' industry movement and actions in relation to the organization

- analysis of the severity of exposure of the organization with regard to changes in the financial markets driven by geographical and geopolitical events or other market forces, how they affect the financial risk profile of the organization, and to what extent they may hinder organizational opportunities

- analysis of the financial environment in which an organization is operating

Guiding principles of geofinance: financial versus political strength

1. Financial strength is as important as political power.

2. Within the current banking system, the United States is, for now, a free rider. However, as finance becomes global, that

country is losing its leadership. Already, the Chinese and Russians are attempting to derail the supremacy of the US dollar, but their actions will remain impotent so long as US Treasury bills retain a high rating. This could potentially change, given the weak public finances of the United States.

3. The biggest consumer market is no longer the United States but China and India.

4. Just as numbers of weapons and soldiers are the best way to win a war, so financial strength—quantity of assets—is the best way to gain market share. The battlefield consists of industries and markets.

5. A new world order is arising through a transformation of the financial world that has never before been witnessed in world history.

6. The competitive factors for a nation are:

   - its technological-industrial strength;

   - its substantial financial reserves (China's reserves are more than $3 trillion, and its debt amounts to $4.3 trillion, compared to the United States' more than $20 trillion of debt);

   - a vibrant, strong culture;

   - a power-projection capacity to send troops quickly to any corner of the globe and to execute military operations effectively;

   - a capacity and willingness to learn from and about the world in which we live; and

   - the existence of a certain sociopolitical consensus in domestic politics.

7. Of the twelve largest stock exchanges on the globe, five are now in Asia, including three in China alone: the Hong Kong

Exchanges, the Shanghai Stock Exchange, and the Shenzhen Stock Exchange. Economic strength has shifted to the East.

8. Some see the new international marketplace as a battlefield and the new world order as a return to the Middle Ages.

9. Do not be fooled by the hype about the knowledge economy and new service sector as superior business strategies for growth. While these are critical, you still need to significantly export to become a financial/economic power.

10. If you do not have large volumes of financial reserves, you will not be respected as a country. Paris gave only 10 percent of the amount that Berlin gave to Central European countries immediately after the Cold War in 1989. Berlin was raised from the rubble to become a global capital in not even ten years. No one had built so much so fast before. Now the Chinese are doing the same thing, only more successfully and faster. (Pudong, China's financial center, was rice fields only seventeen years ago. Chengdu-Chongqing will be the world's new industrial center.)

How to Deal with Geofinance

With the intensification of the globalization of financial markets, itself driven by the increased financialization of economies, causing them to be more vulnerable to systemic crises, one might become dazzled by the fury of these changes. But that may be because we look at things from the perspective of privileging stability. In other words, we look for ways to stabilize whatever is unstable. However, while it might sound counterintuitive, we need to navigate the waves and embrace inherent instability instead.

Similar to a vessel navigating on top of the waves in the middle of the ocean, we need to navigate our organizations. If, instead, we drop anchor in the middle of the ocean, the ship will be hit by many big waves, causing damage and the feeling that we do not control our destiny. In that respect, nature can teach us a lot of valuable lessons on how we should embrace a seemingly destabilizing phenomenon such as geofinance. We can never go back to the past when the economy was not as financialized and international capital flows were more confined within national borders. But we should attempt to control our destiny.

Building resilient financial systems may require policy makers to take cues from biology. Similar to ecosystems, global finance is made up of compound, evolving systems from which unexpected bubbles, crashes, and other surprising behaviors can emerge[120]. Without a doubt, the current financial systems are complex and often hard to predict. And when they swing out of control, these systems tell us much about how they work and how inadequate our conventional approaches to controlling them are. In all their complexity, though, capital markets do not hold a candle to the natural world, with its ten million-plus species—those we know of, not including the millions that have come and gone—evolving and interacting in the world's forests and oceans and the microbiomes of our guts.

---

[120] Levin, "What Can Mother Nature Teach Us about Managing Financial Systems?" 2016

In 1999, Simon Levin published a book[121] about how the biosphere is organized and how complicated it is. And, as with our financial systems, our efforts to intervene in it have often led to confusing results. Puzzlingly, the more orderly a market looks, the less stable it actually is. Think about dominoes standing on a table. If they are distributed randomly, knocking one over has little effect. However, if they are in a line, the whole lot of dominoes will come down.

To use an analogy, for seven-plus decades, the famous icon of Smokey Bear has reminded us how important it is to prevent wildfires. But modern ecological practice acknowledges that suppressing all forest fires merely sets forests up for more extensive and more destructive catastrophes later. In all likelihood, financial systems are no different; small disasters are likely key to preserving their ongoing health.

But how? How might biology provide us with information about our efforts to manage markets? How can we get beyond a metaphorical comprehension of the ways that financial markets and ecosystems are alike to explore, in practical terms, what the scientific world offers our financial regulatory apparatus?

Embrace quantum physics and the immunization theory

The financial markets should be approached as an application of quantum mechanics rather than classical mechanics. Quantum principles are much better at understanding chaotic or random systems like the financial markets. Quantum mechanics explores the micro world, which has very minute scales and what seems to be bizarre, unpredictable behavior.

---

[121] Simon Levin, *Fragile Dominion: Complexity and the Commons* (New York: Perseus Publishing, 1999).

While there is some complexity here, the first analogy between quantum mechanics and the financial markets is relatively straightforward. In quantum mechanics, chaotic elements are grouped into a "black box" to neutralize ambiguity and make the result more predictable. This is not to say that pundits should dismiss the current ways of Wall Street, but they should start to approach the markets in a new, more open-minded way. Once people come around to the idea that they have been dealing with the financial markets in entirely the wrong way, they can start to take steps in the right direction.

Rather than continue to use expensive tools that have been proven to be prone to failures and imprecisions, people should start looking at a new generation of risk tools based on quantum mechanics. So what if, instead of waiting for disaster to happen, we cause a crisis to happen but on a small scale? In other words, we should inject the system with low doses of crisis to create an immunization to a broader crisis. This immunization theory has been adopted by Michael L. Hart, David Lamper, and Neil F. Johnson and labeled as "an investigation of crash avoidance in a complex system."[122]

Indeed, whoever knows the ways of nature will more readily notice her deviations, and whoever knows her differences will more accurately describe her ways. In other words, the system can be immunized by provoking a small response today, resulting in its future resiliency against large changes. In the same way, a small crash induced today can be used to prevent a much more massive crash from arising later.

[122] Michael L. Hart, David Lamper, and Neil F. Johnson, "An Investigation of Crash Avoidance in a Complex System," *Physica A: Statistical Mechanics and its Applications*, 316(1–4) (2002), 649–61, accessed February 20, 2018, https://www.sciencedirect.com/science/article/pii/S037843710201381X?via%3Dihub.

The complex-systems perspective

The "financiosphere" and biosphere are both fascinating in their complexity and have surprising similarities. Both are dynamic systems in which the separate actions of many individuals— whether they be investors or living cells—lead to hard-to-predict consequences at the system level. In turn, these collective efforts and results impact individual actions in endless cycles of evolution, mutation, and adaptation.

To a large extent, evolution is about preparing for the unknown, because the scope of possible modifications in our environments is so massive that we cannot hope to forecast their timing or shape. We can predict, however, that during our lives, we will be affected by a variety of pathogens.

Thus, vertebrates have developed a contingency plan in the form of immune systems and obstacles to infection, such as skin and cell membranes. These systems combine generalized first lines of defense and early-warning indicators that buy time while we populate our immune repertoire with more specialized antibodies tuned to the specific risks. This is akin to circuit breakers in capital markets, which shut down trading activities when volatility becomes too high.

Mammals have created regulatory systems that help maintain the stability of their overall systems. Breathing and human heart rate, for instance, are conditioned by physiological processes that correct deviations from the norm in the time scales needed for survival—kicking them into overdrive when we are being chased by a lion, for instance.

But when our physiological feedback loops are too vulnerable, too sluggish, or too robust, pathologies show up. Regulatory feedbacks that are "just right" help preserve a healthy human. Concomitantly, when the time scale of capital innovation outstrips that of prudential regulation—as in the case of high-frequency trading activities—there are most likely to be unintended results.

But prudential responses that are poorly timed or too strong, such as short-sale restrictions, emergency price controls, extreme capital constraints, and bank holidays, can result in greater panic and uncertainty among consumers and investors, ultimately leading to even less desirable results, such as rapid inflation, recessions, and housing-market crashes. Prudential feedbacks that are "just right" help keep a healthy financial environment.

Self-organized robustness

Complex interrelationship indicates the importance of preserving diversity in capital markets, in part by allowing enough exploration (that is, financial advances) to produce the required variety for a healthy financial system. But what is the adequate amount? As mentioned earlier, evolution has dealt with the diversity issue in part by administrating evolutionary processes themselves: the rate at which mutations take place, and sexual recombination, which helps ensure the production of new variants and the reassortment of genes in a population.

We tend to believe that evolutionary alteration is primarily in terms of natural selection, based on the reproductive success of individuals with desirable traits. But all complex systems, including financial ecosystems and biological systems, also exhibit self-organized patterns at scales more extensive than those at the level of individuals.

Such self-organization also "selects" by producing, from the interactions of individuals, new features that either persist or wane. The self-organized systems that continue (and that we observe) tend to have properties that make them more resilient. Such self-organization does not always result in robust systems, however; self-organized phenomena may also have the seeds of system collapse, as we witnessed during the financial crisis of 2007 to 2008, when financial innovation and unprecedented connectedness, among other factors, combined into a perfect storm to bring the system to the brink of collapse.

Still, some features of biological systems might be useful in shaping self-organized financial systems for resiliency. Redundancy is a form of insurance against unexpected losses. The American chestnut tree disappeared from the forests of the Northeastern part of the United States, but other species came in to take its place. In 2004, though, when Chiron, one of only two corporations delivering flu vaccines in the United States, announced that its manufacturing sites in Liverpool, England, were contaminated, our house of cards was threatened with disaster. We were too reliant on too few suppliers. Modularity (the inverse of connectedness) isolates related variables, restricting systemic threat by decreasing the potential for a local issue to spread to the rest of the globe.

Barriers and quarantines limit movement of infected individuals to help control the distribution of a contagion. Such approaches are used not only for the diseases of livestock but also for those that affect humans, as in the case of hoof-and-mouth disease. Similarly, modularity in financial systems can help avoid problems that show up in one industry or market from spilling over to others and bringing the whole system down.

In biology, breakdowns in size, similar to gigantism, are labeled as not healthy for biological organisms. Similarly, the unchecked development of financial organizations can result in the creation of banks that are too big to fail, which, we now know clearly, can bring down the stability of an entire financial system.

Cues from evolution

Any perspective on financial systems must acknowledge that they are ecosystems connecting stocks, flows, and agents. Similar to an environmentalist who focuses on the cycling of crucial parts in an ecosystem such as nitrogen, phosphorus, and carbon, so, too, can a financial ecologist focus on the sustainable process of cycling vital elements such as labor, financial innovations, and capital.

As we define and refine the levers by which we try to manage tomorrow's financial systems, we need to keep in mind that prudential regulations that focus on specific portions of systems often fail to see the big picture. In the buildup to the 2007–2008 crisis, for instance, bank regulators focused on the banking industry, failing to acknowledge the impact of the rapidly developing shadow-banking system and its consequences to financial stability.

Management of environmental systems in the past usually applied simple interventions, but their failures have resulted in calls for biosphere approaches—in the management of forests and fisheries, for instance. Similarly, our failures to forecast and control financial ecologies should remind us that, if anything, the interconnectedness of global capital systems is ever more critical, and a holistic approach is vital if we want to succeed.

As complex, adaptive systems, financial and natural systems share profound similarities. We should learn from billions of years of evolution. Biology and nature provide solutions to some challenges of financial regulation, not to mention the supervision and control of many other systems crucial to well-functioning societies. Indeed, similar to Mother Nature, some things benefit from chaos and shocks; they grow and thrive when exposed to randomness, volatility, stressors, disorder, adventure, risk, and uncertainty[123].

As already mentioned, immunization is an example in which the stressor is a poisonous substance, and the system becomes better overall from a small dose of the stressor. This principle can be applied in the financial markets and the financial services industry as well. To put it differently, depriving systems of vital stressors is not necessarily a good thing and can be downright harmful. A controlling force or complex-systems manager could intervene at moments when there is little cost to manipulate a winning outcome—times when it may require as little as a single agent to change the path of the system. In this way, the controlling force could prevent the crash with minimal effort or investment.

Not all geofinancial risk events are black swans

Contrary to popular belief, not all geofinancial risk events are black swans, even though interlinked markets are forcing faster asset repricing. Many geofinancial events result from correlations with the consumer-spending deflator or the GDP deflator. And since it's a more dynamic, global marketplace, the difficulty of pricing is part of investing in the worldwide market.

When analyzing countries under pressure, paying close attention to actual inflation rates may reveal clues about where civil unrest could happen next. For example, the Chinese are already exceptionally worried about inflation because in their history, it has always been a catalyst for dramatic unrest.

---

[123] Levin, "What Can Mother Nature Teach Us about Managing Financial Systems?" 2016.

The early stages of inflation throw up specific signals. The first is a gap between perceived and real inflation pressure—highlighted, for instance, by the fact that large companies would start buying raw materials three months out. Another indication is the evolution of sugar prices, which are notoriously volatile and are also being affected by civil unrest around the world. Chinese manufacturers fear a lack of food security in almost the same way as the Chinese government fears inflation. They have been setting up operations in Pakistan and Mozambique for some time, but now they're starting to acquire the companies themselves, as they are worried about inflationary wage pressures.

Elsewhere in Asia, there are indications that Vietnam could be the next Tunisia. Buying peace is expensive; it could translate into higher oil (and other) prices in the longer term. But what's the alternative? Civil unrest leads to drops in agricultural, mining, and oil production, which in turn lead to higher prices for these commodities. And with record indebtedness similar only to the interwar period between 1918 and 1939, sovereign defaults will erupt in various shapes and forms and under clever disguises such as devaluation, debt rescheduling, austerity measures, and inflation, which are ultimately forms of default and which affect a nation's own citizens, as essential services are downsized as a result of its indebtedness.

Following the stability of the past two decades, volatility and politics have again taken center stage, but geofinancial risk events are still not black-swan events. That's why it is critical to look at correlations between real inflation and civil unrest, and it is vital to differentiate between official government figures and actual inflation rates—volatile commodities, such as energy and food, may be excluded from price calculations, as is the case in Europe and the United States. For instance, even the US Consumer Price Index does not include energy and food, and therefore official figures in the United States and elsewhere underestimate the nature of price increases.

The real inflation rate in China is probably a lot closer to 6 percent than it is to 1.6 percent. In India, it is officially at 5.21 percent, while for food it is more likely around 16 percent, and in portions of the country, the real inflation rate is nearing 100 percent for core staple foods. Again, when analyzing states under pressure, paying close attention to actual inflation rates may reveal clues about where civil unrest could happen next. The Arab Spring did not begin by chance, and it was not restricted to the Middle East and North Africa.

In response to widespread unrest, states have provided salary increases, but that may not be enough in emerging markets, where workers are demanding immediate hikes because of uncertainty about the future. If, for example, as a Chinese worker, you are sure you're going to be rich before you get old, that's fine. You will keep on working diligently. But since the GFC, Chinese workers no longer have as much hope. There are probably thirty million unemployed people in China today. Wage demands out of Bangladesh are rising rapidly. Bangladeshi workers recently rioted after a doubling of the minimum wage. They apparently wanted much, much more.

Price pressure started in Mozambique some nine months before Tunisia. Of all African countries, 33 percent are currently experiencing some form of unrest. Asian countries can contain civil disorder as long as they can pay; when they stop paying, all hell breaks loose. So, as I said earlier, following the stability of the past two decades, volatility and politics have again taken center stage. And risk managers can no longer say that if you can't quantify something, it doesn't matter.

Considering the current condition of international markets, both geopolitical and financial, one has to admit that geofinancial risks are going to rise further. While market observers claim that until recently, financial markets have proved resilient to bursts of geofinancial volatility and uncertainty, current events in both

Western and emerging markets suggest that businesses need to be more aware about pricing with respect to geofinancial risk. And this means that safer assets, such as assets denominated in the US dollar, could see higher demand. Overall, businesses need to get used to the idea that a continuously simmering pot of geofinancial volatility is the new reality for the global economy..

Interestingly, the considerable degree of social dislocation and pain caused by the 2007 GFC is one reason for the rise in geofinancial risk, and thus it should be put on the risk radar. Geofinancial risk reared its ugly head after the GFC and over the past several years has become much more pronounced.

Because geofinancial risk is difficult to assess, not to mention price, many businesses and investors choose, out of ease of mind but also because they lack the resources or even the risk awareness, to ignore it. While in some countries, geofinancial instability is usual and can be ignored, in the cases of Ukraine and North Korea, it was vital to pay attention to further developments because of the broader ramifications for emerging markets.

The Crimea and North Korea are, unfortunately, not the only sources of geofinancial tension around the globe. In Asia, a territorial dispute in the East China Sea has soured relations between Tokyo and Beijing, the world's number three and two economies, respectively, not to mention the maritime dispute in the South China Sea. In Venezuela, meanwhile, antigovernment protests go on and have claimed hundreds of lives, and in Brazil the army has taken over the security of Rio de Janeiro. In Thailand, the latest chaos coincides with the rise of close-by nations such as Myanmar and the Philippines, both of which are enjoying a period of political stability and quickening growth. In contrast, rising Thai consumer debt and stalled infrastructure projects are highlighting economic threats in a country that Indonesia overtook as an investment destination seven years ago.

Add to this, interrogations about the strength of US power affected by the leading-from-behind US foreign and defense policies of the Obama era, which add to political risk globally. To some degree, the increase in global geofinancial risk has roots in the financial crisis. By far the leading cause, however, remains the relative demise or retreat of the United States as the dominant superpower. And we are now moving from a world with one dominant power to a world with no dominant force, an inherently less stable situation.

Quantum physics, predictions, and geopolitics

A better understanding of probability and uncertainty will improve the ability of organizations to assess the future state of their geopolitical environments and their ability to respond to emerging events. Many pundits tend to confuse confident predictions with accurate ones, and that can be a problem, as today's world is more complicated and interconnected than ever.

Quantum physics is hardly a perfect metaphor for geopolitics, but it is a higher-caliber one than the prevailing overly simple theories that have dominated international relations for the past several decades, such as realism, Marxism, liberalism, and constructivism. Interestingly, biologists and mathematicians are much more at ease with the reality of indeterminate complexity than social scientists. Indeed, they have accepted that we live in a system of complex systems (politics, economic, geophysical) that regularly intersect, modify, disrupt, and amplify one another.[124] Instead of treating complexity as an exception to rigid rules, quantum physics provides an approach in which everything fits sensibly.

[124] Khanna, "Want to Understand How Trump Happened?" 2016.

Being a social science, political science is by definition not an exact science, but neither is it completely amorphous. While you cannot really predict the likelihood and timing of a geopolitical event in the way that you can forecast the outcome of, for example, a storm brewing over the Atlantic Ocean, you can pick out the signal from the noise, and from that derive the likely trajectory if not the train of events.

Granted, with the advent of quantum computing, humankind can now run complicated calculations and scenarios very fast. But supercomputers will never be able to predict human behavior. Yes, big data is useful for understanding the past and finding correlations that might be useful for the future, but we will always need the agile and experienced human mind to make ultimately labyrinthine decisions, particularly relating to geopolitics.

Quantum theory is a field of theoretical physics that endeavors to understand and forecast the properties and behavior of solids, molecules, atoms, and nuclei. One aspect of the theory is that quantum fluctuations are responsible for the likelihood of all actions, with broad consequences for theories of the universe.[125] In other words, particles do not have traditional properties like position or momentum; instead, there is a wave function that determines a complex number, called the amplitude, for each possible measurement outcome.

One odd feature of quantum physics relates to predictability. Classical mechanics is, in essence, deterministic, meaning that if you know the exact situation as it is now, then you can forecast with precision what it will be at any moment in the future. In other words, randomness plays no role in classical mechanics. In contrast, quantum mechanics is probabilistic; even in the presence of exact knowledge of today's situation, it is impossible

[125] Andy Fell, "Does Probability Come from Quantum Physics?" *UC Davis Newsletter*, February 5, 2013, https://www.ucdavis.edu/news/does-probability-come-quantum-physics/.

to forecast its future precisely, regardless of how much work and care you invest in such a prediction.[126] All these behaviors, such as solutions to the "prisoner's dilemma," which may have seemed irrational under classical probability models, suddenly become explainable through quantum theory.

The uncertainty principle is important

There are so many factors affecting geofinancial events and decisions, including ego and sense of humiliation, that one can never predict with absolute certainty the ultimate scenario that will drive a future geopolitical event. In layman's terms, there is a divide between how good we believe we are at prediction and how good we actually are.

To address that gap, we can improve our forecasting capabilities with new technologies that leverage big data more efficiently and think more holistically. But concomitantly, it might also mean that somehow, we need to lower our expectations and acknowledge the existence of complexity, as jarring as that might be for us.

It is pointless to believe that we can forecast something to a high degree of certainty when we just cannot. Werner Heisenberg's uncertainty principle, a key point in quantum physics, states that the more precisely a particle's position is determined, the less precisely its momentum is known. This principle tells us that there are ambiguity and uncertainty in nature, a fundamental limit to what we can know about the behavior, in the case of quantum physics, of quantum particles (the smallest gradation of nature). We can extend this phenomenon to human behavior as it relates to geopolitics: this is called quantum cognition, a new research area that proposes that the mathematical principles

---

[126] Daniel F. Styer, *The Strange World of Quantum Mechanics* (Cambridge, UK: Cambridge University Press, 2000).

behind quantum mechanics can be used to understand notoriously difficult-to-understand human behavior.[127]

Nassim Nicholas Taleb's *The Black Swan* shows that mathematical models are only as good as the set of assumptions they are based on. You can have highly pristine quantitative models, but they will only work with the assumptions you have set. (Some would describe this colloquially as "garbage in, garbage out.") Look at how wrong the mathematical models of the rating agencies were when they assigned AAA ratings to collateral-debt obligations (CDOs) and mortgage-backed securities (MBS) leading up to the GFC. They implied a 0.1 percent probability of defaulting on a one-year time horizon for structured-finance securities and 2.6 percent PD on a five-year time horizon.[128] And what about similar failures when they assigned high (AA/A) investment-grade ratings to financial institutions in those days, with a probable default rate fluctuating between 0 and 0.2 percent on a time horizon between one and five years?[129] By granting such high ratings, they misled the public. Their mathematical models claimed that these highly rated CDOs, MBSs, and financial institutions were very safe.

Ironically, the same thing has been taking place regarding political predictions that have geopolitical consequences. The most illustrative cases were the 2016 US presidential election and the Brexit vote, in which political scientists failed miserably at predicting outcomes. They failed because pollsters were biased

[127] Julie Beck, "How 'Quantum Cognition' Can Explain Humans' Irrational Behaviors," *The Atlantic*, September 17, 2015, https://www.theatlantic.com/health/archive/2015/09/how-quantum-cognition-can-explain-humans-irrational-behaviors/405787/.

[128] Andrew H. South and Zev R. Gurwitz, "2016 Annual Global Structured Finance Default Study and Rating Transitions," S&P Global Ratings Direct, May 9, 2017, https://www.spratings.com/documents/20184/774196/2016+Annual+Global+Structured+Finance+Default+Study+And+Rating+Transitions.pdf/dd0ac65e-b3ff-4da6-b399-65b8aba5be74.

[129] Stern New York University, "Measured Spread from Treasury," 1997, accessed February 20, 2018, http://pages.stern.nyu.edu/~eelton/working_papers/corp%20bonds/all%20tables%20and%20figures%201.pdf.

and took an arbitrary view based on their own political beliefs on what the results of the elections should be in contradiction to what the voters thought. In other words, the partisan narratives of these political scientists prevented them from polling the proper groups of people. And the failure of the pollsters to accurately predict these election results was not even about ignoring fat tails but merely a question of sampling the wrong population.

There is a big-data bubble affecting the monitoring of geopolitical events

The fallacy of big data is the conjecture that enough of it removes the need for human intervention. While the use of big data in combination with powerful technologies such as supercomputers and machine learning can improve the decision-making process within an organization, big data is not the holy grail for solving everything without human intervention.

As it relates to geopolitics, the key to leveraging big data is streaming (real-time) data. There are already a couple of tools available to track and quantify critical geopolitical trends and their interconnections in the global economy:

- Global Database of Events, Language, and Tone (GDELT) combined with BigQuery (Google) as a real-time, global open database to illustrate geopolitical analysis visually and comprehensively[130]

- a project known as EQLIM, aimed at providing real-time data about human activity in emerging countries[131]

[130] Through this tool, BBVA attempts to understand the social, political, and geopolitical trends in parallel with the dynamics of the global economy. BBVA Research, "Big Data to Track Geopolitical and Social Events," December 2015, accessed January 23, 2018, https://www.bbvaresearch.com/wp-content/uploads/2015/12/DEO_Dec15_Cap4.pdf.
[131] Mike Butcher, "EQLIM Startup Aims to Surface Geopolitical Big Data in the Middle East,"

- other corporate solutions for helping predict geopolitical events offered by Palantir, Recorded Future, and Control Risk[132]

Big data is indeed about what were previously called databases and management-information systems (MIS). Exhaustive and timely qualitative reporting has long been at the core of a robust decision-making process, but the key differentiators between good analysts and bad ones are experience, expertise, and instinct. In other words, it is about an analyst knowing when to trust what the data is saying and when the pertinence of the data has reached the limits of human behavior—such as in regard to geopolitics. Organizations should take these processes steadily and slowly, refine them and get better, and reorient their instincts so they have a better feel for how to read the data.[133]

Organizations have to walk a fine line between miscalculating by trusting their instincts too much and erring by putting too much faith in computer programs, big data, and models. But organizations should always remind themselves that prediction models were designed by people, and people make many assumptions when they build anything.

In a nutshell, organizations should embrace and make the best use of big data, but it should be only one of many tools to help with decision making, particularly as it relates to the complex and interconnected world of geopolitics, where irrational human behavior plays a vital role. The bottom line is that models cannot decide for you. In 2007 and 2008, quantitative models were

TechCrunch, September 3, 2014, accessed January 5, 2018, https://techcrunch.com/2014/09/03/eqlim-startup-aims-to-surface-geopolitical-big-data-in-the-middle-east/.

[132] Katja Muñoz, "The Role of Big Data in Early Warning Conflict Monitoring," LinkedIn, September 5, 2016, https://www.linkedin.com/pulse/role-big-data-early-warning-conflict-monitoring-dr-katja-mu%C3%B1oz.

[133] Nate Silver, *The Signal and the Noise: Why So Many Predictions Fail—But Some Don't* (New York: Penguin Press, 2013).

allowed to dictate to us, showing that they cannot obviate the need for human intervention.

How can we predict geopolitical events?

Along with using big data, we must not forget the fundamentals. The most significant failures of prediction in the past thirty years were that scholars and intelligence services alike could not foresee the fall of the Berlin Wall in 1989 or the collapse of the Soviet Union in 1991. In hindsight, it looks easy to point to the influence of Gorbachev and economic destruction, combined with the problems in Afghanistan. Nowadays, many political scientists claim to know how and when the Chinese Communist regime will fall. But they always make the same mistake; they have learned nothing from history.

First, most political scientists consider local politics junior to geopolitics; they ignore the fact that most geopolitical episodes start at home. But whether unintentional or on purpose, domestic politics are a crucial contextual driver of future events. A regime that falls short of delivering economic success, justice, and good health to its people will eventually resort to nationalism, xenophobia, and fanaticism. Indeed, with its failure to honor the social contract, a regime will face rising political protest and ultimately revolution. This happens when the number of individuals losing hope in their future or that of their children reaches a tipping point, and they feel they can succeed only under a different sociopolitical context.

Alas, governments do not fall solely over questions of political expression and freedom. Those are not nearly as lethal as a collective sense of injustice, helplessness, or outrage over the security or health of a population's children. To fight this revolutionary, anxiogenic situation, a regime will try to distract its citizens from its problems by changing the subject—perhaps by blaming some sort of enemy, either domestic or foreign, or resorting to the traditional tactics of nationalism, xenophobia, fanaticism, and fear of instability.

Second, history itself can help us pick up signals, since there is a perceptible universal trend to events that cuts across borders, whether relating to the politics of energy, economics, or geopolitics. To be clear: while such trends do not determine the future, they help us isolate the most likely scenarios from the noise of the unruly speculations of global opinion, and organizations can decipher better for themselves what is going on.[134]

Third, no matter how unconventional and freakish a country's history may be, filaments of history may repeat through which we can observe what might come next. History does not repeat itself exactly, but we all have heard that those who do not learn from history are doomed to repeat it. All the great empires of the past have been characterized by very strongly centralized rule. They all also had an exaggerated sense of identity and carried what they saw as a civilizing mission and an acceptance of pervasive— even deadly—cruelty toward their own citizens as well as those of neighboring countries. Therefore, it is not surprising that these traits are the bricks and mortar of many of today's autocrats.

Last but not least, keep in the back of your mind the old rivalries supported by traditional power plays. Even if France, the United Kingdom, Germany, the United States, and Japan are currently allies, there have been several periods in history when they fought one another. Alliances can change, and old reflexes never die. For example, if either Germany or France was aspiring to become the most powerful country on the European mainland again, politically and militarily speaking, it would cause London to resort to its old tactics of divide and conquer and containment.

[134] Steve LeVine, "The 14 Rules for Predicting Future Geopolitical Events," *Quartz*, January 7, 2013, accessed January 23, 2018, https://qz.com/40960/the-14-rules-for-predicting-future-geopolitical-events/.

This would prevent any of those powers from emerging and ruling over continental Europe. (Note that Germany is currently an economic powerhouse on the European mainland but politically and militarily weak.)

Most geopolitical predictions fail, often at high cost to organizations and society, because most pundits have a poor understanding of probability and uncertainty. Both experts and laypeople confuse confident predictions with accurate ones, and overconfidence is often the reason for failure in forecasting emerging geopolitical events.

If our appreciation of uncertainty improves, our forecasts can get better, too. This is the prediction paradox: the more humility we have about our ability to make geopolitical projections, the more successful we can be in preparing for the future. The most accurate forecasters tend to have a superior command of probability, and they tend to be both humble and hardworking, relying on experience, expertise, and instinct. They understand the distinction between what we can and cannot predict, and they notice a zillion little details that bring them closer to the truth. Because of their appreciation of probability, they can separate the wheat from the chaff.

Geofinance and behavioral finance

As noted earlier, behavioral finance is a relatively new field that seeks to combine behavioral and cognitive psychological theory with conventional finance to provide explanations for why people make irrational financial decisions. For example, notwithstanding the tremendous geopolitical activities in the world (North Korea, Ukraine, Syria, Iran, Venezuela, China, Congo, Brexit, etc.), markets have continued to show strong performance as if they existed in a bubble, ignoring what has been happening outside it. Indeed, what market actions have demonstrated once again is investors' willingness to set aside considerable unusual uncertainty. They remain deeply comforted by the notion that central banks continue to cover their backs, that corporate cash will continue to be plowed into the markets via dividends and share buybacks, and, to a lesser extent, that the global economy is in the midst of a synchronized upswing. In recent years, such faith has richly rewarded investors who have been conditioned to buy the dip, regardless of its causes.

As valid as these factors may be (and there is room for debate about all three), they do not directly reduce the uncertainties posed by geopolitics and national politics. In effect, rather than trying to internalize them, stock markets essentially ignore them because they are intrinsically difficult to price and because, so far, they have had limited lasting impact. This market attitude is familiar to students of behavioral finance. It speaks to elements of neuroscience and psychology that affect investor behavior and, due to investors' desire to return to a comfort zone, can lead to overly optimistic assessments of risks. But it is also an attitude that is vulnerable to sudden, large tipping points, particularly if one or more of the uncertainties evolve in a significantly unfavorable fashion.

So far, investors have been right to supplement their structural and secular portfolio strategies with a good dose of tactical positioning. In doing so, they have been outsourcing uncertainties to institutions (namely central banks) and an economic and financing paradigm (that of a low-volatility new normal) that has emboldened them to take on more market exposure and greater liquidity risk. To make this approach rewarding over the long term, at least one of two additional factors must materialize over time: an improvement in underlying fundamentals that validates existing asset prices or sufficient investor agility and resilience to enable them to navigate safely the eventual more realistic pricing of the fluid world we live in.

Geography and ego still matter

Washington and its European allies, particularly the Eastern ones, may not like Moscow's position, but they should understand the logic behind it. Great powers are always sensitive to potential threats near their home territory, whether we are discussing the nineteenth, twentieth, or twenty-first century, as much as it may displease former president Obama. Indeed, Ukraine is a huge expanse of flat land that, over the past two centuries, Napoleonic France, imperial Germany, and Nazi Germany all crossed to strike at Russia itself. Thus, not surprisingly, Ukraine serves as a buffer state of enormous strategic importance to Russia, and no Russian leader would tolerate a military alliance between Ukraine and a country that is Moscow's mortal enemy. Nor would any Russian leader stand idly by while the West help install a government there that is determined to integrate Ukraine into the West. After all, if we were to switch their roles, the United States would, understandably, never tolerate distant great powers deploying military forces anywhere in the Western Hemisphere, much less on its borders. (Imagine the outrage in Washington if China built an impressive military alliance and tried to include Canada and Mexico in it.)

Logic aside, Russian leaders have told their Western counterparts on many occasions that they consider NATO expansion into Georgia and Ukraine unacceptable, along with any effort to turn those countries against Russia—a message that the 2008 Russo-Georgian war also made crystal clear. And now, we have the unfortunate Ukrainian episode. But again, the Russians have steadfastly voiced over and over their opposition to NATO enlargement, especially into Georgia and Ukraine. And, at the end of the day, it is the Russians, not the West, who ultimately get to decide what counts as a threat to them.

To understand clearly why the West, especially the United States, failed to understand that its Ukraine policy was laying the groundwork for a major clash with Russia, one must go back to the early and mid-1990s, when the George H. W. Bush and Clinton administrations, respectively, began cornering Russia. Indeed, why did neither the Bush nor Clinton White Houses embrace postrevolutionary Russia in the same way the States did post-WWII Japan and Germany? Why did the West, generally speaking, not allocate tens of billions of dollars in investment to help restore the former USSR's economy? And why did Clinton and George W. Bush advocate ongoing NATO expansion? Pundits advanced a variety of arguments for and against enlargement, but there was no consensus on what to do. Most Eastern European émigrés in the United States and their relatives, for example, strongly supported expansion because they wanted NATO to protect such countries as Hungary and Poland. A few realists also favored the policy because they thought Russia still needed to be contained. But some wise realist voices, such as US diplomat George Kennan, articulated that NATO expansion would actually trigger an adverse reaction from Moscow and affect its policies. Kennan sensed rightly that the West was committing a tragic mistake, as there was no reason for it whatsoever; no one was threatening anyone.

Realpolitik dictates that a humiliated, formerly great power would only view a NATO enlargement as an incentive to cause trouble in Eastern Europe. And nowadays, in light of the tension in southeastern Ukraine and given that most Western leaders continue to deny that Putin's behavior might be motivated by legitimate security concerns, it is unsurprising that they have tried to modify it by doubling down on their existing policies, punishing Russia to deter further aggression. But these sanctions will, economically and financially speaking, hurt more European than Russian interests, as Moscow is already successfully switching gears to the benefit of Chinese businesspeople. Evidencing this, for instance, is the recent $400 billion energy deal between Gazprom and China's CNPC and the construction of the Power of Siberia pipeline, which will be the world's biggest

construction project. Generally speaking, Moscow is diversifying
away from Western markets by attracting investments from
Chinese companies that are to be concentrated in Siberia, the
Russian Far East, Moscow, and Saint Petersburg, with a
prominent role in the natural-resources-related sectors, including
not only oil and gas but also forestry and agriculture.

Although Washington has maintained that all options are on the
table, neither the United States nor its NATO allies are prepared
to use force to defend Ukraine. The West is relying instead on
economic sanctions to coerce Russia into ending its support for
the insurrection in eastern Ukraine. Instead, it should make
Ukraine a neutral country in the same way as Finland and Austria
during the Cold War. And Moscow would be fine with that, as one
need only consider the Soviet and US experiences in Afghanistan,
the US experiences in Vietnam and Iraq, and the Russian
experience in Chechnya to be reminded that military occupations
usually end badly. Putin surely understands that trying to subdue
Ukraine would be like swallowing a cactus. His response to events
there has been defensive, not offensive. (Had his response been
the latter, Kiev would already have fallen.)

The United States and its European allies now face a choice on
Ukraine. They can continue their current policy, which will
exacerbate hostilities with Russia and devastate Ukraine in the
process—a scenario in which everyone would come out a loser.
Or they can switch gears and work to create a prosperous but
neutral Ukraine, one that does not threaten Russia and allows the
West to repair its relations with Moscow. With that approach, all
sides would win.

Now, this does not mean that NATO should not reinforce its rapid-
deployment force to reassure the Eastern European NATO
members, such as the Baltic states, Poland, the Czech Republic,
and Hungary, that there is strong commitment behind Article 5.
NATO's credibility is also at stake and hence, ultimately, Europe's

security. This crisis should also be viewed as an opportunity for the European Union to define a strategic vision in relation to its foreign policy; with the decline of France and the United Kingdom distancing itself from the EU, Germany will try to reconnect with its *Drang nach Osten* coupled with its *Ostpolitik*.

But concomitantly, sticking with the current sanctioning and isolation policy would also complicate Western relations with Moscow on other issues (Syria and Afghanistan, to name but a couple). Looking even further into the long term, the United States will also someday need Russia's help to contain a rising China. Current US policy, however, is only driving Moscow and Beijing closer together—so here, too, Western countries have studied Geopolitics 101 badly. Ultimately, in the long term, the great beneficiary will be China.

Physical or dematerialized geopolitics?

We all currently live in physical space, where geography matters. Our round world defines us, and geography is back with a vengeance. (See Kaplan's *The Revenge of Geography*.) It has always been here, even though former president Obama claimed that geography was something from the nineteenth century. With the full-speed advent of AI, machine learning, big data, and robotics, some futurists argue that our future will be very dematerialized. But, like culture and economics, technology is just another layer of the geopolitical onion.

Throughout history, geopolitics has relied on different critical resources. Food, water, and energy (coal, oil, uranium, gas) have been some of the vital resources that have spurred economic growth but, alas, also conflicts over access to and control of them. Another intangible support has been ideology, and yet another is geography like that envisioned, for example, by Halford John Mackinder in his concept of the heartland. Robert Kaplan states that Russia under Vladimir Putin has had no inspiring ideas to offer, no ideology of any kind, in fact; what it has in its favor, he claims, is only geography.

However, Kaplan is wrong. Putin does offer an ideology, but it is not liberal democracy, Marxism, or fascism. It's a new political ideology that fuses elements of these three prior doctrines to create something that opposes globalism. This new principle, the Fourth Political Theory,[135] is aimed not only at the people of Russia but also at Europe and, foremost, at Asia. In other words, it was conceived as the ideology of a new Eurasian Union. The brain behind this ideology is Alexander Dugin.

Nowadays, data is the new oil. It is the quintessence of modern development and increasingly shapes political and economic lives. As more information is stockpiled and processed digitally, the administration of this data affects geopolitics just as the politics of oil has done over the past hundred years. Recent developments (not the least due to a particular unruly NSA contractor) have affirmed that geopolitics and its extension, geo-economics, still rule the roost when it comes to the physical framework that is the mainstay of the Internet. Data still lives in a round world, it seems.

One of the reasons for this is that the possession and transmission of and access to data are still very much controlled by nation-states and their instruments. Physical proximity to servers and data centers and their location remain very important as more and more data is collected. Additionally, there is the case of submarine cables that carry the data across the seas between continents. The physical criticality will most likely be a leading issue of contention among economic powers.

The other reason is that US internet powerhouses (such as Facebook, Apple, Amazon, Netflix, and Google's parent company,

---

[135] Alexander Dugin, *The Fourth Political Theory* (Seattle: Amazon Digital Services, 2012).

Alphabet, a.k.a. FAANG) believe that leaders of nation-states are minor nuisances at best and immaterial obstructionists at worst. Concomitantly, political leaders across most of the world think of applied science as an on-off partner at best and a force to be either managed or unleashed against their enemies at the right time. Despite this apparent gap, there is an intimate complicity of the technology giants with instruments of state power. And this is the reason that American Internet giants are increasingly locating their data centers in countries that have had, historically, very proximate ties with the United States. But there is a darker side to it—namely that the US government has potentially allowed several monsters to breed within its own borders.

Indeed, judging by market-research figures, Alphabet Inc.'s Google gets about 77 percent of US search-marketing revenue; Google and Facebook Inc. together control around 55 percent of the mobile-ad market. Amazon takes about 70 percent of all e-book sales and 30 percent of all US online commerce. And Facebook's part of mobile social-media traffic, including the company's WhatsApp, Messenger, and Instagram units, is at 75 percent.

But then again, this complicity is nothing different from that seen in what in the West can be called the military-financial-industrial complex. So on top of this complex, a new one is being created— we can call it the data-driven complex. This complicity taints not just the United States but also China, which, as we know, is a rising power and intends to challenge US global domination strategically. And one way for the Chinese to challenge US supremacy is by creating technological giants that are absolute leaders in these fields.

In China, there is the BAT—a trio of China's (and the world's) biggest Internet firms, which are becoming increasingly prominent and share some similarities with their counterparts in the States. These are Baidu, China's version of Google; Alibaba, the country's response to Amazon (although it is much more than that); and Tencent, which owns the social-messaging platform WeChat, which is similar to Facebook. Knowing China's aspirations for ultimate power, the United States is particularly concerned about Beijing's interest in research fields similar to machine learning and artificial intelligence, both of which have increasingly attracted Chinese capital in recent years.

The concern is that the newest technologies spearheaded in the United States could be used by China to reinforce its own military capabilities and perhaps even push it ahead in strategic industries. Therefore, Washington is now looking to strengthen the role of the Committee on Foreign Investment in the United States (CFIUS), the interagency committee that reviews foreign acquisitions of US companies on national-security grounds. Alas, the Trump administration has proposed a 10 percent cut to the National Science Foundation's spending on intelligent systems. And, tragically, this could present a potential opportunity for China, through strong government support and financial incentives, to attract US talent to set up AI labs and conduct pilot projects there. Granted, Beijing has some work to do before it successfully harnesses the potential of AI. But it has the resources and talent to reach its goal—and now it has the political will to make this a national priority.

The combination will be a challenge to beat. Despite the significant interest in the development of intelligent systems, these systems will always remain, one way or another, dependent on geography. In other words, while we are living in an ever more dematerialized world with the advent of massive data collections and flows, our society remains round. For example, critically strategic physical points, such as the Suez Canal and Straits of Malacca, remain as relevant today as they were in the past; most of the data traffic between Asia and Europe goes via Egypt (Alexandria, the Suez Canal). Other critical physical points include Luzon and Hormuz.

Another illustration is how the diversity of data-traffic routes is increased via terrestrial cables. As already mentioned, submarine cables are increasingly supplemented by other physical ones. Then there is the Digital Silk Road, part of China's One Belt, One Road initiative, aiming to span Euro-Asia with fiber-optic cables laid along newly built railroads and energy pipelines.

And what about the Internet-traffic hubs that are critical points for global data traffic? Most Internet traffic converges on a few primary centers. In Europe, most data traffic goes through Frankfurt (Deutscher Commercial Internet Exchange) and Amsterdam (Amsterdam Internet Exchange). For traffic across the Atlantic, the critical point is the London Internet Exchange. In Asia, the key Internet-traffic hubs are Hong Kong (Hong Kong Internet eXchange) and Singapore (Singapore Internet Exchange). Most Latin American cables reach land via the Internet hub in Miami (Network Access Point [NAP] of the Americas). Finally, let's talk about satellites and their physical location in space. Approximately two thousand artificial satellites orbiting Earth relay analog and digital signals carrying voice, video, and data to and from sites worldwide.

The enduring importance of physical constraints on data as illustrated by the examples above does not reduce in any way the growing influence of data as a critical commodity that will spur more rivalry among nations. Now, to be quite clear, data, as a symbiosis of information and knowledge, has always been at the heart of geopolitics. In their daily work, diplomats, politicians, and military and intelligence officers collect, analyze, and communicate data, information, and knowledge. The difference is that shortly, we will be able to extract even more knowledge and information from existing data.

Atlas of Geofinancial Risks

Geofinance cannot be one-sided

Winston Churchill famously stated that "history is written by the victors," arguing that winners overwhelmingly influence historical accounts. When studying the importance of geofinance, it is paramount to have the facts straight, particularly as they relate to history.

In essence, this talking point asserts that the truth about the past is not defined by rational interpretations of academic research or a factual understanding of history but by the might of cultural and political leaders who have the power to shape historical narratives through school textbooks, public iconography, movies, and a range of other media. And, to be sure, these media are great venues for establishing political ideologies and shaping personal assumptions about the way the world works. And governmental or "official" entities can and do exploit this power to achieve their ends. These official cultural expressions aim to shape how people remember the past. They originate from social leaders and official authorities who seek to shape society's historical understanding in ways that promote "social unity, the continuity of existing institutions, and loyalty to the status quo."[136] In other words, those in power have an interest in maintaining their power, and a "usable past" that conforms to their vision of present-day conditions can be a reliable tool to uphold their status.

Naively, many now believe that the Internet offers enormous potential for people from any walk of life to build robust platforms from which they can convince others of their beliefs and opinions. It is true that one may spout whatever one likes, but this underestimates the strength of the current of dogmatic thinking, as the media and other establishment groups will

---

[136] Andrew E. Kersten and Kriste Lindenmeyer, eds., *Politics and Progress: American Society and the State since 1865*, (Santa Barbara, CA: Praeger, 2001).

quickly claim that anyone contesting the official "truth" is a vector of fake news. See how the 2016 US election campaign and Brexit were conducted and how opposing protagonists threw loads of propaganda at one another. Look at how those who dare to contest globalism, migration, and the European construction dream are labeled as bigots, racists, and populists.

Even more illustrative would be to delve into the history of WWII. While it is quite clear that the Axis forces were the aggressors, and no one will try to excuse or justify the atrocities that the Axis countries committed in the name of their ideology (particularly the atrocious Holocaust), the Allied forces were not innocent of crimes against humanity. For example, the way the Axis occupation forces exerted their powers on the countries they governed was not very different from the way the French and British imposed law and order on their colonial empires. (Again, I am not talking about the Holocaust, which is a different and tragic matter.) Look at the Sétif massacre that took place in French Algeria on May 8, 1945, the day of the capitulation of Germany. In a span of merely twenty-four hours, some fifty thousand Algerians, including women and children, were massacred by the French occupation forces. What is so different from the massacres committed by the SS on the Eastern Front or by the Gestapo/SD in Western Europe? Both French and German occupying forces were imposing law and order in a very harsh and arbitrary way, and any resistance was dealt with swiftly.

Or what about the Bengal famine caused by the British in India in 1943 and 1944 as they diverted food supplies from Indians to feed British troops? Indeed, the famous Winston Churchill, as part of the Western war effort, ordered the diversion of food from starving Indians to already well-supplied British soldiers and stockpiles in Britain and elsewhere in Europe, including Greece and Yugoslavia. This caused the death of nearly three million Bengali. What is so different from the famine caused by Stalin in Ukraine in the 1930s or Mao in the 1950s and '60s in China?

Everyone mentions the fact that the CIA and SIS both hired former Nazis (German scientists such as Werner Von Braun), Gestapo (Klaus Barbie), and Abwehr staff (Reinhard Gehlen) and how they helped Nazi dignitaries evade prosecution and execution after WWII. Operation Paperclip is a famous shorthand for this chapter of contemporary history. However, the Soviets did precisely the same thing through various Soviet operations, including Operation Osoaviakhim, which took place during 1945 and 1946 in Austria, Germany, and Czechoslovakia, and whose targets were the exploitation of German atomic-related facilities, intellectual materials, tangible resources, and scientific staff for the benefit of the Soviet nuclear-bomb project. At gunpoint, the NKVD and Soviet Army troops recruited more than two thousand German technical specialists and scientists from the Soviet occupation zone of post-WWII Germany for employment in the Soviet Union. Where do you think the AK-47 comes from? (Hint: see the Sturmgewehr 44.) Or the SU-76i? (See the Panzer III.) Also, Heinrich Müller, supreme head of the Gestapo, fled to the Soviet Union after WWII and worked for the NKVD/KGB.

The so-called neutral countries were not that neutral—quite the contrary, as they collaborated much more with Germany than with the Allied powers. Neutral Sweden allowed Nazis to use its railways to occupy Norway and transfer Jews to death camps. Switzerland was Berlin's Alpine vault, and here, too, Swiss railways permitted German troops to cross the country to reach the borders of Italy, particularly after 1943, when after the fall of Mussolini, Italy fell into the Allied camp, prompting a German invasion of the Italian peninsula.

Franco's Spain and Salazar's Portugal also tacitly collaborated with the Nazis (e.g., the Blue Division sent to the Eastern Front and the supply of tungsten to the German war machine). Thailand allowed Japanese troops to cross its country to reach the borders of Burma. And, even prior to WWII, Western colonial powers committed atrocities in a fashion not entirely different from how the Germans fought resistance fighters in the occupied countries.

Indeed, what about the repression of the Mau Mau uprising in Kenya between 1952 and 1960, when more than five thousand Kenyans were tortured and abused by the British occupation forces? And did you know that Hitler did not invent concentration camps, although he put them to use on a massive scale, leading to the massacre of six million Jews in Europe? Long before WWII, the British used a secured camp where civilian "enemies" (children and women) were placed. This was from 1899 and 1902, the conflict was the Boer War, and the victims were Dutch settlers in South Africa. Of the 107,000 people concentrated in these harsh camps, some thirty thousand were Boer women and children, along with an unknown number of black Africans.

The French, with their imperial ambitions, associated empire with national worthiness, and while they were less racial in their attitude than the British, they spared no efforts to achieve their goals. For example, as in Africa, the French taxed the Vietnamese and drafted them to labor on public works. On one such project in 1908—the Hanoi–Yunnan Phu railway—twenty-five thousand Vietnamese died. Conditions in Vietnam, in general, created a decline in Vietnam's population.

The Americans, too, were involved in massacres. Although the United States achieved victory in the Spanish-American War, gaining new territory and establishing itself as an imperial power, it soon found itself engaged in another conflict as the Philippines began to rebel against its new American rulers. US president McKinley made it clear that the Philippines would not be granted independence, fighting broke out, and the subsequent war cost the lives of more than five hundred thousand Filipino civilians. And nearly everyone associates the term *slave trade* with the Western colonial powers that captured millions of Africans to ship them mostly to the American colonies in the eighteenth and nineteenth centuries. But the Islamic slave trade was even more massive. Some fourteen to twenty million Africans are estimated to have been killed in the trade between the eighth and nineteenth centuries, and between 1 and 1.25 million[137] Europeans were captured between the sixteenth and nineteenth centuries by Barbary corsairs. So European powers did not have a monopoly on terror.

Many "snowflakes" believe that the Muslim presence in Spain and Portugal between 711 and 1492 was an age of tolerance and peace, in which Muslim rulers treated Christians and Jews respectfully. They portray al-Andalus as an enlightened society that combined religious belief with humanism and artistry. However, that is a fairy tale. The occupation of the al-Andalus was the result of a vicious jihad against the local Spanish and Portuguese inhabitants, resulting in the massacre of Jews and Christians, particularly during the reigns of the Almoravids and the Almohads between 1147 and 1492.

And the Chinese are not immune to glorifying certain aspects of their own history. Indeed, party history is a sensitive subject in China, as much of the party's legitimacy rests on its claims of great historical achievements, such as leading China to victory over Japan before and during WWII. Dissenting views, such as those of historians who point out that much of the fighting against the Japanese was done by the then-Kuomintang (KMT) government, are not welcome. More sensitive topics, like the chaos of the Cultural Revolution, the Great Leap Forward, the occupation of Tibet, and the Tiananmen massacre remain mostly taboo. The Chinese Communist Party refers to those who stray from its line as practicing "historical nihilism."

---

[137] Robert Davis, "British Slaves on the Barbary Coast," BBC History, February 17, 2011, accessed March 4, 2018, http://www.bbc.co.uk/history/british/empire_seapower/white_slaves_01.shtml.

So, as we see, the past is full of historical events that are kept behind closed doors—an insult to real historiography. And for sure, the Internet allows no more excuses for not delving into history or for not challenging the official storyboard of history. The Internet and the greater access to historical documents should provide support for interpretive historical scholarship or, at the very least, a more thorough and factual understanding of the past. Therefore, when analyzing historical events, historians should take a 360-degree vision and put things into perspective. Yes, Germans, Italians, Japanese, and their Axis brothers were evil—no doubt about it. However, do not think that the Allies were necessarily all that respectful. We know that the Soviets under Stalin committed a lot of atrocious crimes, such as the 1940 Katyn massacre of the Polish intelligentsia committed by the NKVD, but the Anglo-Saxon powers as well as the French have done the same.

Atlas of current geofinancial risks

The realities of a world with a so-called emerging vacuum of power (a.k.a. a G-Zero order), a geofinancial world without global leadership, are evident. Many believe (wrongly) that this power vacuum has been created by a demise of Western influence and the local focus of the governments of the developing countries. But nothing could be further from the truth, as highlighted by tensions in the South and East China Seas, a widening popular dissent in Asia and South America, Moscow playing hardball in neighboring Ukraine and beyond, and never-ending Arab revolutions in the Middle East. Some things never change.

One could summarize the atlas of geofinancial tail risks as follows:

- The emerging markets no longer represent a homogeneous group, such as the BRIC countries, for instance. While one can find as a common trait their surfing on the wave of cheap money (thanks to prevailing US QE that is very slowly being unwound) and thus not taking the opportunity to restructure their economies, their respective fates are now diverging. Those diverging markets saddled with current account deficits are triggering a range of political legitimacy crises as local voters become disillusioned with policies and their economic results. And some major markets that can have elections will hold them this year (well, China does not—and Russia does not count): Brazil, Colombia, India, Indonesia, and more. Not one of those states enters its electoral cycle with popular, strong leadership. Add empowered middle classes that demand greater accountability from their governments, whether in Latin America (Venezuela, Brazil, Mexico, and Colombia) or Southeast Asia (Thailand, Malaysia, Cambodia, the Philippines, Indonesia). The stakes are rising, and some of the world's key economies are in for a rough ride.

- Fragile Abenomics and its "three arrows" could reverse and potentially trigger a huge Japanese sovereign-debt crisis, thereby causing a contagion in the rest of Asia. According to the rating agencies, Japanese government debt totals 250 percent of its GDP, by far the highest in the developed world. And if you add in corporate and private debt, total Japanese debt equates to an astonishing 500 percent of GDP. If growth suddenly stalls, Japan may respond with even more monetary stimulus and bigger budget deficits, potentially leading to a collapse of the yen as investors lose faith, followed by excessive domestic inflation. For now, economic progress has been reassuring, with an annual GDP growth of 2.1 percent for 2017, but the recovery is fragile. Then again, the Bank of Japan has not implemented the full extent of its QE measures. But if markets and investors eventually become convinced that PM Abe cannot definitely turn the tide, yields will go up, making the refinancing of the Japanese sovereign debt highly exposed.

- On the one hand, oil prices could go down by as much as 10 or 15 percent due to supply-side-driven factors (overcapacity), such as increased production, a normalization of Iran's relationship with the world, and/or the recently discovered benefits of the shale-oil revolution. For instance, the supply of oil in the United States, in Iraq, off the coast of Africa, in Brazil, and elsewhere continues to rise. Even places like Russia and Mexico, which have been neglecting their oil-production infrastructures, are making plans to reinvigorate output. But demand-driven factors could also come into play as demand from emerging markets and China falls. The same phenomena can be observed for mining resources as well. For commodity-driven economies, such as the petrostates—Bolivia, Indonesia, and Russia, for example—falling prices may potentially cause deficits, leading to disruptions in growth and possibly even political stability.

- After the ongoing revolutions in the Arab world, here comes the dissent in Southeast Asia. As the cheap printed money that has fed the emerging market boom dries up, long-running social, ideological, and political feuds are reigniting and feeding off urban, middle-class protest over corruption. Although each situation has its own dynamics, the common theme of fundamental stagnation colliding with the chaos triggered by the commodity bust seems to hold. Look at the situations in Thailand, Cambodia, and Malaysia. And one can imagine that, with the coming elections in some other countries of the region, popular dissent will become even more apparent.

- Due to fiscal mismanagement, the political leadership in both Europe (causing the rise of nationalist-populist parties) and the United States (the rise of the Tea Party) is becoming vulnerable to a legitimacy crisis and thus the risk of failing to make courageous decisions when navigating these troubled nations through dangerous waters. Interestingly enough, while US political leaders look down with contempt on the way that the European crisis was handled, it seems that Washington is also prone to dysfunction, as evidenced by the lack of across-the-aisle, consensus-building measures, itself the result of small lobbying groups that dictate their radical agendas to the mainstream political parties. And the longer this inability lasts, the more radical politicians voters will elect.

- The never-ending Arab Spring—or the current and ongoing instability in the Middle East in countries such Libya, Tunisia, Syria, Egypt, and Bahrain—is now also spreading to Yemen, Lebanon, and Jordan. The Arab Spring is now in its sixth season. Some uprisings are against dictators; others are the result of the centuries-old Sunni-Shiite conflict. These revolts are not linear, either, and will last for many more years. As of now, Tunisia remains in a kind of limbo; Libya lacks a government that can control the militias. Syria is still in rubbles, Egypt is under military control, and so on.

- Russia is back with a vengeance—not just in the Middle East (Syria and Egypt), but also in Asia, South America, and most recently in Eastern Europe and former USSR states. Moscow is playing hardball not just in Ukraine but also in the Baltic states, and Russia's increasingly unpredictable and assertive foreign policy will generate risks. Europe's worst nightmares are the events that shaped the 1930s with the rise of fascism, while Russia's nightmares are the 1990s and the fall of the Soviet Union. Brussels eurocrats see the answer to their problems in transcending power and the nation-state. For Moscow, the underlying solution is in bringing them back to life. So what happens when a twenty-first-century country faces a threat posed by a nineteenth-century power? The contours of the conflict are already emerging—in diplomatic standoffs over Serbia, Georgia, the Baltic states, and Ukraine; in conflicts over oil and gas pipelines; in nasty diplomatic exchanges between Russia and Britain; and in the return of Russian military exercises of a kind not seen since the Cold War. Europeans are apprehensive, with good reason.

- The corruption scandal affecting Turkey's AKP government and President Tayyip Erdogan has developed into a full-fledged regime crisis. Additionally, the Fed's tapering is also hurting the Turkish lira and its economy. Erdogan has been ruling the Turkish state for more than ten years, and his rule is hegemonic in the real sense of the word. His utilization of Islamic conservative values has successfully convinced entire sections of the popular classes. His alliances with businesspeople and capitalist entrepreneurs have helped finance the AKP party. In turn, strong economic growth has left some bread crumbs for those at the bottom of Turkish society. The crisis unfolding in Turkey goes beyond a governmental crisis. It truly is a regime crisis that will shape Turkey for years to come.

- Conflicts in the Democratic Republic of Congo, South Sudan, and the Central African Republic are threatening—to varying levels—to engulf the region. Rebels fighting in one state use another as a haven. Should tensions persist or worsen in any of these countries, Central Africa could see a dramatic security vacuum due to refugee flows and weak state authority. Despite inadequate infrastructure and at times even poorer governance, the continent has been attracting more and more interest from American, European, and Chinese investors, targeting such countries as Kenya, Nigeria, South Africa, Angola, Tanzania, and Rwanda, to name a few. Today, half of the world's thirty fastest-growing countries are in Africa, which is quickly losing its image of hopelessness and despair.

- China's more assertive foreign policy in both the South China and East China Seas versus Japan's and the Philippines' apparent willingness to push back against it increases the likelihood of sparking a wider conflict, albeit perhaps by accident rather than design. China's military modernization, coupled with the potential decline in US power caused by sequestration, is modifying the balance of power in the region and reducing the deterrent effect of the rebalancing policy. The risk is increasing that China's coercive approach to its sovereignty claims will lead to greater conflict in the region. China is using its military forces to coerce Japan into giving up claims to the Senkaku Islands, and it is also pressuring the Philippines to renounce its claims to the Spratly Islands in the South China Sea. Both regions are believed to harbor valuable undersea oil and gas reserves.

- The 2003–2017 period was supposed to be the decade and a half when Latin America would catch up with emerging Asia, thanks to high commodity prices, a low-interest-rate environment, and beneficial demographics. Instead, the Latin American region has fallen further behind. Peru, Colombia, and Uruguay should be applauded for keeping their commitments to reform in spite of difficult times and political obstacles. However, the scope and pace of reform in Brazil, Argentina, Chile, and Venezuela has proven disappointing. Further exacerbating the problem of political risk is the electoral calendar of the coming years. Brazil and Colombia face national elections, and both nations remain vulnerable to falling commodity prices. In Colombia, most analysts continue to focus on the longevity of FARC peace agreements as the determinant for coming elections. However, voter frustration stems, in much larger part, from the perceived lack of fulfillment of government promises in areas such as education, basic utilities, and infrastructure. And in Venezuela, Caracas continues to dangle on the edge of the precipice with the risk of systemic sovereign default.

- China's policy makers are aggressively clamping down on what some experts are calling a credit bubble. This comes as China's economy slows, and incoming data continues to disappoint. All this has economists upping their odds of a hard economic landing, a scenario in which growth slows to a point that causes unemployment to spike. The experience of 2008 showed that the Chinese economy is vulnerable to trade shocks. A hard economic landing could be provoked by either an intended credit deleveraging going out of control or insufficient public investment from Beijing. Whatever the spark that ignites the cataclysm, the excess capacity in the manufacturing sector—estimated at 50 percent in 2016 by the IMF—would be exacerbated by a sharp slowdown of economic growth. This cataclysm would result in corporate margins falling sharply, making profits dive and triggering a downward spiral in local demand. Bankruptcies, unemployment, and social unrest would occur on a large scale, threatening social, financial, and political stability. One aspect that could accelerate the downward societal spiral is the high leverage of China's corporate sector and local governments, which was estimated to have reached more than 200 percent of GDP by the end of 2017.

- Israel and Iran are already waging war, mainly executed via proxy forces and covert operations. The conflict is bound up in the religious and political struggle of Iranian religious leadership against Israel, while Israel's counteraim is to prevent the use of nuclear weapons by the Iranian government and to downgrade its allies and proxies, such as the Hezbollah party in Lebanon and the Syrian government in Damascus. However, they have potentially taken a step closer to a direct conflict, as Iran's nuclear deal could shake up the Middle East after generations of conflict. Granted, the nuclear deal with Iran presents a chance of changes in alliances and rivalries that have dominated the region's politics. But the deal creates new tensions in a Middle East already challenged by the upheavals of the 2011 Arab Spring. Washington's decision to sideline its allies Israel and Saudi Arabia in the secret bilateral negotiations with Iran that began in August is, in some respects, as significant for the future as the nuclear deal.

- Local officials have blamed violent attacks in southern Xinjiang, located in northwest China next to the Pakistan-occupied Kashmir border, on terror outfits with links to Pakistan-based groups. Following attacks in Hotan over the past few years, Xinjiang's governor, Nur Bekri, claimed that members of the separatist East Turkestan Islamic Movement (ETIM) and terrorists in neighboring states have a thousand and one links. Xinjiang officials have also blamed knife and bomb attacks in Hotan on groups with links to Pakistan-based outfits. But Beijing has appeared keen to play down terror concerns in light of its all-weather ties with Islamabad.

Scenarios for upcoming geofinancial crises

What would an upcoming geofinancial crisis look like in the immediate future? 1) China's economic transformation and slowdown would cause the jittering of commodity economies, posing refinancing risk to the US Treasury bill; 2) there would be an EU regime crisis due to 2.1) a European sovereign-debt crisis reentering through the back door, 2.2) the rise of large-scale anti-EU sentiment, and 2.3) the Kremlin fragilizing EU crisis-management skills; 3) South and East China Sea maritime disputes would gain momentum due to the effects of US foreign policy; 4) a nuclear arms race would occur in the Middle East (Israel and Saudi Arabia versus Iran); and 5) the unwinding of QE would translate into monetary tightening, suppressing the grassroots of an economic recovery.

This is how it would look in more detail:

- Commodity-driven economies: As the Chinese economy is slowing faster than expected, with annual GDP growth for 2017 well below the magic number of 7.2 percent (most likely in the high 6 percent), investors now realize that the past demand for commodities is unsustainable. Combined with the massive oversupply that built up during the boom, this will gradually lead to a sustained collapse of commodity prices. Having borrowed to finance expensive development projects, the commodity-rich countries in Latin America and Africa and also, to some extent, Australia (and some of the world's leading mining companies, such as BHP, Rio Tinto, etc.), will become the focus of a debt-refi crisis.

- Refi risk for the US Treasury: China held $1.2 trillion in US Treasury bills as of December 2017. China, with its current unbalanced trade policies, especially those that have resulted in its overreliance on exports for its economic growth, large savings rate, and accumulation of huge foreign exchange reserves, is eager to transform its economy by boosting consumer demand and to improve domestic living standards, leading to an appreciation of the renminbi (RMB) against the USD. Such policies will lessen China's need to buy US securities in the future, posing a refi risk for the US Treasury as it seeks to finance its deficit, although its size has been reduced drastically—from 10 percent of GDP in 2009 to below 4 percent by the end of 2017.

- Eurozone debt problem: Granted, while the sovereign risk in the eurozone is still systemic, several mitigating factors have since been put in place with the advent of the Long-Term Refinancing Operation (LTRO) facility from the ECB, the recent move to bail in rather than bail out bank creditors, and the improved understanding of banks' capital needs derived from stress-testing initiatives. While the near-term risk of a eurozone default has subsided, the debt burden for Greece, Italy, Portugal, and France will remain a major drag on economic growth as governments continue to report high deficits. Current bullishness for euro debt will be replaced by resurfacing bearishness.

- EU regime legitimacy crisis: There was relative economic boom in 2016 and 2017 after the euro's existential crisis of the previous years, but a distinct type of crisis started to emerge—rising anti-EU sentiment and collapsing political confidence. Across the European Union, politicians have realized that they can no longer dismiss parties that fundamentally dislike the European Union as fringe movements. Prevailing issues are hostility to immigrants; the euro-debt-crisis mismanagement, which caused widespread socioeconomic calamity in Southern Europe; youth unemployment; and so on.

- The Kremlin testing European Union resolves with the current crisis in the Ukraine: The EU has shown that it not only miscalculated the reaction of Moscow while stirring up the crisis in Kiev, but it also failed to respond adequately after the annexation of the Crimea by Russia. Without the United States, the EU is a toothless and embarrassing geopolitical joke. And now, Russia is testing the waters with the eastern part of Ukraine and potentially later the Russian region of Moldova—perhaps with the Baltic states (in particular Estonia and Lithuania) shortly. The Eastern European members of the EU are particularly nervous, as they still have negative memories of the USSR.

- South and East China Seas maritime disputes: With Beijing gaining vocality in the region, it is challenging the status quo of international maritime borders, particularly in the South and East China Seas and involving predominantly the Philippines and Japan. Granted, the United States has security agreements with both countries, but President Obama's foreign policy was not overly convincing as to whether it would translate words into actions. Its leading-from-behind policy, most dominant during the Libya and Syria crises, has shown that the United States prefers a back-seat approach and will not back up its threats if breaches are voluntarily undertaken by opponents such as Syria, Iran, and so on.

- Iran nuclear talks: Despite a signed TNP with Iran, hostilities remain between Tehran and Washington, in part fueled by a distinctly negative outlook for the real aftermath, namely Israel and Saudi Arabia. Already, the former has several times openly threatened to preemptively strike the nuclear research facilities within Iran, and Tehran has threatened the destruction of the State of Israel while Riyadh is working with China—through Pakistan—to obtain nuclear tactical and ballistic missiles aimed at counterbalancing Tehran. Despite Israel and Saudi Arabia not being friends, they could find a common cause in launching an attack against Iran.

- Impact of the QE exit strategy: Unwinding the vast enlargement of the Fed's balance sheet and liquidity greatly increases the usual risks in monetary policy aimed at price stability, growth, and employment.

Greater uncertainty means navigating uncharted waters, with heightened chances that tightening will lead to a significant downturn. A slow exit raises the threat of inflation, and the massive expansion of bank reserves that the Fed has fostered could spark an excess supply of credit. Unconventional monetary policy and stimulus can be part of a successful economic program for a period, but they are no alternative to public investment, structural reform, and fiscal discipline.

The Interplay between Global Finance and Geopolitics

The role of financial markets in geopolitics

While the materialization of new geopolitical risk is often met with an increase in the risk denominator, causing financial markets to drop, this market effect is usually short lived as investors continuously reevaluate the impact of the perceived risk on their cash flow and earnings hypothesis. If an event is localized and unlikely to spread or affect global economic growth, its risk premium will quickly disappear. To use a metaphor, this dissipation of the additional risk premium looks similar to the wave that spreads in a pool of water after a pebble is dropped in it. The size of the roller (i.e., the risk premium) is significant when you are close to the core of the event, but as you move away from the source in either time or distance, the wave dissipates quite quickly.

We are all somewhat familiar with how geopolitical events can lead to significant or persistent global-market reactions, such as how a naval war can lead to a rise in the price of commodities or a terrorist plague can affect long-term market sentiments, thereby reducing the appetite for investments and consumption. However, in contrast to the extent of media coverage or the level of emotion that we as empathetic humans exhibit, most geopolitical events do not lead to significant or persistent global market reactions. We could even add that unless there is a substantial spike in volatility, financial markets are relatively complacent about geopolitics.

The former British prime minister William Gladstone expressed the importance of finance for the economy in 1858 as follows: "Finance is, as it were, the stomach of the country, from which all the other organs take their tone."[138] According to cross-country

---

[138] Aziz Gulhan, "Financial Literacy Matters," *Sanford Journal of Public Policy*, November 8, 2013, https://sites.duke.edu/sjpp/2013/financial-literacy-matters/.

comparisons, individual country studies, and industry- and company-level research, a positive correlation exists between the sophistication of the financial system and economic growth. While some gaps remain, I would say that the financial system is nowadays vitally integrated into the economic environment.

Nevertheless, economists still hold conflicting views regarding the underlying mechanisms that explain the positive correlation between the degree of development of the financial system and economic development. Some economists just do not believe that the finance-growth relationship is important. For instance, Robert Lucas asserted in 1988 that economists badly overstress the role of financial factors in economic growth.[139] Moreover, Joan Robertson declared in 1952 that "where enterprise leads, finance follows."[140]According to this view, economic development creates demands for particular types of financial arrangements, and the financial system provides automatic responses to these requests.

Other economists firmly believe in the importance of the financial system for economic growth. They address the issue of how the optimal financial system should look. Overall, the notion seems to have developed that the optimal financial system, in combination with a well-developed legal system, should incorporate elements of both direct-market finance and indirect, bank-based finance. A well-developed financial system should improve the efficiency of financing decisions, favoring a better allocation of resources and thereby economic growth.

[139] Robert E. Lucas, "On the Mechanics of Economic Development," *Journal of Monetary Economics* 22 (1988), 3–42, accessed February 18, 2018, https://www.parisschoolofeconomics.eu/docs/darcillon-thibault/lucasmechanicseconomicgrowth.pdf.
[140] Willem F. Duisenberg, "The Role of Financial Markets for Economic Growth," Speech delivered to the economics conference The Single Financial Market: Two Years into EMU, Vienna, May 31, 2001, accessed February 18, 2018, https://www.ecb.europa.eu/press/key/date/2001/html/sp010531.en.html.

Market events can yield geopolitical consequences

What is less known is how market events can lead to geopolitical responses. An excellent example of this is the recent and still lingering eurozone crisis—in particular, the Grexit, and how if a default by Greece had been allowed, Athens would most likely have turned to Moscow for help, thereby leaving NATO and fragilizing its southeastern flank. Indeed, Greece has long been an anchor of the Western world against external threats. So Athens's departure from EU institutions, or even a significant weakening of the Greek polity, would deteriorate security in the Balkans and the Southern and Eastern Mediterranean at a time when regional threats have been arguably at their highest peak for decades.

Another illustration is how the fall in commodity and energy prices can significantly affect mining and energy producers. For example, North Africa and the Middle East contain the highest concentration of oil-dependent economies in the world. The region represents nearly a third of liquefied natural-gas exports and seaborne crude oil. The Middle East—particularly the Persian Gulf—also represents the majority of OPEC oil exports and production. Therefore, the Middle Eastern region is the most vulnerable zone in terms of volatility in global energy markets— and the geographical area that can trigger the most instability as well, as seen recently by Libya's production fluctuations. A sustained fall in the price of oil could jeopardize the economic stability that many of the region's energy exporters have enjoyed following the tumult of the Arab Spring.

Asia, too, is exposed to instability. Indeed, the apparent weakness in the economy of China is radiating out into the world as authorities in Beijing look for a means to deflect popular anger from domestic ills and transpose it into nationalistic overseas ambitions. China is an entirely different country from the one often portrayed by outsiders—an emerging superpower with global economic reach and goals to challenge American predominance, at least regionally in Asia. The real China, the one its citizens are most accustomed to, is facing severe, long-term challenges at home. China's global ambitions divert us from the reality that Beijing's leadership must cope with political, social, economic, and environmental problems on a scale that necessitates the reallocation of a significant share of the country's resources and prestige. Counterintuitively, China's overseas adventures expose its weaknesses and vulnerabilities and underscore the leadership's insecurity when it comes to dealing with them. And this makes China's neighbors very nervous.

Geopolitics traditionally focuses on foreign policy and military might, resources, and demographics as measures of national influence. Meanwhile, finance focuses on funding activities, trading commodities, financial securities, and other fungible items of value that can be transacted at low costs and at prices that reflect supply and demand. But geopolitics and finance have intertwined throughout history. Indeed, from a historical viewpoint, if we go back before the end of the Cold War (the 1980s), tail risk already loomed large in the financial markets as it did in the decade following the end of the Cold War.

Figure 10: History of Financial Crises, 1930–2011

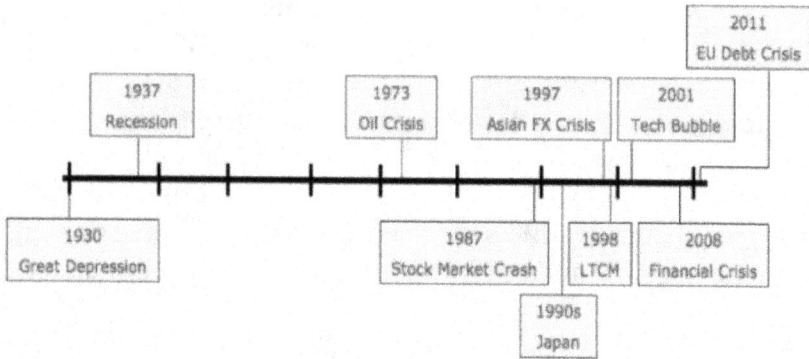

Indeed, while the world is becoming a global village due to faster communication channels, (relatively) free movement of capital, and more efficient logistics, this same world has in fact always been prone to tail events, whether driven by geopolitics, financial market disruptions, or a combination of both.

Referring to a more contemporary illustration of the nexus between geopolitics and finance, let's talk about the eurozone crisis and its connection to the power games in relation to Moscow and Tehran. In essence, Berlin needed a deal with Moscow (the Crimean crisis) to be able to manage the existential crisis for the eurozone (Grexit and the domino effect). And Moscow needed an agreement with Washington to restrict US encroachment on its sphere of influence. (This is the reason that the United States never sent substantial military assets to Kiev.) In turn, Washington needed a deal with Tehran to refocus its attention away from Russia.

A financial crisis can lead to a military crisis

Though on a different scale, a financial crisis is never divorced from a military one. Both German and Russian issues bring the United States back to Eurasia. A distracted Germany will compel the United States to go beyond NATO boundaries to encircle Russia. Rest assured that Russia—even under severe economic stress—would find the means to respond. Generally speaking, as the Cold War ended, an era of universal norms ushered in global financial markets.

Now, more than twenty-five years after the fall of the Berlin Wall, strategic competition is returning to the foreground in Europe. The world is juggling with a seemingly accelerating dynamic between finance and geopolitics. Today's realpolitik is not ideologically driven; instead, it includes new players and takes place in the context of financial integration. Will international capital, the efficiency of international markets, and the win-win logic of global finance be undermined by geopolitics? How will financial decisions and spheres of influence affect the global balance of power? What kinds of global risks could emerge when countries use financial rather than military tools to advance their national interests?

These questions have been brought to the foreground as a result of the following trends:

- the recent heightened tensions in East Asia
- the acceleration of regional integration in Southeast Asia
- the rise of alternative financial markets and financial tools more generally
- the turbulence in the Middle East and Ukraine
- the shale-gas-and-oil revolution in the United States

- competing integration mechanisms in Latin America
- China's assertion of leadership in global banking
- acts of terrorism and violent strife that are redrawing borders and sending financial markets backward

Global interconnectedness and the increasing speed at which information is being transmitted have reinforced the interdependence between finance and geopolitics, with cyberspace representing an essential new front in the geopolitical equation as cyberattacks grow in potential to inflict financial collateral damage. This raises the risk of unintended consequences.

The interplay between geopolitics and finance can create, reinforce, and modify the nature of the interconnections between these global dangers, affecting many areas of international cooperation and public policy. Businesses and governments alike must conduct geopolitical audits to avoid being caught off guard. Failing this, significant disruptions to international finance and threats to political cooperation and the global rules-based system could take place through prudential regulation.

A driver of the intensifying interplay between finance and geopolitics is the growing direct role of the state in world finance, which is affecting traditional financial markets and investment flows alike and potentially enabling countries to exert geopolitical influence through financial dependency. This phenomenon is manifest in the increasing state-sponsored investments in other countries' infrastructures, such as in the case of Chinese investment in Asia, Africa, and Latin America. Another example is strategic investments by state-owned enterprises and sovereign wealth funds in businesses' ventures and land acquisitions in other countries, as seen in the case of investments made by Gulf countries in Africa and Australia, not to mention government purchases of other governments' debt.

Figure 11: Allocation of US Debt

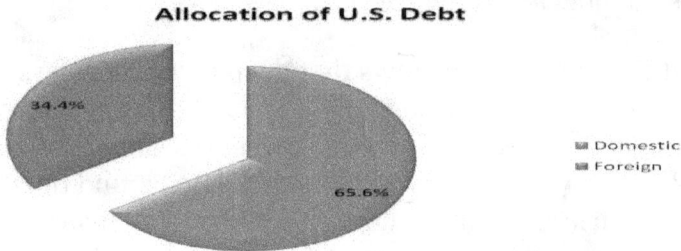

Allocation of U.S. Debt

34.4%
65.6%

Domestic
Foreign

Source: Forbes[141]

To strengthen their geopolitical positions, countries have also reverted to measures that survey access to financially critical national resources or control the prices of commodities over which they exert monopoly power to undermine other states' financial and economic performance. These potential ways to leverage power over other countries through financial and economic links are increasingly becoming an explicit part of foreign-policy thinking. In today's interdependent global economy, whenever countries focus on their domestic/regional market—even if the decisions are made by central banks rather than by the political leadership—there is always a potential for unintended effects on other countries to spill over into the geopolitical sphere. For instance, one side effect of Japan's expansionary monetary policies to reinvigorate its national economy has been the devaluation of the yen, which has lost half its value in recent years, much to the detriment of the country's neighbors. Another example is the quantitative easing in the United States that has affected international capital flows into

[141] Mike Patton, "Who Owns the Most US Debt?" *Forbes*, October 28, 2014, https://www.forbes.com/sites/mikepatton/2014/10/28/who-owns-the-most-u-s-debt/#6a85ffc3819c.

emerging markets. When confronted with political and financial volatility at home, countries often revert to protectionism under the guise of policies to reduce risk.

A recent OECD report[142] shows that despite their professed commitment to free movements of capital, G20 economies have increasingly reverted to protective measures since growth slowed in 2012 in the wake of the global financial crisis, and thus Donald Trump's policies are not outliers either. Protectionism exists in different shapes. It can be related, for instance, to the protection of strategic industries, state bailouts, or local-content necessities in the case of external investment.

Economic sanctions are another type of punitive geofinancial measure, such as the pingpong game engaged in by Russia and the West, which indicates that some countries are ready to countenance an extended period of economic hardship and diplomatic woe to achieve their political goals. And the same can be said between the West and Iran up until the TNP between the P5+1 and Tehran was signed in 2015, resulting in the lifting of financial sanctions.

The underlying risk is that if the use of punitive geofinancial measures becomes more widespread, a growing number of countries will then revert to protecting national markets. Such protectionism would in turn affect global capital flows considerably. The financial consequences of sanctions can include increased unemployment, slower growth, and heightened fiscal pressures.

Taken together, a slowdown in globalization and a rise in protectionism, not to mention an increasing popularity of sanctions, could result in slower growth in both developed and

[142] World Trade Organization, "Report on G20 Trade Measures: Mid-October 2016 to Mid-May 2017," June 30, 2017, accessed February 20, 2018, https://www.wto.org/english/news_e/news17_e/g20_wto_report_june17_e.pdf.

developing countries. In turn, slower growth in emerging economies could translate into local political instability and social unrest if the aspirations of large groups of the population cannot be met adequately.

Much of the interplay between finance and geopolitical interests plays out not only in the financial arena but also in the Bretton Woods institutions, such as the World Bank and IMF. Indeed, countries' inability to agree on an institutionalized, closer coordination of fiscal policies to decrease global imbalances gives an interesting example. Some commentators see the failure to mitigate these shortcomings, combined with the return of strategic competition in an era defined by erosion of trust, as raising a tail-risk possibility of undermining the Bretton Woods institutions themselves, not to mention the international rule-based system more generally speaking.

These developments are reflected in the recent alternative structures being established by some countries. For instance, as an alternative to these Western-controlled multilateral institutions, rising powers such as Brazil, Russia, India, and China decided in 2014 to establish the New Development Bank, a so-called BRICS bank. Its objective is to provide lending sources up to $34 billion globally,[143] particularly for infrastructure projects. And, in the same year, together with twenty other countries, China also created the Asian Infrastructure Investment Bank for the Asia-Pacific region.

In the eyes of the West, as much as a retreat from global multilateralism could be deemed worrisome, stronger regional multilateralism is not necessarily a bad thing. Many times, local solutions are better tailored to addressing regional problems. At a time of highly interconnected issues that we are told can only be

---

[143] Stephany Griffith-Jones, *A BRICs Development Bank: A Dream Coming True?* (New York: United Nations Conference on Trade and Development, 2014).

resolved through international cooperation, eliminating the obstacles to international collaboration is deemed crucial, as no cooperation at all would be the worst possible outcome.

What can stakeholders do to strengthen international collaboration while simultaneously reducing the risk of the harmful effects of geofinancial measures? Faced with competing strategic pivots and governments' growing tendency to look inward and prioritize their own domestic/regional markets and with an increased reliance on financial levers as a means to gain geopolitical influence, the coming decades will see competitive relationships among the major powers develop into finance and currency wars requiring geofinancial diplomacy.

When markets sleepwalk into geopolitical crises

It seems that notwithstanding the difference in investment horizons, investors remain oblivious to extreme global geopolitical and heightened global economic-growth risks. Granted, risk perceptions evolve for investors in capital expenditures, while risk perceptions among portfolio investors usually change suddenly and dramatically. Indeed, though extreme global geopolitical risk and high global economic-growth risk have undermined capital expenditures around the world, equity and bond investors continue to pump money into increasingly risky investments. Stock markets in developed countries are trending higher, mainly since Donald Trump came to power early in 2017. Stock markets in many developing countries are likewise flirting with record high levels.

However, bond yields worldwide do not reflect weak underlying economic fundamentals—look at the euro crisis. Yields on Spanish and Italian bonds are low notwithstanding the public finances and economies of these countries remaining problematic. Finally, emerging-market stock markets are recovering slowly from the gradual unwinding of the US quantitative-easing measures.

The combination of the Ukraine crisis, the war in Yemen, and the euro crisis, not to mention the military standoff in the East and South China Seas, should be a vector for creating unprecedented instability. However, none of these events are causing any stress in terms of government yields, oil prices, interest rates, or FX rates. While this tendency is worrying, it is not new in the sense that, in the past ten to fifteen years, capital as well as commodity markets have remained as oblivious to geopolitical risks as ever before. Indeed, already in those days—despite the effects of 9/11—researchers had been taken aback by the fact that investors did not yet link extreme global geopolitical risk with high global economic-growth risk.

This complacency was evidenced by the very modest impact that these rapidly rising risks had on the world's financial markets. (As a reminder, the GFC was not caused by a geopolitical flashpoint but rather by financial mismanagement.) Thus, given today's resurgence of the threat of geopolitical risk, it is reasonable to question why global financial markets continue to remain so buoyant.

But first: What is geopolitical risk? *Geopolitik*—a term coined around the turn of the twentieth century by the Swedish political scientist Rudolf Kjellén—has the following standard definition of geopolitical risk: the risk of one country's foreign policy affecting or upsetting domestic social and political policy in another country or region. Alas, this definition does not fully encompass the scope of today's geopolitical risks. Some types of risks fit this description (e.g., Russia's annexation of Crimea and support for separatists in Ukraine, China and Japan's dispute over various islands, and Iran's support of Hezbollah), while others do not.

Indeed, an increasing number of groups are aligned with an ideology rather than with a traditional country (e.g., Boko Haram in Nigeria or Islamic State in the Levant [ISIL]). These groups represent a significant geopolitical threat. Additionally, as a collector of old maps, I see constant reminders of how unstable nations and their spheres of influence can be affected. The establishment and subsequent fall of the world's great empires resulted in changing political structures and, more often than not, armed conflict. Military conflicts may, but do not necessarily, affect markets. Pronounced and prolonged market reaction seems to depend on where the conflict takes place, whether it spreads out, and how much it affects globally vital commodities, such as oil, gas, and gold.

So what causes this inertia of investors toward geopolitical risks? The answer may partly be the ongoing nature of geopolitical risk itself, paraphrased as "the more things change, the more they stay the same." It only takes a cursory Internet search to retrieve statements from ancient philosophers dealing with the certainty of uncertainty. For example, Pliny the Elder, a Roman author born in AD 23, is credited with saying, "In these matters, the only certainty is that there is nothing certain." It is always hard for investors and entrepreneurs to build a portfolio of investments or business assets that allows for the small likelihood of one of these geopolitical threats to escalate into a major crisis affecting yields and returns in the markets. Consequently, the more important query might be, "Has the nature of geopolitical risk changed that much, thereby raising the probability of market disruption?"

An analysis suggests that, despite their levels of atrocities, armed conflicts confined to areas far away from significant world economic activity have a tendency not to affect markets unless they threaten energy supplies or global trade flows. Observe, though, that there might be brief anxiety as business investors assess these criteria. The ability of conflict to spread out to geographic zones of higher economic activity or rather, the fear of a domino effect, appears to be affected by the involvement of a superpower or regional power. Countries that immediately come to mind are the United States, a pretender to the title of superpower, and also China and Russia as regional contenders for this role. We should not forget the European Union, which also wields significant influence in world affairs.

Granted, the United States is the only country that controls or influences approximately 20 percent of global GDP while concomitantly maintaining both a significant military capability and the ability to project that military power globally. While the European Union is, politically speaking, punching below its weight, the EU's economic and financial influences affect faraway geographic zones such as China. Russia does not have sufficient global reach, but its regional attempts to reassert the degree of influence the Soviet Union enjoyed back in the day are apparently a source of growing geopolitical risk. As for China, its importance is growing by the moment in the Asian region, evidenced by the rising tensions with Japan, the Association of Southeast Asian Nations (ASEAN) countries, and India. All three of these major countries have significant military strength, while the EU has a limited military impact, except within the scope of NATO. And China cannot project power on a global level due to the country's relatively small global naval presence, although the People's Liberation Army (PLA) navy's military presence is noticeable regionally. It is hard to act as a global superpower without air and maritime power that can be projected into different geographical areas simultaneously.

Consequently, the United States is the only current major power meeting all three superpower criteria: a 20 percent GDP, significant military capability, and significant global power-projection capacities. It is evident in their actions that Moscow and Beijing are unwilling to accept the status quo as their geopolitical appetites are growing, while the EU prefers to rely on Washington for its security. Both Moscow and Beijing are apparently seeking to assert more influence in the regions bordering their homelands and also in the broader global arena.

China will continue to significantly expand its maritime presence, which in turn will cause the potential for higher tension with the United States as well as fellow Asian countries. In the interim, China is confined to but increasingly assertive in its territorial claims in the South and East China Seas, the Indian Ocean, the Himalayas, and so on.

Although regional in scope, these actions create potential global geopolitical risk by increasing tensions with several neighbors, including Japan, India, Vietnam, Malaysia, Indonesia, Singapore, and the Philippines. Both Japan and the Philippines are likely to call on US naval support if the tension with China escalates to armed conflict. (Note that we even do not talk about the enduring hidden tension between Taiwan and China.) While Russia has significant naval and air resources, it is clear that these need to be modernized and upgraded. Russia has embarked on a military program to rearm and modernize its military forces while concomitantly, Moscow has launched a campaign to reassert economic and political influence over the former Soviet republics (Ukraine, Georgia, Moldava, the Baltic states, etc.).

Until recently, the principal venue used to unlock resistance was hindering access to energy. The virtual regional monopoly that Moscow enjoys in the supply of gas to Europe via Gazprom allows it to reassert influence surreptitiously. Still, the escalation of events in eastern Ukraine has raised the visibility of Russian intentions and thus posed the risk of the spread of conflict. Russia is testing NATO and EU responses, but we do not believe it intends to engage in an all-out military battle in the traditional meaning of the term. More likely, we will see increased hybrid warlike activities (for example, cyber war and the use of local militias as well as paramilitary forces) that have equally global consequences for the levels of defense spending.

Already in Asia, a looming arms race is taking place. Indeed, from the Arabian Sea to the Pacific Ocean, countries fearful of China's growing economic and military might—and worried that the United States is less likely to intervene in the region—are hurtling into a new arms race. However, in Europe, the picture is astonishingly entirely different as NATO members, Western Europeans in particular, push defense budgets to the brink. Indeed, while the Russian bear is showing more aggressive rhetoric corroborated by a succession of provocative actions (violations of sovereignty in Sweden, Finland, the Baltic states, Moldova, and Georgia and prodding Great Britain and France, for instance), the European NATO countries seem to continue to show complacency, except for some rhetoric during an election campaign. History will tell whether Europe has once again been sleepwalking into a geopolitical conflict.

To go back to the premise embedded in the title of this book, the risk to the capital markets may not be through an escalation of a military conflict in Ukraine, the Philippines, or some other place. Instead, the risk might be through a reallocation of financial resources toward a buildup of military capabilities, which may not have the same multiplier effect on global economic growth as other forms of investment.

A significant fear for businesspeople is the fragile momentum in global economic growth, and anything that undermines confidence in increasing risks may affect market valuations. Recent geopolitical events have illustrated how the nature of geopolitical risk is changing. The nature of US military involvement in various crises is a critical factor for change. Washington continues to demonstrate its willingness to commit naval and air resources. However, as first seen during the civil war in Libya, again in Syria, and in combating ISIL, the United States has become less and less willing to commit troops to resolve global conflicts, which is forcing other countries, such as Japan and those in the EU, to reconsider their role in addressing military conflicts.

When you think about it, part of the problem in analyzing geopolitical risk is the word *risk*. It is widely acknowledged that geopolitical risk also offers opportunity. For instance, the fall of the Berlin Wall in 1989 and the collapse of the Soviet Union in 1991 raised significant uncertainty but ultimately yielded an enormous peace dividend. While we can discuss how appropriately the dividend was distributed and how lasting the peace will prove to be, it is difficult to frame these as adverse events.

Of course, to use a metaphor, a risk is similar to matter: it can be transformed, but it rarely disappears. Capital markets tend to overreact to the end of a crisis, assuming tensions are over. However, in most cases, a given risk has merely been transformed into another one. The disappearance of Gaddafi in Libya may have been the fall of a tyrant, but concomitantly, it created a conflict among the factions that the dictator had previously forced to cohabit. It also caused the creation of a failed state on the shores of the Mediterranean Sea. We witnessed a similar phenomenon in the Balkans in the wake of the dismemberment of the Federation of Yugoslavia back in the early 1990s. While few in the West mourn the loss of Muammar Gaddafi, Josip Tito, or Saddam Hussein, we can trace several of the current geopolitical risks to the overthrows or deaths of these dictators and the subtle changes that occurred subsequently (i.e., vacuums of power).

The ugly truth about business attitudes toward geopolitical risk is that we are amoral in our assessment of the consequences to our business portfolios. Consider the death toll in the civil war in Syria, estimated to exceed two hundred thousand; markets have remained mostly unaffected. I do not wish to imply that entrepreneurs and investors as individuals are not profoundly affected by these tragedies. However, the narrow parts of our egos that we use as investors are focused on the impact on the earnings and profits of the corporations we invest in, not the injury, loss of life, or dangerous living conditions that people endure.

Therefore, as already highlighted, geopolitical events do not always lead to significant or ongoing international market responses. That may be in contrast to the extent of media coverage or the level of emotion that we, as empathetic humans, exhibit. However, investors cannot and should never entirely ignore these events, as a few of these geopolitical risks do escalate. We should also observe that the nature of a crisis is chaotic, and therefore the level to which a disaster may increase is hard to predict, especially given the interconnected, conflicting ambitions and sometimes historical antipathy of the antagonists.

Additionally, the current level of central-bank interventions is unprecedented. Over the past few years, various experiments with quantitative easing (QE) have caused enormous liquidity pools to erupt. Therefore, the complacent investor reaction to the current plethora of geopolitical threats may be the result of the blind confidence investors have that central banks will just do whatever it takes to soften the impact of the possible escalation and spread of current threats. If QE ever ends, then business sensitivity to potential shocks may arise.

If the reality is that a geopolitical risk rarely results in a significant, persistent threat to the global financial markets, why do we spend so much time trying to understand it? The human element will always draw attention, but the most intriguing part of a geopolitical risk to investors is the opportunity it creates.

There have always been and will continue to be investors who overreact to events, and that volatility creates an opportunity for those with cooler heads. One might hope that the rise of behavioral finance—aimed at understanding some of the anomalies—will also encompass a higher interest in the impact of geopolitics on capital and commodity markets. (As a reminder, behavioral finance is a relatively new field that seeks to combine behavioral and cognitive psychological theory with conventional economics and finance to provide explanations for why people make irrational financial decisions.)

More importantly, geopolitical risk may lead to change. While general market indices rarely show significant reaction, there may be opportunity in specific asset classes and sectors. If the conflict in Ukraine were to lead to a return to Cold War conditions, what is the chance offered to investors?

Defense spending at NATO is not evenly spread across all states. Will municipal-bond investors benefit in the US states where defense spending is important? These are the kinds of questions we should focus on when considering geopolitical risk.

From precarious heights occur the most significant falls—an aphorism that can easily be applied to the world's equity markets, where valuations offer zero premium for extreme global geopolitical and high global economic-growth risks.

A sudden change in risk perception among portfolio investors, bringing perceived risks into closer alignment with actual threats, may well push the world's financial markets sharply lower in the months ahead. This sudden loss of investor capital could easily trigger a global economic recession.

Overall, unless the energy of a crisis is reinforced by items that threaten global economic growth, such as the involvement of a superpower (with the increased risk of a more significant military conflict and a drop in consumer confidence), a threat to energy prices (and therefore increased transport costs to industries and a decline in consumer spending power), or a risk to the global financial system (with a resulting reduction in lending, leading to a decrease in economic activity), the risk premium reduces quickly.

Geopolitical tensions and carefree financial markets

Opinions differ on the significance of geopolitical threats to the capital markets. On one hand, you have the movement that considers geopolitical risks to have no enduring consequences for global capital markets and to therefore be unimportant. In this regard, the Yom Kippur War of 1973 is the only geopolitical event since WWII that has had a lasting impact. This geopolitical crisis resulted in oil embargoes and a structurally altered energy market. While all other geopolitical events (9/11, the Tiananmen Square massacre in 1989, the Arab Spring in 2015, Iraq's invasion of Kuwait in the early 1990s, the revolution in Tehran in 1979, etc.) resulted in short-lived reactions in the capital markets, they more than recovered within a few months.

In recent times, too, the financial markets seem to have been affected very little by geopolitical unrest. The Brexit vote led to much commotion initially: the day after the referendum, most shares indices in the developed economies fell by more than 5 percent, and the pound devalued by 8 percent against the dollar. Bond prices and corporate credit spreads strengthened, but the markets recovered rapidly, and now the UK markets are booming.

When US presidential candidate Donald Trump was elected in November 2016, things went even faster. Stock prices dropped sharply during the initial opening, but after only a few hours, markets realized that the new president-elect would be responsible for lower taxes, more government spending, and deregulation in various economic sectors. Since early 2017, the S&P 500 and Dow Jones indices rose to levels never before achieved.

Even now, the markets are not responding much to recent geopolitical tensions. For example, the missile launches in North Korea, the increasing tension between Riyadh and Tehran, the upcoming elections in Italy, and President Trump's domestic political disputes—none of these have made the markets nervous. There is a definite signal from the primary indicator of uncertainty on the financial market that corroborates that sentiment: namely, the VIX index.

On the other hand, not everyone is so carefree. Professor Eswar Prasad of Cornell University warns that the financial markets tend to underestimate geopolitical risks.[144] In this, he draws particular attention to the consequences of the recent cyberattacks affecting all kinds of businesses and the economic dangers of increasing protectionism. His concern is supported by the Bank for International Settlements (BIS). In its recently published annual report, the BIS pointed to the discrepancy between geopolitical tensions on one hand and low market uncertainty on the other.

In this regard, the BIS is looking for signals that the market is starting to factor political risks indifferently and is slowly starting to become more nervous. For the BIS, the first sign was the diminishing correlation of the yields of the various submarkets on the stock market. The underlying reason for this change in correlation is that recent geopolitical developments have created winners and losers in the financial markets.

Since Trump's election success, the financial services sector has been characterized as a winner, given the expected interest-rate increase as well as the proposed deregulations. Conversely, the import-intensive sectors have been regarded as losers due to the announced aggressive trade policies that will herald a return to some form of protectionism. The appraisal of the various risks has therefore led to diminishing sectoral correlations of the yields. The same assessment can be applied to regional yield correlations. Countries with close trade relationships with the United States see their exchange rates and share markets

---

[144] Marcel Baartman, "Geopolitical Tensions and Carefree Financial Markets," *Clingendael Magazine*, July 13, 2017, https://www.clingendael.org/publication/geopolitical-tensions-and-carefree-financial-markets.

weakening in general, while other nations expect to profit from the improving world economy.

The BIS's second signal concerned the financial markets' factoring in of very improbable events (a.k.a. tail events). Here, the Basel Committee pointed to the increases in the CBOE SKEW (an index derived from the value of S&P 500 tail risk)[145] and RXM indices (the CBOE S&P 500 Risk Reversal Index, or RXMSM Index, a benchmark index designed to track the performance of a hypothetical risk-reversal strategy).

Although the Basel Committee is doing its best to see to the responses to geopolitical risks in the capital markets, its arguments come off as a little feigned. Perhaps the rationale for the discrepancy between geopolitical tensions and complacency in the capital markets needs to be found somewhere else entirely. The extraordinarily accommodative monetary policies of recent years that have led to significant liquidity surplus in the financial markets (and even to negative yields in some cases) have disrupted many normal market fluctuations.

Risks are therefore not adequately priced, given the current extremely offhand liquidity ratios. This disruption could also apply to the VIX index. The markets, in this case, assume that the central banks will mitigate any adverse impacts of geopolitical tensions by facilitating monetary policies, so capital markets remain unconcerned. Such a thing took place days after the Brexit vote in 2016: the Bank of England lowered its base rate to mitigate the uncertainty. However, the day that the normalization of monetary policies becomes the norm again, liquidity will become scarcer. As a consequence, geopolitical tensions will start to translate into increasing uncertainty in the financial markets, possibly sooner than expected. In this case, the main thing will be

---

[145] Similar to VIX, the price of S&P 500 tail risk is calculated from the prices of S&P 500 out-of-the-money options. SKEW typically ranges from 100 to 150.

to keep a close eye on inflation expectations. After all, higher inflation leads to normalization of monetary policy and therefore to the fair pricing of risks, including those of geopolitical tensions.

Geofinance: "He who licks knives will soon cut his tongue"

As usual, markets continue to underprice political risk in a desperate search for some yields, particularly in a low-interest-rate environment. Those same markets are betting that economic relationships will trump political ones. Financial and trade markets may be treating the international shouting match as a nothing more than a little local difficulty for Russia and barely even noticing the killings in Syria or Yemen or the military escalation in the China Seas. And, granted, money always speaks louder than words. But eventually, the fire will spread and cause economic disruptions, pushing awry the markets' invisible hand.

Generally speaking, while political-risk analysts have been speculating for the past two years about a new cold war involving the West and Russia and/or China, particularly in the aftermath of claims of Russian involvement in a recent air crash in Ukraine and China's aggressive stance toward its neighboring countries, investors and business entrepreneurs continue to see barely an icicle forming. Apparently, as already mentioned, the central banks' quantitative easing has acted as an anesthetic for the capital markets as a whole, thus helping to suppress volatility and perceived uncertainty. As the US Fed removes the blanket of monthly asset purchases and steadily increases interest rates, volatility will progressively increase, and geopolitical events will most likely represent a bigger toll on financial markets. In practice, without the anesthetic of the central banks' asset-purchase programs, the capital markets will transition back to allowing free markets to set interest rates.

The scope for immediate economic contagion from any default in Ukraine, Russia, China, Thailand, and so on is, as I write this, relatively limited, although the relatively large exposures of some European banks, mostly through subsidiaries, may raise a few eyebrows. The geopolitical significance is apparently much more substantial.

But here, too, one struggles to see as likely a scenario in which increasingly acrimonious relations between the West and the Moscow-Beijing tandem would lead to severe repercussions for the global economy beyond, say, higher energy prices for Europe.

But these events are occurring against a backdrop of a steady stream of negative stories in emerging markets—from Turkey's ongoing alleged corruption tapes and the lingering protests in Thailand to China's constant struggle to rein in credit without destroying growth.

And, notwithstanding growing tactical underweights by many investors, emerging markets—along with all other high-yielding assets—in strategic terms have been the darlings of asset allocators over the past ten years and have seen substantial institutional inflows that have yet to reverse entirely.

Each additional headline and each downward revision to emerging markets' growth prospects take the markets closer to the point at which investors reevaluate the risk-reward of their emerging markets' assets to their portfolios, as has already taken place with gold and silver and is happening now with commodities more broadly as well.

And today, with US interest rates steadily creeping up, yields are likewise increasing in the developed countries, making emerging-market yields fear for competition.

At best, this will result in drastically reduced inflows toward the emerging markets, making refinancing of the large volume of corporate and sovereign emerging-market debt that has been building up in recent years challenging. In the worst case, it could result in a panicky rush of outflows. In the long run, even the developed markets will be exposed to a similar portfolio reassessment. Indeed, in a global world in which the run-up in asset prices owes more to central-bank monetary largesse than it does to the underlying macro fundamentals, it feels almost ineluctable. But we have to give the last word to the Ukrainians: "He who licks knives will soon cut his tongue."

Financial markets and the mirage of geopolitics

If you want to fish for geopolitical risk, you can easily find it, and markets know it. When geopolitical tensions flare and the investor class sits up at attention, the character of the stock market tends to change almost immediately.

Growing geopolitical risk has been on everyone's radar for several years now, but it's always helpful to have this reminder: the only time since WWII that a violent conflict has had a medium-term adverse impact on markets was in 1973, when the Israeli-Arab war led to a Saudi oil embargo against the United States and a quadrupling of oil prices.

Nevertheless, some find it striking that many financial markets are at, or near, all-time highs (or lows, depending on the indicator) despite this diet of bad news. The Dow Jones Industrial Average (DJIA) is gaining points day by day; despite the Greek crisis, bond yields seem to fare relatively well; the US dollar appears to strengthen on an ongoing basis; and oil prices seem unmoved by geopolitical tensions.

Figure 12: **FX Rate—USD per Euro**

USD to EUR Chart

3 Feb 2008 00:00 UTC - 30 Jan 2018 03:05 UTC   **USD/EUR** close:**0.80837** low:**0.62597**
high:**0.96231**

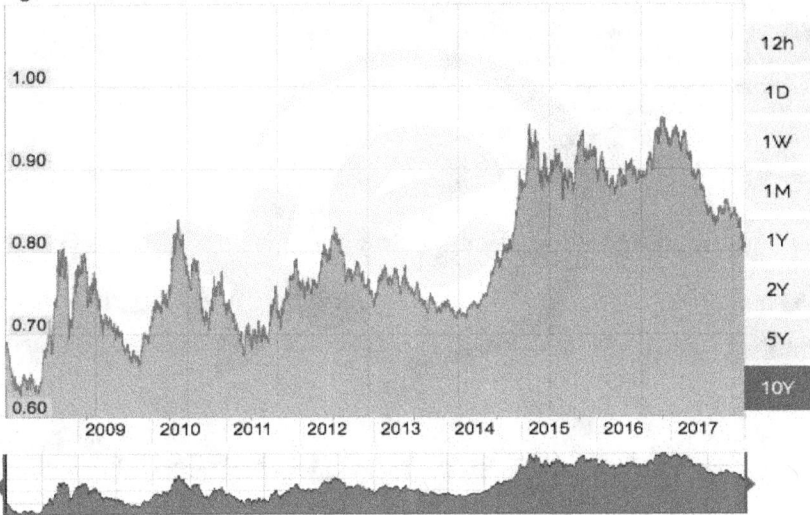

Source: XE[146]

[146] XE.com, "XE Currency Charts: USD to EUR," accessed January 30, 2018,
https://www.xe.com/currencycharts/?from=USD&to=EUR&view=10Y.

Figure 13: Oil Chart

Crude Oil Prices - 70 Year Historical Chart

Interactive charts of West Texas Intermediate (WTI or NYMEX) crude oil prices per barrel back to 1946. The price of oil shown is adjusted for inflation using the headline CPI and is shown by default on a logarithmic scale. The current month is updated on an hourly basis with today's latest value. The current price of WTI crude oil as of January 29, 2018 is **$66.26** per barrel.

Source: Macro Trends[147]

[147] Macro Trends, "Crude Oil Prices—70 Year Historical Chart," accessed January 29, 2018, http://www.macrotrends.net/1369/crude-oil-price-history-chart.

Even the volatility is low. This index mirrors investor sentiment and expected levels of market volatility, tracking the volatility of S&P 500 (VIX) option prices as a way of surveying anticipated levels of near-term volatility in the US equity market. However, one should not overstate this absence of bearishness; in the spring of 2018, most significant indices (including the Dow) are exhibiting all-time highs on the year. Even Japan and Australia are performing very well, not to mention the entire European continent and even the United Kingdom, notwithstanding Brexit. Perhaps the capital markets would have been even more bullish but for geopolitical factors. And, granted, the prospect of a still-possible Grexit (even though Athens will most likely step out of the bailout scheme this summer) is putting some pressure on European government-bond yields but not to the extent one would envision given the systemic consequences of Greece defaulting on its debt.

Consequently, notwithstanding the following, markets seem to have remained unnervingly calm:

- the tit-for-tat sanctions against Russia
- Islamic jihadists still spreading terror in Iraq and Syria and also threatening Libya and Afghanistan
- Israel recently confronting Hamas and potentially Hezbollah again
- Boko Haram kidnapping children and burning down villages in Nigeria
- the Congo still being in turmoil
- North Korea launching an increasing number of missile tests
- China and Japan rattling sabers over uninhabited islands

It is as if sudden geopolitical tensions never erupted and nothing happened in the past twenty-five years (like two Gulf wars, a Balkan war, and 9/11, for example).

Maybe investors' insouciance in the face of lingering geopolitical risks is a result of their experience that change can be positive, as we've witnessed over the past thirty years: the shredding of the Iron Curtain in 1989, the demise of the Soviet Union in 1991, the emergence of China as an economic power since the 2000s, and so on. However, the current reemergence of nationalism, whether in the extreme (Russia/Ukraine), moderate (Japan/China tensions), or mild form (populism in Western Europe) points in the opposite direction.

Still, observation shows that geopolitical risk has rarely affected markets over the medium to long term. Indeed, analyzing sixteen serious geopolitical crises since 1950, only four saw the S&P down one month later. Similarly, four events saw markets lower over the next six or twelve months. The leading contender as a consistent, primary driver of significant structural alteration in levels of global geopolitical anxiety is the rise and fall of the world's leading power: namely, the United States.

In general, one could argue that periods of single-superpower world dominance have been times of relative structural geopolitical stability, while times of equal and competing great powers have been times of structurally high geopolitical instability. Hence, the question is, are we still in a period of *pax*, or are we entering the waters of a wild river whereby geopolitical tensions will ultimately be adequately priced?

To highlight this question, then, let's go all the way back to the tumult that followed the passing of Alexander the Great— although that might seem a bit of a stretch. Alexander only ruled for thirteen years and spent much of his time waging war against rival empires. He was a one-person-show source of geopolitical tension, and after his death, the whole region was in turmoil.

Two other illustrations are the Roman and British Empires, a.k.a. the Pax Romana and the Pax Britannica. In each case, the realms peaked at more than 20 percent of global output, and the alpha power had a substantial incentive to foster economic activity backed by military muscle (naval in the case of Britain, and legions in the case of the Romans) to impose its will. The regions they occupied were in relative peace, except the areas bordering the rival empires. Rome fell in AD 476, together with the last of the Roman emperors in the West who were overthrown by the Germanic tribes.

The order that the Roman Empire had brought to Western Europe for a thousand years was no more. For the British Empire, the Pax Britannica lasted more than three hundred years—from the 1600s to 1914 with the advent of WWI. (Some claim that the empire continued until 1997, with the handover of Hong Kong to China.) And after WWI, the United States eventually took over the role of superpower, along with the high portion of global GDP. But this is where the reasoning faces a bit of a juggle. The periods of Pax Americana have been very short lived, as its empire only started after 1918. First, the threats from Germany and Japan had to be seen off. And then, after 1945, Washington faced a rival superpower in Moscow, which may not have matched it in economic power but did so in military might. So the shortish period of American "hyperpowerdom" can be dated only from 1990. However, that lasted only ten years, as since the 2000s, China has been the rising power, together with the reemergent Russia.

Indeed, the period of the 1990s was a time of investor abundance and prosperity. But the perception of Washington's global dominance lured the George W. Bush administration into the Iraq invasion of 2003, from which much subsequent instability and chaos have flowed. In any case, the United States has now dropped below the 20 percent of global GDP ratio that marks global ascendancy. And its ability to leverage its economic and financial power into political power has also waned. There may be three underlying reasons for this:

- First, since the global financial crisis, the United States and the West in general have lost their appetite for policing global affairs. It is not so much that they have lost confidence; it is more that the fake reasons for invading Iraq and the vast costs and chaos that this war brought with it reignited some isolationist tendencies. In other words, the wars in Afghanistan and, in particular, Iraq, have left Washington far less willing to gendarme the world. One of the major lessons that the United States seems to have learned is that it can no longer solve all the world's problems alone—and, in fact, can often make them worse.

- Second, the apparent demise of laissez-faire economics, combined with the United States' weak public finances, has pushed the country into a more protectionist mood. As this retreat into "America First" has grown, so has American willingness to convince the rest of the world that the country should follow the Western liberal-order model.

- Third, the rise of intractable partisan politics in the United States has left the American people with ever less faith in its government and with a democratic system that can no longer build a consensual strategic vision. China has emerged as the rival superpower and is flexing its muscles in all sorts of ways.

If these reasons are well grounded, then the rise of global geopolitical tensions in the past five years (and most notably in the past twelve months) may well prove not short lived but fundamental to the current global system. And the world may continue to undergo more frequent, longer lasting, and further-reaching geopolitical tensions than it has over the past thirty-something years. If this is the case, then financial markets might have to price in a higher level of geopolitical risk in the years to come.

To this, one might also add the domestic tensions that have resulted from the unequal distribution of wealth that has led to a rise in votes for extreme populist parties. We must emphasize that all these factors are structural rather than issues that should trigger an immediate sell-off in the markets.

Thus, one should be even more cautious about those who argue that "this time, it's different"—that the fifty years of the twentieth century when stock market valuations were lower are irrelevant because of the occurrence of the two world wars.

Today's period is "normal" in the sense that rival powers are competing for resources and influence as every empire has done in past centuries; tension, and thus conflict, are ineluctable. The Muslim world may be going through a series of religious wars similar to those that plagued Christian Europe from the 1600s to the start of the Age of Enlightenment in 1701. All this will disrupt investment and commerce, and thus, geopolitical risks are not going to go away.

The illusion of geopolitics that the markets portray is something we all need to think about. But what is truly important is not what markets say but instead what information they hold that we do not know. Therefore, we need more thorough analysis of the best way to mine the data we need. No, the situation is not ideal, but it's not as bad as we might think.

Global finance is not only about the capital markets; it is also about risk management. Credit risk, market risk, liquidity risk, operational risk, interest-rate risk, FX risk, and geopolitical risk are critical vectors for better understanding the exposure of a financial institution to movements in the markets, a given geopolitical context, and how the financial system itself is adjusting to these changes.

The key to sound risk management is solid underwriting. Therefore, organizations need to strategize on how to reach these goals in this day and age of geopolitical and market turbulence and lack of commitment from individual leaders to conduct proper underwriting.

Mathematical models are useful but should merely be viewed as tools for better understanding of the geopolitical and market environment in which a financial institution operates. Overreliance on mathematical models delegates decision making away from the bank executive to the models, which is not acceptable, as models are only as good as their assumptions. What goes in must come out.

The connection between geopolitics and financial markets is not random

Geopolitical hotbeds, from North Korea to Ukraine through the Middle East and the China Seas, are interconnected, in essence, with financial market pressures. Therefore, geopolitics as a tail event is not random and should not be seen as an unknown unknowable (as most tail events are, by the way).

Geopolitical tensions are also the result of continuing globalization. But unfortunately, risk analysts and investors alike are mostly unable to analyze the connection between these two dots, and the evidence is that international financial markets typically fail to respond to geopolitical developments until they culminate in graphic headlines.

Once again, given the current lingering threat of geopolitical risk, it is reasonable to question why global financial markets remain so buoyant.

Figure 14: S&P 500 Index around Military Conflicts

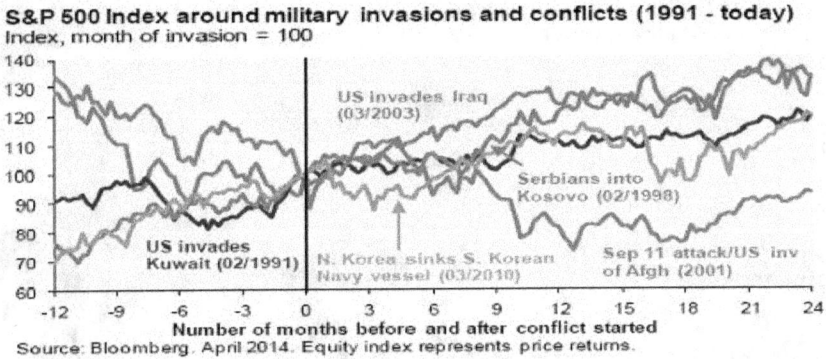

S&P 500 Index around military invasions and conflicts (1991 - today)
Index, month of invasion = 100

US invades Iraq (03/2003)

Serbians into Kosovo (02/1998)

US invades Kuwait (02/1991)

N. Korea sinks S. Korean Navy vessel (03/2010)

Sep 11 attack/US inv of Afgh (2001)

Number of months before and after conflict started

Source: Bloomberg. April 2014. Equity index represents price returns.

A sharp increase in Middle East geopolitical tensions, first with the resurgence of a radical al-Qaeda affiliate now called the Islamic State and, more recently, with escalating military flashpoints in the Palestinian territories, has barely caused a blip in global markets.

And the same can be said about the turbulence that North Korea is creating. Concomitantly, the border conflict between Ukraine and Russia—one of the largest oil producers globally—has reached a more dangerous level, as no end seems in sight, and also has resulted in little oil-price response. Indeed, it is difficult to identify another flashpoint of which the markets would not be too dismissive.

Figure 15: Brent Crude Oil Prices and Conflicts

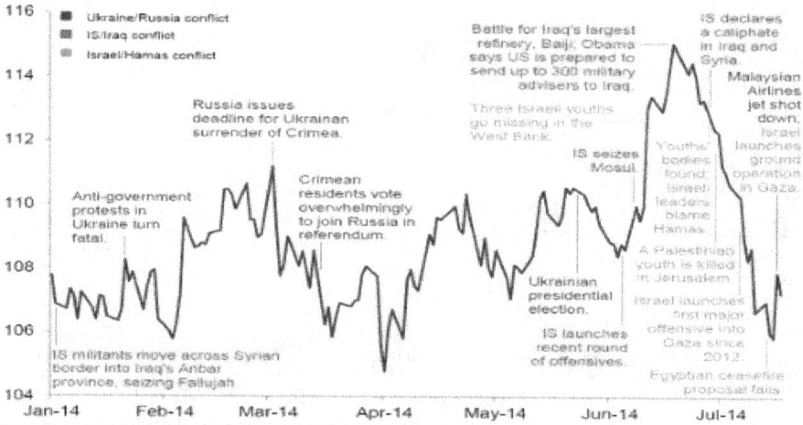

Source: Goldman Sachs Global Investment Research, various news sources.

Figure 16: Gold Price and Conflicts

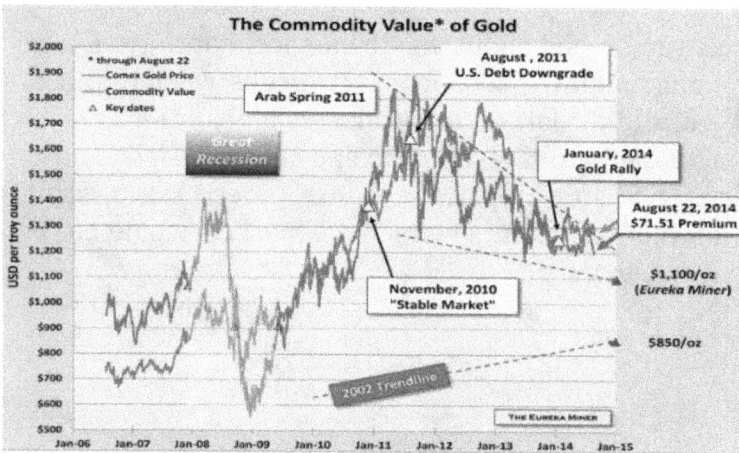

Source: Kitco—The Eureka Miner Gold Value Index

Western governments are deliberately defaulting on their
mountains of debt without officially calling it a default. They are

doing so by manufacturing price inflation through unprecedented monetary expansion, thereby lowering the purchasing power of creditors, which include some of the most influential countries in the world, most notably China. But are we experiencing inflation at a time of warnings about deflation? Price increases are not adequately being reflected in the statistics published by central banks in the West, but they are very much there. The rising prices of essential items—such as wheat in the Middle East, pork in China, and onions in India—are causing ripple effects in those societies.

Even though inflation indicators published by the central banks may suggest low numbers, it is a misconstruction that price inflation will not matter in the advanced economies. Indeed, even though deflation risk was, until recently, on the radar screen of many investors, the rising cost of living reflected in the prices of real estate, utilities, food, health care, education, and so on remains a top issue for households in these developed economies.

In response to the Western quasi-default on sovereign debt through manufactured inflation, international creditors, including China and Russia, are buying strategic assets around the world, including those in food, infrastructure, telecommunications, and energy. The Chinese and Russians are also aggressively pursuing their claims to disputed territories, such as in the China Seas (South and East) for China and the European hinterland for Russia.

The nature of the geopolitical power game is changing, as boots are no longer necessarily required on the ground. Modern-day conflicts are conducted in a hybrid way, such as by using paramilitary forces or local militias, space satellites, cyberspace, monetary policies, or financial instruments. China's military PLA forces train to operate without GPS, and Beijing is testing destructive antisatellite systems. Why? Because by controlling satellite systems, an army can deny its enemy the ability to operate the weapons that rely on satellite technology. Cyber hacking has emerged as a tool of modern warfare; the laptops of high-ranking US defense officials have frequently been breached from within the Pentagon. It's not just satellite technology and cyber hacking, however; monetary policy and financial instruments themselves have become power-projection tools in conflicts.

But why is it that risk analysts are unable to notice and analyze such developments thoroughly? Many analysts today grew up in a post–Cold War era and have thus not yet observed any war between major military powers. They also have not yet experienced the ravages caused by price inflation. These analysts need to read history to realize that what they have experienced is not normal. Alas, it is normal for the world to experience major geopolitical conflicts, substantial inflation, and changing borders—events in which fortunes are lost and won.

So, what should risk professionals do to manage geopolitical risk? I do not think the answer is holding gold, mainly because governments can expropriate gold in one way or another. The record-high prices for diamonds suggest that people are turning to them to protect their wealth. To manage geopolitical risk, buy or invest in strong business brands that can pass on the effects of inflation—just as the Chinese and the Gulf States are doing now.

The contagion effect of sovereign risk on the banking industry

The global financial crisis (GFC) has, not surprisingly, emboldened authorities, mainly those in developed countries, to implement prudential measures designed both to lower the risk of banks failing and to decrease the burden on taxpayers should that failure occur. Much debate about future support has taken place and new legislation passed in several countries, but coordinated and comprehensive legislation and structural reforms that would be most defining in the evolution of bank resolution have not yet become law or been implemented in most of these countries.

Large banks have usually been bailed out by taxpayer money when necessary (the too-big-to-fail syndrome), and as a result of the last GFC, new legislative and supervisory processes are underway in critical markets to reduce both bank risk and sovereign support for banks. But depending on the country, there will be challenges in implementing effective bank-resolution mechanisms. Nations differ in the extent and pace of their change, depending on legislative developments, practical aspects regarding bank resolvability, and politics.

And, as many risk managers and analysts know, bailout support is a critical input in determining the creditworthiness of banks, and this kind of support has historically had a considerable impact on senior-level default risk. More often than not, governments with the ability to do so have extended extraordinary support to systemically important banks that had become or were on the point of becoming nonviable (Dexia, ABN AMRO, UBS, Fortis, Citibank, etc.). This government support was evident not just in the most recent financial crisis (2007 onward) but in previous ones also. Until the events in Cyprus in the first quarter of 2013, cross-border support had even been provided within the euro area (e.g., bank or joint bank/sovereign bailout packages for Spain, Ireland, Greece, and Portugal).

By contrast, small banks are often not supported because contagion risks arising from a small-bank default are considered limited, and other measures, including deposit-insurance schemes, are usually in place to look after depositors up to a point. However, this approach ignores the theory of network whereby one weak link can weaken the entire chain. There have also been cases in which systemically important financial institutions, mostly domestic ones, have been allowed to default. However, assuming they have the ability, governments are usually reluctant to sanction a senior-level default if the systemic cost (the impact in the broader banking sector or more general financial stability) is higher than the cost of an individual bailout.

Governments are also more likely to be supportive where banking sectors are highly politicized, with a government-owned national champion or policy bank often likely to be looked on especially favorably. In China, for example, the banking sector is mostly state owned or affiliated and highly politicized. The government remains focused on a stable banking system due to the critical role it plays in financing state-owned corporations, governments, infrastructure programs, and economic growth. Banking sectors in parts of the Middle East, notably most GCC countries, also share some of these characteristics.

Government and regulatory responses to financial crises have been highly varied and can be split very broadly into two areas: those aimed at addressing idiosyncratic and systemic financial-sector risks, primarily by enhancing banks' capitalization and reducing their market/liquidity risks and those aimed at facilitating the orderly resolution of banks that do fail while minimizing the cost to taxpayers, placing the expense on shareholders and creditors by implementing more formal and effective resolution frameworks. Generally speaking, over the medium term, the interplay of these two themes is critical for banks whose creditworthiness is underpinned by support rather than intrinsic factors. At the forefront of the "making banks stronger" agenda, and spanning well beyond the US/European epicenter of the crisis, is Basel III. This essentially has a "more and better" agenda: more and better-quality capital and more and better-quality liquidity. In many cases, Basel III still needs enactment into local countries' regulations, but it has very broad buy-in and is positive for inherent bank risk and financial stability.

One may expect that improvements to banks' financial profiles prompted by the Basel III agenda will most likely lead to further developments of creditworthiness over the next year or two as capitalization and liquidity profiles improve, for example, for European banks recovering from the crisis. But the related structural and behavioral initiatives vary in their size, scope, and geographical reach.

They range from central clearing of swaps in order to reduce counterparty and thus contagion risk to the ring-fencing of activities (in the United Kingdom and France and under consideration across the broader EU) to the EU Banking Union proposals to the Volcker Rule and restrictions on proprietary trading to changes in compensation structures, bonus deferrals, clawbacks, and so on. Assuming no unintended consequences, these, too, ought to be net positives for bank creditworthiness profiles over the medium to long term.

It is evident that the bank-resolution agenda does not have the same level of priority across the banking world, especially in many emerging markets. This means that support propensity is likely to remain high over the rating time frame in many jurisdictions. However, over time, even a number of these countries may face external pressures to fall into line with most major developed markets.

Where there is intent to reduce the implicit and sometimes even the explicit support for banks, it comes down to the severity of the roadblocks to determine when/whether it will be useful and thus when/whether senior creditors might become more exposed to losses. Legislative roadblocks exist where legislation or regulation is far from optimal. Such issues should not be viewed as insurmountable, noting, for example, the Financial Stability Board (FSB) opinion that the EU's Bank Recovery and Resolution Directive (BRRD) represents substantial progress with respect to its suggested framework. In any case, Cyprus is a recent example in Europe of legislation being drawn up quickly if needed.

These points are most relevant for large and complex banking groups operating in multiple jurisdictions, across various business lines, and through numerous legal entities. However, operational issues can also represent roadblocks to sufficient resolution for purely domestic players.

As already mentioned, complexity can indeed represent a significant hurdle to resolution for several reasons, including the difficulty of identifying and segregating core or "utility" functions such as payments processing, intragroup exposures that can rapidly transmit risk across multiple entities, inadequate resolution-funding mechanisms, and the difficulty of coordinating with resolution bodies across domestic sectors or borders in a resolution scenario. These make a useful resolution not only technically hard but also potentially dangerous from a systemic-risk/financial-stability perspective.

Ring-fencing of utility functions, resolution plans or living wills, minimum "bail-in-able" debt plans, and the creation of ex-ante resolution funds are examples of initiatives to address these problems. These are concepts that are taking shape, to varying extents and at different paces, in places such as the EU and the United States, but they often have minimal traction elsewhere.

Historically, it is unlikely that policy makers and regulators in most of the markets eagerly and willingly sought to commit vast sums of taxpayer funds in the name of shoring up the banking system. But with no active circuit breaker in place to address financial contagion, faced with a choice presented to them as either 1) write a large government-issued check to the banking system or 2) suffer the imminent collapse of your financial system and likely economy as a whole, the decision has almost always been number one.

Politics can—and often do—hinder the introduction of new legislation or mean that perfectly good legislation is not used to its full theoretical capacity. The full implications of actions proposed tend to be fervently debated, and this is more protracted the more complex the matter, such as in cross-border situations. Even with all resolution tools and technical safeguards in place, invoking resolution powers that hit senior creditors of large banks involves considerable uncertainty as to the consequences. Choosing not to do so when the choice is yours may still be a legitimate option.

Among other political challenges are cultural sensitivities, which tend to be more common in emerging-market countries but are also found in developed markets in Asia, such as Japan, Korea, and Taiwan, which have a history of varying degrees of support for large banks. In countries that exhibit a high degree of state ownership in the banking system, such as China, India, and Taiwan, a default by any state-owned bank—whether a systemically important financial institution or not—would raise questions about the financial health or stewardship of the federal or provincial government and be received poorly by the broader population, who expect government banks to be safely managed.

Another concern, especially in emerging markets with underdeveloped bank-resolution infrastructures, is the degree of integration across sectors and state ownership of entities, including corporations. Defaults by systemically important financial institutions may pose systemic/contagion risks, depending on the degree of exposure that counterparties, often state owned themselves, have to those banks. Loss of employment through bank-insolvency administrations is politically sensitive; hence, the state may choose to provide necessary support to a failed bank or orchestrate a merger between a failed bank and a more extensive/stronger bank.

Even within the EU, it would undoubtedly be folly to assume that all national authorities are equally resolute in their desire not to use taxpayer money to support their banking systems or bail out senior bank creditors. This means that some EU governments may still look to stabilize banking sectors or even individual banks before the point at which conditions for resolution are met and resolution authorities can intervene. EU state-aid rules could still be relevant in such circumstances; it would depend on whether any banks are advantaged or disadvantaged from a competition perspective. But these would not represent a threat to senior creditors, only junior ones.

Key to facilitating an orderly resolution is being able to do so without harming the required payments architecture of the affected bank and without triggering direct or indirect prolonged contagion risks to other banks, counterparties, and depositors within a sector. Even when all the practical adjuncts to resolution tools, such as resolution plans and sufficient resolution funds, are in place, resolution of a large bank by way of a business sale, asset separation, and bridge bank tools is likely to be fraught with complexity and risk.

Overall, the bail-in tool, while still potentially posing considerable general funding market-contagion risks, probably represents the most credible threat to senior debt just because it is burdened with fewer practical hurdles than other resolution tools. Despite this, there remains a lingering skepticism among some market participants as to the sustained efficacy of any bail-in mechanism.

Individually, if an entity is expected to hold significant amounts of loss-absorbing debt in its new incarnation, and—particularly for systemically important financial institutions with a large and diverse global investor base—those debt investors have just been bailed in, it does beg the question of which investors are reasonably expected to lend to the newly restructured entity. If not, in practice, a restructuring under resolution may be little more than a rest stop on the way to liquidation.

Advanced economies have to play the geofinancial game

Despite having the most powerful economies on earth and given the current trends in globalization and integration of markets, many advanced economies, such as the United States, Japan, the United Kingdom, France, and Germany, need to add one more item to their arsenal of power tools. Indeed, next to geo-economical tools, these advanced economies should also embrace the systematic use of financial instruments to accomplish geopolitical objectives. None of these developed nations have outgrown their need for military force, however, which will remain a central component of any foreign policy. But this large-scale failure of collective strategic memory regarding geofinance denies the capitals of these advanced nations potent tools to accomplish their foreign-policy objectives.

Geofinance has been used for decades, though perhaps it has not been labeled as such specifically. We could focus on the use of geopolitical or military power for financial ends, or we could define geofinance more broadly as "the entanglement of international finance, geopolitics, and strategy" in a kind of catchall definition, but this obscures more than it clarifies.

In the particular context of foreign policy, those who use the concept have primarily confined themselves to traditional examinations of international finance and sanctions. Typically, these inquiries depart from a narrow understanding of foreign policy but have no single geopolitical aspect, apart, perhaps, from a widely held belief that expanded finance relations promote peace. It is mostly finance for finance's sake.

Many interpretations of geofinance are useful, but they are also incomplete. Strikingly, none of the existing definitions of geofinance succeed in comprehensively capturing the phenomenon that, as an everyday empirical matter, seems most responsible for the term's recent resurrection: the use of financial instruments to produce beneficial geopolitical results. With this in mind, here is a definition of geofinance: "the use of financial instruments to promote and defend national interests and to produce beneficial geopolitical results, plus the effects of other nations' financial actions on a country's geopolitical goals."

The United States is an excellent proponent of geofinance, as illustrated by the various antiterrorist laws enacted in the aftermath of 9/11 that particularly focus on money and banking transactions. There is the Financial Anti-Terrorism Act providing, among other things, federal jurisdiction over foreign money launderers and money laundered through foreign banks. All financial institutions were forced to form anti-money-laundering programs. And then there was the notorious USA Patriot Act, focusing on international money laundering. The State Department also imposed financial sanctions on foreign banks providing support to rogue regimes such as North Korea, Sudan, Iran, and so forth. The same was also implemented vis-à-vis Russia, Venezuela, and more.

It is the Office of Foreign Assets Control (OFAC) of the US Department of the Treasury that administers and enforces, among other things, financial sanctions based on national security and US foreign-policy objectives against terrorists, targeted foreign countries and regimes, global narcotics traffickers, those engaged in activities related to the dissemination of weapons of mass destruction, and other threats to the foreign policy, national security, or economy of the United States.

China is also often described as one of the world's leading practitioners of geofinance. It is also the primary underlying reason that regional and global power projection has become such a financial exercise, as opposed to a military one. China makes investments, grants loans, and provides financial guarantees, for example, in the scope of its Silk Road project. It invests enormous sums of money in Pakistan and Sri Lanka, to the detriment of India. It financially rewards countries that have abandoned the recognition of Taiwan as a sovereign country. It promises trade and business with several African as well as South American nations in exchange for access to their commodity and energy markets. It reduces financial advantages to European governments that host the Dalai Lama. It initiated the establishment of the BRICS group, consciously excluding Washington. It promotes the Chinese-led Asian Infrastructure Investment Bank to compete with the Washington-based World Bank. In its financial assistance to Africa, it privileges nations that vote with China at the United Nations. It provides more loans to Latin American countries than the World Bank and the International Monetary Fund combined. Its financial assistance props up the economy of Venezuela, the most anti-American regime in South America. The White House has no coherent foreign policies to deal with these Chinese geofinancial actions, many of which are aimed squarely at America's allies and friends in Asia and beyond.

In addition to this rise of Chinese geofinancial power[148], witness the return of Russia's systematic destabilizing geofinancial policies in Eurasia and beyond. Russia is waiving and forgiving loans in countries such as Algeria, Cuba, and Venezuela. To deprive Kiev of crucial transit payments, it occasionally shuts down the gas pipes flowing from Russia to Europe. It promises massive financial assistance to the annexed Crimea. It financially bribes the weaker, cash-strapped members of the EU in hopes of provoking a defection from the US-EU sanctions against Russia.

---

[148] Nicholas Burns et al., *America's National Security Architecture: Rebuilding the Foundation* (Washington, DC: The Aspen Institute, 2016); Robert D. Blackwill and Jennifer M. Harris, *War by Other Means: Geoeconomics and Statecraft* (Cambridge, MA: The Belknap Press, 2016).

For all the readiness drills and military commitments being undertaken by NATO leaders, the United States has no consistent policies to deal with Russia's resurgent geofinancial coercion.

The donor states of the Arab world's economic powerhouse, the Gulf Cooperation Council, are equally uninhibited in their use of geofinancial instruments. The Gulf states pledged $12 billion in 2015 as financial aid to Egypt, adding to the more than $20 billion already contributed since the military ouster of former president Morsi. Oman commits $500 million in financial aid to Egypt. Riyadh continues to provide financial support to Iraqi Sunni tribes fighting ISIL and al-Qaeda. Saudi Arabia and the United Arab Emirates together supply Jordan with more than $2 billion in annual financial aid, leveraging Amman to contain and dismantle the Muslim Brotherhood. With sums of money like these, the Gulf states have necessarily set off a new Great Game in the region; the rules are geofinancial, and once again, Washington does not appear to have any foreign policy to respond.

So it is for many nations—the theater of foreign-policy engagement has for some time been predominantly the financial markets. Many governments today are as likely or more likely to voice disagreements with foreign policies through restrictions on trade in critical minerals or the buying and selling of debt than through military activities. Most nations today blow their foreign-policy trumpets mainly to economic rhythms.

Nowadays and across the political spectrum, Washington instinctively debates the application of military instruments to address these complex challenges. There is no comparable discussion in Washington of any of the following:

- Prioritizing financial-denial strategies in the fight against ISIS

- Returning Ukraine to financial viability as a way to check the Kremlin's designs for a *Novorossiya* (New Russia)

- Building a Middle East coalition to blunt the financial transmission lines that Iran relies on to project influence in the region

- Making reform of the Egyptian economy a primary US foreign-policy objective

- Strengthening Jordan to withstand the effects of the Syrian conflict

- Mounting a significant, patient financial effort to bolster the faltering Afghan economy, a prerequisite for defeating the Taliban over the long run

- Building into a new multilateral agreement (or into the Asia pivot more broadly) defenses to help US allies steel themselves against financial bullying from Beijing

One of the US founding fathers, Thomas Jefferson, would have regarded this as exceedingly odd. He did not send the newly minted US Army to conquer French territory between the Rocky Mountains and the Mississippi River; instead, in an exquisite geofinancial enterprise, he bought it. To prevent London from assisting the Southern Confederacy, the Lincoln administration threatened Great Britain with the loss of billions of US dollars invested in American securities. Government support for overseas private investment drove both American engagement with Latin America and the rebuilding of Europe in the 1920s. In the 1930s, the Roosevelt White House deployed finance as a way to preempt Nazi encroachment into the Western Hemisphere and tried to utilize the US Export-Import Bank to blunt the rise of Tokyo.

Eighteen months after the start of World War II in Europe, the US Lend-Lease policy of 1941 allowed Washington to supply Allied nations with military assets required to win that war. In July 1944, delegates from the Allied countries, led by Washington, signed the Bretton Woods Agreement that was explicit in its belief that strengthened global financial cooperation, built on British and US terms, could help prevent the horrors of another global war. US secretary of state George Marshall put in place the famous Marshall Plan in the period from 1945 to 1947, whereby Washington assisted in the European economic recovery with direct financial aid amounting to $13 billion (a current value of nearly $140 billion as of January 2018).

American experts in finance tend to resist putting financial policies to work for geopolitical purposes, in part because the notion of subjugating finance in this way challenges some of the most profound assumptions of their discipline: the heart of politics is always power; the aim of finance is wealth. Power is inherently limited. The quest for power is therefore competitive. It is a zero-sum game. Wealth, by contrast, is limitless, which makes finance a positive-sum game. Because many US finance experts and policy makers tend to view the world through positive-sum logic and have little understanding of the realities of power competition among states, they tend to be skeptical of using financial policies to strengthen America's power projection vis-à-vis competitor states.

The notion has also encountered ambivalence from foreign-policy strategists. Although they are steeped in traditional geopolitics and are not averse to viewing financial instruments of statecraft with zero-sum logic, most strategists fail to recognize the power and potential of finance as an instrument of national purpose. Thus, embraced by neither most finance experts nor most foreign-policy strategists, the use of financial instruments as tools of statecraft has become an orphaned subject. For a time, it seemed of no great consequence. In the years following the Cold War, the United States faced no powerful geopolitical rival, no real struggle for international influence or in the contest of ideas. Liberal economic consensus prevailed.

And, as it did, what began as a set of progressive financial prescriptions aimed at limiting the rightful role of government in the market morphed over time into a doctrinal unwillingness to accept economics as subject to geopolitical choices and influence. Thus, specific liberal financial policy prescriptions, such as trade liberalization, that found favor initially at least in part because they were seen as advantageous to US foreign-policy objectives, became justified predominantly on the internal logic of laissez-faire liberalism, not on the basis of (perhaps even in spite of) US geopolitical grounds.

Given the persistent use of geofinance instruments by China, Russia, the Gulf countries, the Western nations, and others, there is no reason to expect that the issue or the stakes will diminish any time soon. These countries' focus should, therefore, shift to a new organizing question for their foreign policy: How do they maintain global or regional leadership in an age importantly defined by geofinancial power?

The defense departments of these countries should shift some of their funds to promote national interests through geofinance instruments. These advanced economies will also need to develop a more mutual understanding of geofinance across all their executive-branch agencies with responsibilities in foreign policy and national security. Such a conceptual framework should, at a minimum, be capable of distinguishing geofinancial from nongeofinancial instruments and influencing, as well as determining, what makes them more or less useful; it should also offer policy makers a means of evaluating geofinancial policy options against other policy alternatives.

The Nexus between Geofinance and the Business World

Following the end of the Cold War with the fall of the Iron Curtain and the demise of the Soviet Union,[149] market participants focused mainly on "normalized" macroeconomic and political trends[150] when attempting to determine financial market outcomes. Black-swan[151] events and geofinancial, as well as country risks were treated as afterthoughts, mere blips on the radar screen.

And before the eurozone crisis in 2009, no one had predicted that the countries of Southern Europe would eventually fall into financial disarray. Most companies, whether they were financial institutions, corporations, or government agencies, had not allocated significant resources to fat-tail risk management[152] and lacked the vision to adopt a holistic approach that would have embedded, for instance, country and geopolitical risks in an investment, business, and lending process. Now, however, geopolitics and country risks are viewed as much more potent forces that can undermine global financial markets. Not only can fat-tail events shape the economic environment and fundamental investment outlook, driving economic growth and asset returns, they can also potentially blindside a business model and an investment portfolio.

In this environment, understanding geofinancial risk is vital for determining outcomes for the economy and financial markets. The type of geofinancial event can drive the way financial markets

---

[149] The Cold War ended with the dissolution of the USSR on December 26, 1991, by Mikhail Gorbachev. The Eastern European revolutions of 1989 combined with the dissolution of the Soviet Union led to the end of decades-long hostility between NATO and the Warsaw Pact, which had been the defining feature of the Cold War.

[150] *The End of History and the Last Man* is a 1992 book by Francis Fukuyama, in which he argues that the advent of Western liberal democracy may at one point signal the "endpoint of humanity's sociocultural evolution and the final form of human government."

[151] Nassim Nicholas Taleb's black-swan theory is a metaphor that describes a low-probability, high-severity event: in other words, an event that comes somewhat as a surprise, has a significant impact, and is usually inappropriately rationalized after the fact with the benefit of hindsight.

[152] A fat tail is a probability distribution that forecasts movements of three or more standard deviations from the mean that is shown by a normal distribution. Typically, periods of financial stress are represented by fatter tails.

behave and whether the reaction is temporary or sustained, localized or global. But since probability, causality, timing, magnitude, and impact are difficult to assess, market participants rarely give fat-tail events the full attention they deserve.

Geofinancial and country risks, for instance, are fat-tail events—in other words, they are low-probability but high-impact incidents. They are the proverbial bolts out of the blue and are unpredictable and highly uncertain. The 9/11 terrorist attacks and the global credit crunch took nearly everyone by surprise. *Fat tail* is industry shorthand for a fat-tailed distribution (as shown by a curve on a graph), a probability distribution that exhibits extremely large "skewness," meaning that a number, sometimes a large number, of data lie outside a standard distribution pattern. Tails can be skewed negatively (meager prices, to the left of normal) or positively (extremely high prices, to the right).

While market observers claim that up until recently, financial markets have proved resilient to bursts of geofinancial volatility and uncertainty, current events in both Western and emerging markets suggest that entrepreneurs need to be more risk aware about pricing in geofinancial risk. And this means that safe-haven assets, such as assets denominated in the US dollar, could see higher demand.

Overall, entrepreneurs need to get used to the idea that a continuously simmering pot of geofinancial volatility is the new reality for the global economy. The dollar, the Swiss franc, and the yen will be treated very differently by both entrepreneurs and global investors. Safe dollar assets, along with gold, silver, diamonds, and other fear-based assets, will enjoy large inflows and rising prices.

Interestingly, the considerable degree of social dislocation and pain caused by the 2007 GFC is one reason for the rise in geofinancial risk and thus should be put on the risk radar.

Geofinancial threats reared their ugly heads after the GFC and, over the past several years, have become much more pronounced.

Hey, entrepreneurs and investors: brush up on geofinance

If you had asked people five years ago what they thought was the most prominent risk to their business and finance portfolios, they would not have said, "Geopolitics." Today, if it is not the first thing they mention, then, apparently, they have not been paying attention. Not only do we have the usual wars going on, but now we also have unrest across Ukraine, the Korean peninsula, and the China Seas as well as the usual suspect—the Middle East and its Islamic threat—pretty much everywhere else. And, given rising global interconnectedness, combined with a worldwide benign interest-rate environment and the lead-from-behind US policy leaving a power vacuum, geopolitical conflicts and sustained higher volatility are bound to play more important roles in shaping business and finance investment outcomes during the next decade.

The key to assessing the business and investment implications of geofinance lies in understanding how they affect the primary drivers of business and financial investment returns. Fortunately, the same variables that are relevant in any generic investment context are relevant here. To illustrate, assume that a military conflict erupts between two neighboring states; diplomatic solutions are exhausted, and military action looms. Such news, if unexpected, is likely to affect the following market drivers:

- Influxes of flight to quality, not to mention that increased liquidity preferences and risk aversion would tend to depress real interest rates
- Prospects for higher defense spending would most likely push inflation expectations higher.

- Increased uncertainty would be expected to raise the risk premium, at least among the affected countries. Meanwhile, a sustained military offensive could lead to:

  o A decline in labor, investment, and trade flows, which would decrease economic growth prospects in more than just the affected countries, and

  o Higher commodity prices (for example, energy), which would put a burden on economic growth and increase inflation expectations, potentially affecting the global economy.

All too often, investors spend their time incorporating quantifiable variables into their investment process when deciding which assets to own and in what proportion. Typically, geofinancial risk only enters the discussion as a sort of catchall caveat about things that can go wrong. Rarely do investors reflect on geofinancial risk at the outset of the investment process along with all the other quantifiable variables to create a view of the investment environment and the associated level of risk that is priced into financial markets.

The difficulty for investors is that it is not easy to distinguish between noise and an unfolding game-changing event. Full-blown geopolitical conflicts can take a while to play out. At each stage of the investment process, it is not necessarily clear whether further escalation is avoidable, a peaceful resolution is possible, or outright confrontation will result. Investors need to remain aware of the critical and ever-changing geopolitical landscape, understand how these shocks can affect various assets within a portfolio, and regard geopolitics as central to the investment decision rather than merely as an afterthought. Investors and entrepreneurs would be better served by following a more pragmatic approach based on diversification across countries and uncorrelated assets, ongoing risk assessment, actively managing exposure, and making tactical investments.

The belief that financial markets can assess the future is false

Why do we continue to believe that financial markets can assess the future? And how can we learn from history? Well, unfortunately, we will not learn—and even worse, maybe we never will. Financial markets can give it a shot, and sometimes, yes, they are right, but almost every time, they miss the magnitude and spillover effects of geopolitical tensions, as these types of risks are usually low-probability, high-severity events (a.k.a. tail risks).

Interestingly, as the centennial of the end of WWI is commemorated, scholars will take notice that financial markets did not account for the run-up to the first global war, even though global geopolitical risk had evidently risen dramatically in the period from 1904 to 1914. During those years, an incongruity emerged in which financial risk (as measured by global interest rates) diminished at precisely the same time that geopolitical risk (as measured by arms buildup, nationalist problems at the fringes of the big empires, and vulnerability at the core of those empires) rose.

The key is to remember, however, that just as the 1930s are not a mirror of what we are experiencing nowadays, the run-up to WWI is not necessarily a reliable indicator of what will happen in our contemporary near future. But, then again, it would be foolish not to learn from history, and hence it is irresponsible to not prepare ourselves in a "keep calm and carry on" way, as preparedness will avert panic. Indeed, when doing a fast-forward to today, one could arguably claim that the same anomaly is emerging across the globe: financial risk is diminishing, evidenced by continuously falling yields due to an anesthetized, volatility-free environment, while geopolitical risk—whether in the Ukraine, Iraq, China, or the price of oil—appears to be rising.

Figure 17: Crude Oil—NYMEX

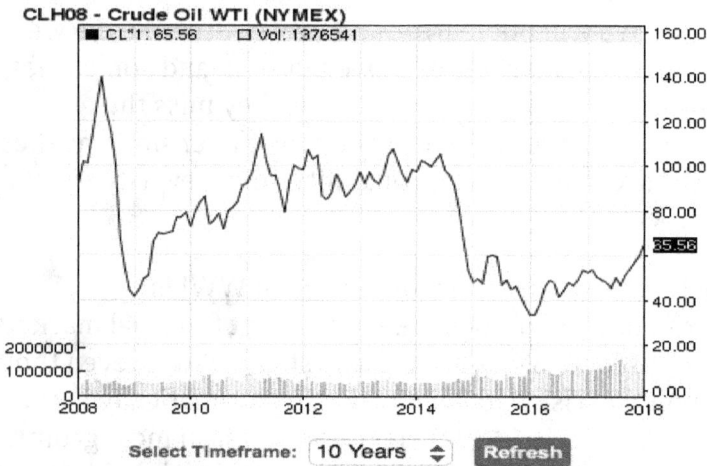

WTI (NYMEX) Price

End of day Commodity Futures Price Quotes for Crude Oil WTI (NYMEX)

Source: NASDAQ[153]

The potential for a geopolitical deflagration, while perhaps not on the scale of 1914 or 1939, is there. Indeed, the surprising voluntarily orchestrated abstinence of the world's superpower, the United States (with its "leading from behind" and "America First" attitudes), from intervening in the South and East China Seas, Northern Iraq, Syria, Libya, North Korea, or Ukraine and its weakness in its fundamental ability to pay its bills without having

[153] NASDAQ, "End of Day Commodity Futures Price Quotes for Crude Oil WTI (NYMEX)," accessed January 29, 2018, http://www.nasdaq.com/markets/crude-oil.aspx?timeframe=10y.

to borrow heavily from the rest of the world is increasing our current geopolitical risk.

And it is not just the United States that is faced with unbearable government debt levels but also Europe and Japan. Indeed, excessive debt fed by incessant profound deficits imperils national sovereignty and power projection, be it soft or hard power. Naturally, this raises the question of how much debt is too much. At what point are the economic consequences regarding inflation, higher interest rates, slow growth, or a collapsing dollar (euro, yen, etc.) so severe that everyone recognizes that radical action is required?

Now, as a reminder, while WWI and WWII were very different from each other, they also had one striking similarity. Before each war, economic recessions hit several of the countries involved. WWII famously brought most of the world's economies back from the Great Depression, and WWI helped the United States recover from a two-year mini recession that had already slowed trade by 20 percent. While correlation does not imply causation, it is still worth noting which economies recovered earlier than others, which may have had a significant impact on the way things turned out.

By 1933, Japan had taken moves to devalue its currency, which led to increased exports and a resulting growth in its economy. It pumped the extra money into the acquisition of combat assets, which gave it a decisive military edge in the years leading up to the war. Germany, on the other hand, entirely crashed as a result of the Versailles Treaty, making the Nazi Party take similar steps and earn overwhelming support among the populace. Germany's massive internal spending in the 1930s pulled it out of the Depression faster than America or the rest of Europe. And, in recent years, the GFC hit Russia less than much of the remainder of the world, due in part to the fact that Moscow supplies a quarter of the natural gas imported by the entire European continent. And then there's China. The US government is close to $21 trillion in debt, and China owns 5 percent of that, or about $1.1 trillion.

China recently flew past Japan to become the world's second-largest economy, and if it were to keep growing at this rate, its GDP could potentially match America's within twenty years. (However, China might also be in a middle-income trap or even worse, as its house of cards might falter.) The risk, while remote, is that if China decides to dump the US debt and/or starts to diversify away from USD assets, which it is already doing on a small scale, it could be a crippling blow to the American economy—and to much of the world, since the US dollar is still held in reserve by most foreign governments.

Like today, the financial markets claimed to be assessors of risk prior to WWI and WWII. They continue to claim to be able to digest all the relevant information about the investment environment and price the risk accordingly. And the financial markets believe that the best instrument to assess future risk is the yield, right? In the run-up to both world wars, yields were low as if geopolitical risk was being ignored, although there had been several signs of deep and growing tensions.

It reminds me of the excellent book *The Sleepwalkers: How Europe Went to War in 1914* by Christopher Clark. And when comparing the world between 1900 and 1914 and in the 1920s and '30s with today's world, we can observe some similarities, even though there are also distinct differences. Capital and goods were likewise highly mobile, and thus, given the communication systems of those days, there was already a sense of some global economy. Europeans in particular were migrating in huge numbers, not only to the United States, Canada, and Australia but also to Argentina, Brazil, and South Africa, while today it is populations from the south that are migrating, within the Southern Hemisphere and to the Northern Hemisphere.

Back in the day, railroads in Russia were financed by Anglo-Irish gentry, many of whom invested the proceeds of land reform in rural Ireland into the Tsarist empire. And in the interlude period, massive railroad investments were conducted in China, Mexico, Brazil, Peru, and so on. Both periods were the first ages of globalization, so when you think about it, there's not much different from today's global finance. During the twenty years preceding each of the wars, interest rates fell progressively all around the world and ended up in a range between 2 and 4 percent.

Between 1895 and 1914 (a.k.a. the Belle Époque), from Turkey, Russia, Germany, France, Japan, India, and Mexico, the story was the same: interest rates fell because the world had entered a "happy-clappy" period of globalization when countries did not go to war, geopolitical risk was ignored, and all investments were safe, except maybe the during the two-year US mini recession ending in 1912.

And by mid-1930, after the Great Depression, during the interbellum, interest rates had dropped to low levels, although expected deflation and the continuing reluctance of people to borrow meant that consumer spending and investment were depressed. Equally striking is the fact that the stock markets in Europe and the United States continued to rally throughout July 1914 as well as up to the summer of 1939.

Only on July 22, 1914, did the European markets begin to get jittery. Until August 1, when German and Russian armies were mobilizing on the continent, the *New York Times* was still suggesting that war could be avoided. On August 3, the world's stock markets just shut down and did not open again for months and months. How's that for the financial market's legendary foresight? If there was a war coming, the financial markets certainly did not see it! And with respect to WWII, up until the German invasion of Poland on September 1, 1939, markets didn't seem to anticipate an upcoming war—particularly after the signing of the Munich Agreement on September 29, 1938, as both Édouard Daladier and Neville Chamberlain were convinced they had put Hitler back in the closet and that peace had been safeguarded and war averted.

Again, no one is saying that we are on the cusp of a major world disaster. However, it does appear logical that the risk-management departments of banks and businesses, as well as their respective boards of directors, should spend much more time looking at tail/geopolitical risk when making their decisions regarding clients or shareholders' monies. It is not because there is no more volatility in the markets that the latter is correctly pricing in risk. The financial-versus-political-risk paradox is now evident, with the financial markets telling us everything is fine when patently, it is not.

Thus, the lesson for risk managers, investors, and entrepreneurs is that we need to step outside the risk-management comfort zone (no more sleepwalking) and think about managing tail risk by devising scenarios that consider extreme what-ifs, which can act as a flight simulator so that they are better able to cope with tail risks when they crystallize. And there is indeed a need to redirect our focus to the catastrophic events—the low-frequency, high-impact incidents that can cause companies to fail and the compounding of sequences of extreme risk—and propose approaches to tackle them.

But, quite honestly, if I may say so, I am not sure where the real risk is, as no one can predict the future. Geofinancial risk is probably somewhere below where it was in July 1914 or August 1939 and somewhere above the chance of winning the lottery. However, it is key to be prepared by conducting reverse stress-testing scenario analyses as well as building early-warning systems.

Many people still believe that tail/extreme-risk events are exclusively those that are triggered by exceptional and fundamentally unpredictable reasons (i.e., things that happen out of the blue). The reality is different. Unfortunately, extreme-risk events (low-likelihood, extreme-severity events) are often created as a result of key and preventable actions like human stupidity or the reckless behavior of, for instance, states and governments.

The paths to WWI and WWII were already very clear from their beginnings, but human ego helps financial markets remain blind and deaf up until destiny's stroke. As previously mentioned, claiming that the next global conflagration is just over the horizon is as bizarre as it gets, but the condition of the world today does show some eerie similarities to the pre-WWI and WWII global pictures. And history is a creature of habit.

As with many other significant events, neither WWI nor WWII suddenly flashed into existence; they both edged their way into the world's consciousness one bit at a time, like a rusting bicycle, until war was officially declared. While it's straightforward enough to put the conflict into layman's terms, a lot of different elements came to the surface concomitantly to make up what we now view as single wars. The years leading up to each of the two wars war held a lot of indicators, revealed in hindsight, that aggressive countries were testing the waters for what they could get away with:

- The WWI crisis came after a complicated and lengthy series of diplomatic clashes among the great powers (Italy, France, Germany, Britain, Austria-Hungary, and Russia) over European and colonial issues in the decade before 1914 that had left tensions high. In turn, these public clashes can be traced to changes in the balance of power in Europe from 1867. The more immediate cause for the global conflict was tensions over territory in the Balkans.

The Austro-Hungarian empire competed with Serbia and Russia for territory and influence in the region, and they pulled the remaining great powers into the conflict through their various alliances.

- As for WWII, the three leading Axis contenders—Japan, Italy, and Germany—were all involved in minor military disputes that the League of Nations could not stop, such as Italy's invasion of Ethiopia in 1935, the Spanish Civil War between 1936 and 1939, and Japan's chemical-infused invasion of China in 1937, not to mention the ravages that the 1919 Versailles Treaty had caused in Germany, planting the seeds of populist-nationalist resentment.

These days, China is reversing the balance by threatening an invasion of its own. The territories in question are groups of rocks situated in the South and East China Seas. The issue at hand, of course, is that China on the one hand and Japan and the Southeast Asian countries on the other side each feel that these islands belong to them. Whoever controls the islands also controls shipping lanes, fishing waters, and a potential oil field. As a war only becomes a world war when the United States gets involved, and given that around 50 percent of its naval force is stationed in the Pacific, if China makes a move on any of the islands, the US Navy has to retaliate, or it will break the conditions of the existing mutual-defense treaties with, respectively, Japan and the Philippines.

As for Russia, the problem is not that the United States and the United Nations will start tossing bombs into it; the problem is that Vladimir Putin knows they will not. He is a man who once said that the fall of the Soviet Union was the most significant geopolitical catastrophe of the twentieth century, a viewpoint that harkens to the days of Stalin's Great Purge and Khrushchev's missile diplomacy with Cuba. The situation in Ukraine may not be the spark that ignites the fires of the next major war, but it's a nod to the prevalent superpower that Moscow has free rein to do whatever it wishes to do. While, again, correlation does not imply causation, if you give a mouse a cookie, it's going to ask for a glass of milk.

The influence of geofinance on financial business decisions

As mentioned in the beginning of this book, clearly (and unfortunately), literature on the impact of geofinance on businesses and how firms react to geofinancial events is relatively scarce. Still, one can shed some light on the best practices that corporations can execute to manage geofinancial challenges and opportunities.

For instance, a particular geofinancial event in another part of the world, such as an increase in commodity prices as a result of a crisis in Northeast Asia, will likely lead to diverse responses from firms. Some firms active in the region affected by the emergency might minimize spending and conserve their financial resources for tough times ahead. Other businesses might take an opposite view and, in anticipation of further price increases, decide to purchase a lot of inventory. Another firm might decide just to wait and see.

In the same vein, when firms invest in a foreign country, approaches to the geopolitical terrain can be very different. In a country with an inefficient legal system and poor protection of property rights, one firm may take a risk-minimization strategy and refrain from tangible business engagement, while another firm might do as the Romans (i.e., the locals) do and join the illegal bandwagon, and a third firm might choose to live with the inadequacy of property-rights protection and reinvent its business model to succeed in that market.

Here is a nonexhaustive list of best practices on how to manage and mitigate geofinancial challenges and opportunities.

- *Monitoring of geofinancial events*: Obviously, the need for such monitoring varies according to the size of the company and its operational location and depends on the existing employee skills. Typically, this type of monitoring is more critical to oil- and commodity-type industries as well as investment companies. However, there is a growing interest in geofinancial risk across industries due to international volatility, uncertainty, and complexity.

- *Geofinancial data mining*, either through in-house operations or outsourced to a third party. Some companies will rely on news sources for their data mining, depending on the prevalent corporate budgets; others will use consultants as experts for assessment and benchmarking of geofinancial risk.

- *Conducting a holistic review of the geofinancial challenges and their impact on the firm*: Companies must know what to look for and how to analyze the information and understand the interplay of all factors. Challenges can include the lack of international awareness and the absence of cultural education on local customs, not to mention the relevancy of the firm's products and services in foreign markets.

- *Seizing new business opportunities arising from geofinance*: There are several business opportunities that can result from globalization. Consulting is in demand, especially in the assessment of risks and the need to build market awareness, not to mention the growing interest in the development of business-growth strategies.

- *Incorporating geofinancial risk into the business strategy of the company*: To achieve this goal, a company needs to look at the impact on controlling and corporate planning of the business. Someone in the company must be the central internal authority or responsible party on geofinance who will also be accountable for mitigating the risk arising from geofinance. Taking into account the geofinancial context, that person will assist in the coordination of the careful placement of corporate assets and business sustainability. It is critical to have a geofinancial understanding of the business environment in which the company is operating when setting the vision and leading. In other words, there is a need for a knowledgeable public face on geofinancial issues.

- *Measuring the geofinancial impact on the financial bottom line*: The price of oil and other commodities, as well as interest rates and spreads in one part of the world, affects product pricing and sales in other parts of the world and thus, the company's bottom line. Geofinance affects business in the same way weather affects farming.

- *Improving geofinancial risk management*: Detailed analysis and thorough underwriting that go beyond models and theories are necessary, as are awareness and proactive action. Assign ownership of and responsibility for this subject within the firm. You need timely risk identification, competent monitoring of risk events and exposures, and mitigation of risk strategies.

- *Knowing the resources needed for geofinancial risk management*: Both in-house executives and outsource consultants need clear, concise information and analysis relevant to the project or business opportunity. You must identify the real issues, and you need to bring in qualified professional service or have a substantial internal capacity.

- *Using best practices in geofinancial risk management*: These include robust analysis, clear responsibility, heightened employee awareness, operational safeguards, the management team's geofinancial awareness, and the strategic utilization of experts.

- *Seeing that geofinance will grow in importance*: It will be more critical to business in the coming years, so you need heightened market awareness and to manage increasing complexities. Take the opportunity to create competitive differentiators and corporate agility to meet any shifts in global economic, financial, and political dynamics.

- *Understanding that geofinance is highly relevant to businesses*: Those who engage in risk assessment are poised for success; negative public relations have an adverse effect. You must be proactive regarding culturalization and just-in-case risk management and understand the operating environment well. Aim for deeper market understanding through corporate indigenization, localization, real adaptation, and enhanced communication.

The following best practices suggest that firms are well served by pursuing a four-point strategy.

- *Geofinancial awareness*: Senior managers as well as lower-level employees need to be geofinancially curious and to understand the geofinancial implications of international events fully. A culture of information sharing needs to be cultivated within the organization so that valuable cross-border data can be transmitted in a timely fashion.

- *Organizational preparedness*: Firms need to create a corporate architecture that is well aligned with the challenges and opportunities brought by geofinance. Organizations need to implement a just-in-case risk-management culture and policy, assign ownership of and responsibility for it, and hire consultants to assist in geofinancially sensitive projects and endeavors.

- *Proactive thinking*: Firms need to plan for geofinancial issues. Thinking through the critical issues in advance will prevent potential pitfalls.

- *Corporate indigenization*: Businesses need to think globally but act locally and implement well-conceived adaptive measures in foreign environments.

While the geofinancial terrain is often unpredictable and chaotic, organizations need to stay the course of their business agendas by taking on organizational behavior that optimizes their strengths and expands market opportunities.

Why political risks still matter for small- to medium-size businesses

International politics is everyone's business, and global financial markets are more interconnected than ever before. Outsourcing and offshoring have radically changed industry cost structures, compelling more and more organizations to relocate overseas. Even companies without intentions of expanding abroad rely on international flows of capital and commodities. Evaluating a company's exposure to risky political events and assessing their impact should be critical components of any company's enterprise risk-management (ERM) strategy.

Today, four trends dominate the global investment environment: increased reliance on offshoring, the interconnection of financial markets combined with the financialization of advanced economies, energy dependence, and deteriorating national security. Anticipating the types of risks associated with each of these four trends demands asking the right questions about how institutions' and leaders' preferences influence policy choices and, in turn, financial outcomes.

Politics can make many economic decisions look stupid in hindsight. This is especially true in countries where autocratic leaders seem to drive policies and where quantitative data is often adulterated deliberately. It also applies to developed nations where targeted lobbying efforts can modify policy decisions.

How does one separate newspaper hype from the underlying forces that affect a business environment? When do financial figures fail to tell the whole story? How does an organization predict the severity of shocks, such as the unforeseen transfers of political power or the 2004 tsunami, on its overseas holdings? Running a geofinancial risk analysis turns uncertainty into a quantifiable threat.

Because companies are often affected by geopolitical decisions in the countries where they operate, both abroad and at home, all organizations need to factor the geopolitical environment into their planning scenarios. However, geopolitical risk can seem so amorphous that many corporate leaders lack a framework for assessing their exposure. But, like other elements of enterprise risk, geopolitical risk has systematic components that can be isolated by analysts who understand variation across political systems.

The interrelation and interdependencies of global markets will continue to increase. Businesses that reach for new manufacturing and sales opportunities in countries far from their home bases and experience are indeed at the forefront of globalization. While many companies have developed metrics that estimate how their profitability might be affected under various financial scenarios, most have struggled to find a similar and rigorous means of incorporating the range of outcomes that might arise from the political risk inherent in their international business activities.

Political risk relates to the preferences of political leaders, parties, and factions, as well as their capacity to execute their stated policies when confronted with internal and external challenges. Modifications in the regulatory environment, local attitudes toward corporate governance, reaction to international competition, labor laws, and withholding and other taxes, to name but a few, may all be influenced by hard-to-discern shifts in the political landscape. Political risk is the threat of political decisions or events hurting your business. Political risk primarily affects companies doing business in multiple countries or operating in countries other than their own. Political risks can range from war and revolution to corruption and changes in tax laws. Managing political risk involves researching it beforehand, taking steps to minimize it, and ensuring that you have legal recourse.

Nationalization, or takeover by a government, can constitute a serious political risk, especially in countries where governments are not democratically elected or where there is an unstable political situation. For example, following the Cuban revolution, the Cuban government expropriated a large number of American businesses. Even in democracies, states can decide to take over industries and companies. Another illustration is when in 2008, the Dominican Republic expropriated bauxite belonging to the American mining company Sierra Bauxita Dominicana. In response, the firm decided to halt operations in the Dominican Republic to avoid losing even more money if such expropriations continued.

Political protests by local groups can represent a geopolitical risk in some industries. One notorious example of this took place in Brazil in 2004, when a group of foreign companies planning to build a hydroelectric power plant was hit with large-scale protests from Brazilian environmental groups. The consortium, headed by US-owned Alcoa, responded by agreeing to spend more money on compensating people who were being resettled and on mitigating ecological damage. By deciding to spend more money, Alcoa managed to avoid significant delays from protests. Another example of how to handle those kinds of risks is, for instance, the way that Royal Dutch Shell helps mitigate risks from environmental demonstrations by consulting with Greenpeace on ecological issues in areas where it operates.

Geopolitical risk can take the shape of violence against employees, as in the oil-rich region of the Niger Delta in Nigeria. Local groups regularly launch attacks against company compounds and kidnap foreign oil workers, demanding that more oil revenue be spent locally. Oil companies operating in these areas, such as Shell Oil, often manage these risks by hiring security firms to protect workers and by negotiating to create hospitals, schools, and jobs for the local population.

Financial changes can also be a form of geopolitical risk for companies. For example, a government may decide to raise taxes on a specific product, sector, or business; an economic recession or changes to the currency can also affect a firm's ability to earn a profit. In 2000, nearly twenty years ago, telecommunications company Econet decided to invest in the unstable economy of the inflation-prone and poorly managed country of Zimbabwe, and this represented a considerable business risk. The organization responded to this business risk by diversifying and entering neighboring African markets. To mitigate the very high inflation in the country, Econet sent some of its Zimbabwean technicians to work in the new states where Econet was also operating. This enabled the technicians to save money and allowed Econet to keep its best people.

Practical Cases of Geofinance

Europe unwilling to face its own geofinancial demons

Europe is unwilling to face its geopolitical devils; if the United States is unprepared to use force, no common European resolve will ever be found. In other words, Europe's collective defense guarantee is effective only if Washington will actually fight. Still, the question of whether the United States will always protect Europe can be raised, mainly since isolationism is rising among Americans and budget restrictions are forcing the White House to make hard choices, to the benefit of Asia. Europeans have been hedged from a large-scale war thanks to a US security blanket, but they might be forced to face their ghosts sooner than expected.

Granted, Europeans have proven their ability to address postwar conflict situations and mount peace-building operations, primarily (but not exclusively) in their neighborhoods. Europeans—individually, bi-, or multilaterally—may indeed be able to respond to a range of different challenges, from a low-level instability around the European periphery to the invasion of an overseas territory. What is less clear, bearing in mind the relative shrinking of many European militaries and also the cacophony of the EU leadership, is whether they would be able to respond to the new challenges that will manifest themselves in ten years, such as a Russian awakening, without the US security umbrella.

Since 1945, Europe has been spared a massive war except in the former Yugoslavia, mostly thanks to its incorporation into the American empire that shielded Europeans from a potential invasion via the Warsaw Pact. After the Berlin Wall fell (1989) and the dissolution of the USSR (1991), so-called experts were claiming that it was the end of history and that Europe would finally be able to collect the peace dividend, leading to a gradual decrease of its military forces. However, the NATO structure was maintained, guaranteeing ongoing protection by the United States even though no significant menace was then threatening the survival of Europe. Twenty-five years later, a new, multipolar world is forming where US and European leadership is being contested by rising regional powers—in particular China, India, Indonesia, and Brazil but also Russia. It's the latter that could threaten the greater part of Europe.

If one raised the question of whether Moscow could threaten Europe militarily, even in the wake of the crisis in Ukraine, most Western Europeans would shrug their shoulders. However, Eastern Europeans, who were liberated from Soviet occupation some twenty years ago, still recall negatively the days when the Kremlin decided the fates of millions of Balts, Poles, Hungarians, Czechs, and more.

Europeans can, from both a logistic and weapons-systems point of view, project power and take command in non-European theaters. But the question is still whether a direct threat to the European homeland could be dealt with in the complete absence of US intervention. Many will argue that Washington would never let Europe sail away, given the deep and massive bilateral trade, investment, political, and cultural ties between both shores of the North Atlantic. However, history has shown that nothing is irreversible or meant to last forever. Therefore, it is about time that Europeans prepared themselves for such contingencies with the assumption that the United States will not support them.

Granted, notwithstanding Europe's minimalist military efforts, its forces still far outrange Russia's reach. By mid-2017, the other twenty-six NATO members (excluding the United States and Canada) had spent a combined $242 billion on their militaries,[154] compared to a mere $52 billion by Moscow. With a collective GDP more than eight times that of Russia, the Europeans could do far more if they desired. However, these are merely numbers as,

---

[154] NATO, "Defence Expenditure of NATO Countries (2010–2017)," June 29, 2017, accessed January 29, 2018, https://www.nato.int/nato_static_fl2014/assets/pdf/pdf_2017_06/20170629_170629-pr2017-111-en.pdf.

again, we don't know what the European resolve would be if the United States stayed out of a conflict.

Maybe the United States should trigger awareness by cynically refraining from redeploying forces and weapons systems to the Central and Southeast European theater (the Central European plains and Black Sea), forcing Europeans to coordinate themselves and face the Russian bear on their own. Obviously, such a scenario would result in a massive NATO legitimacy crisis and most likely also in the collapse of the EU architecture, which is already facing a regime crisis. But sometimes, one must combat fire with fire: if you want Europeans to stand up for themselves, put them in a situation where they have no other choice.

Could renewed Russian encroachment on Europe eventually be stopped by the Europeans? As we've seen, purely based on defense spending, the answer seems affirmative. But what stands in the way is the absence of political will and a lack of leadership. And while some naively deplore Moscow's power politics as "so nineteenth century," this type of politics has never been out of fashion, especially in our energy-hungry world.

To justify maintaining its existence in relation to Europe, NATO is now intervening in theaters that have nothing to do with the North Atlantic: for example, in Afghanistan, Libya, Iraq, and the Gulf of Aden. So, provocatively, one could ask the reverse question: "From a European security-architecture perspective, if NATO did not already exist, would Washington invent it?"

Additionally, linking an EU enlargement to a NATO expansion is a dangerous game and means that Moscow will always view Europeans as hostile. So, what should be done? The Western European Union, the security arm of the European Union, should replace NATO as the primary guarantor of European security, and thereby, Brussels should undo the link between NATO and the EU. A robust Western European Union (WEU) would have some advantages over NATO. WEU member states have many shared security interests, in contrast to the increasingly divergent US and European perspectives that already have produced severe disarray in NATO. The West European countries have ample financial resources and are capable of taking care of their own defense without US subsidy. Finally, the Kremlin is likely to view the WEU as less provocative and less threatening than a US-dominated NATO, especially an enlarged version that expands to Russia's borders.

As the Ukraine crisis shows, maintaining NATO as the primary European security institution is drawing the United States into military entanglements even when no vital American interests are at stake. Replacing NATO with a Western European Union would emphasize that most flashpoints in Eastern and Central Europe are more relevant to the European nations than to America and that dealing with such problems is appropriately a European responsibility. Moreover, once the West Europeans develop a full, independent military capability, the WEU will be a reliable partner for the United States in the event of a future threat to mutual US-European security interests.

After Berlusconi's party pulled the rug from under PM Letta's government, Italy is once more lurching toward another political crisis that is likely to cause instability in financial markets for the remainder of the year, until markets get clarity. Rome had only recently regained its footing with financial markets and its European Union partners and was able to walk a fine line on the international stage. Granted, since the time that European Central Bank President Mario Draghi vowed to do "whatever it takes" to save the euro, and thereby quickly institutionalized that pledge by establishing the ECB's outright monetary transactions program to buy distressed eurozone members' sovereign bonds, the risk for a disintegration of the monetary union seemed to have been removed for a while. The recent federal election results in Berlin provided some relief as well. However, what the current crisis splash in Italy is evidencing is that the factors that fueled the monetary crisis in the eurozone remain primarily unaddressed as, once again, the whole dark picture of the fundamental problems of the eurozone resurfaces.

Indeed, while the eurozone waters remained calm, mirrored by lower spreads as well as lower tail risks, its fundamental problems have never been resolved:

- Given aging populations combined with low productivity, actual economic growth—even once the peripheric countries exit the recession in 2018—will remain below 1 percent for the next few years, implying that unemployment rates will remain very high.

- Deficit as a percentage of GDP remains in the red, above 3 percent—suggesting that, failing cost-cutting measures and higher economic growth, government debt will continue to increase.

- Levels of public and private debt—both domestic and foreign—are still way too critical, and they continue to rise as a share of GDP (above 90 percent at the end of 2017 versus 66 percent at the end of 2007). This means that the problem of medium-term sustainability is still unresolved.

- Competitiveness remains very weak due to low domestic demand, a high euro (hurting exports), and still-high unit-labor costs and low productivity. (As an aside, Germany and many Nordic countries do not seem to suffer too much from a high euro, as they remain competitive thanks to the manufacturing of high-added-value products.)

- The fiscal drag on growth continues, and its effects are amplified by an ongoing credit crunch, as under regulatory pressure (Basel III), undercapitalized banks still need to deleverage by selling assets and shrinking their loan portfolios.

The primary safeguard for the eurozone is mostly political will, although Germany, for instance, is resisting the risk-sharing elements of a political, banking, and fiscal union: common deposit insurance, a joint fund to wind up insolvent banks, and direct-equity recapitalization of banks by the ESM. Understandably, Berlin fears that risk sharing would become risk shifting and that any fiscal union would likewise result in a "transfer union," with the wealthy core permanently subsidizing the more impoverished periphery. Concomitantly, the entire regulatory process for the financial sector is procyclical.

Moreover, the policies of the ECB—unlike those in the United States and Japan, for instance—are also a drag, as its mandate is not to support economic development but solely to preserve price stability (inflation) as well as stable exchange rates. Hence, the ECB's policies also fuel the credit crunch. Indeed, unlike the US Federal Reserve and the Bank of Japan, the ECB is not engaging in quantitative easing, and its "forward guidance" that it will maintain interest rates at a low level is not very credible. Quite the opposite: interest rates remain too high for individual eurozone countries and the euro too strong to jump-start faster economic development in the eurozone.

From a sociopolitical perspective, austerity fatigue is rising in the eurozone periphery, fueling social and political unrest. Look at how the Greek, Spanish, Portuguese, and now again the Italian governments remain on the verge of collapsing under intense strain as they seek further budget cuts.

If the Italian government were really to collapse, thereby triggering new elections and then complicated coalition negotiations, renewed waves of financial turbulence would be expected, once more weakening the eurozone's fragile economic recovery. But these kinds of waves are sure to resurface over and over as long as the fundamental challenges of the eurozone are not adequately addressed. Tail risk in the eurozone is bound to stay active for a long while.

China's reform plan and the impact on financial markets

As China has become more prosperous, it has become more unstable. Senior Beijing executives now face the dilemma of all reforming authoritarian regimes: economic success endangers their continued political control. Sustained modernization is the enemy of one-party systems. Revolutions occur under many conditions but mainly when political institutions do not keep up with the social forces unleashed by economic change.

Nothing irritates a rising social class like inflexible leaders. Despite Beijing's recent so-called reform policies, the gap between the people and their government will continue to widen, thereby ensuring greater instability in the coming years. Today, there's unimaginable societal change at high speed, thanks in large part to government-sponsored economic development and social engineering. At the same time, the Communist Party remains in the way of meaningful, deep political change. Because senior officials don't allow change of any substance, the authorities must resort to force to stop the spread of unrest and put in place make-believe anticorruption policies.

But the use of the coercive power by the state is only a short-term solution; police force just makes protests harder to control the next time. The leadership cannot come to terms with the cause of unrest. While it is true that Beijing is haunted by the reasons for the fall of Soviet Union, the Chinese authorities want to pretend that they have taken a different route to rejuvenation than the Soviets. Granted, China's economic restructuring has solved some problems that the Soviets could not handle, but it remains stuck in one irreformable obstacle: the existence of the Chinese

Communist Party supported by a police apparatus whose ideological icon is history's worst mass murderer—Mao Zedong.

The renewed emphasis on Marxism and Maoism by Xi Jinping, China's current supremo, substantially reduces the possibility of peaceful transformation of the Chinese political system. Today's leaders may make modifications here and there, but Mao Zedong's policy remains in place, and, to borrow his infamous words, politics remains in command of society. No one wants to see the chaos and bloodshed that goes with upheaval. The Chinese have suffered enough in the past two hundred years. Nonetheless, when political leaders rule out the likelihood of peaceful change, people eventually resort to effective tactics.

Already, not even four months after the Third Plenum of the Nineteenth Central Committee, Chinese authorities realize that they are in a catch-22: either they implement the proposed economic reforms immediately, causing short-term pain to the Chinese people, or they take half measures, and long-term pain will fall upon the Chinese. Not to mention that the elite, privileged class would rebel against anticorruption actions while at the same time, the middle class expects an unfulfilled political liberalization.

Beijing is focused on its 7.5 percent growth target but fears of not achieving it due to lower global demand for Chinese products while concomitantly transforming the economy is pushing authorities to ease lending to buoy growth. China aims for an economy less based on property and infrastructure investments and based more on banking, health care, telecommunications, and energy. But easing credit (M2) encourages more borrowing, further aggravating China's massive debt problem as well as, ultimately, its balloon risk in an environment of increasing interest rates.

Domestically, Beijing is already tightening security by increasing police monitoring of the Internet, as apparently, the Chinese government is worried that a slipping economy could trigger higher unemployment and corporate failures, further aggravating already high social tensions.

While loosening the credit supply would give a short-term boost, it would, further down the road, also worsen the credit problems plaguing local governments as well as corporations and households, not to mention bubble up to the shadow-banking market.

Questions are rising about the commitment and capacity of the Chinese Communist Party and its leaders to reform the country. The challenge ahead includes easing land, labor, and capital controls—a cultural shift for a communist government with a penchant for centralization and control. And many of China's younger generations are tired of delayed gratification.

Not only is China facing a crossroads as its investment-led growth model flags, but foremost, the communist regime and its corrupt leaders must meet a legitimacy test. On a global level, as manufacturing is gradually being re-sourced to Western economies (look at the United States and the positive impact of shale gas on production costs), there will be less demand for Chinese products, even when Western economies are growing more sustainably.

The Chinese Communist Party's biggest obstacle is the party itself, as the success of China's economic reforms depends on whether Beijing can honestly let go.

Remember the prophetic words of the former party general secretary Zhao Ziyang at the time of the Tiananmen massacre in June 1989? "Political reform has to be a priority," Zhao said, and if it isn't, "not only will economic problems get harder to handle, but all kinds of social and political problems will only get worse."[155]

Granted, notwithstanding the fact that the Chinese people have a lot more freedom to travel, communicate, study, and so on than they did during Mao's communist rule, the strong party apparatus still reigns supreme, and the realms of economic reform and political liberalization remain more or less distinct. But the underlying problem has never really gone away. The party still thinks that China can be increasingly competitive and innovative without the type of political reform that many in the West would consider required for any advanced economy. However, the more the Chinese economy advances, the more the needed changes undercut the party's ability to control the nation.

In line with China's make-believe model, China's leaders are much more into big-bang announcements than big-bang reform, and thus the rollout of many of these new policies is expected to be slow. Chairman Xi Jinping's reforms will fail because of an unwillingness to cede political authority to economic need. And he and his senior staff already know this, which is why they rush into overseas bullying and strong army rhetoric as a way to distract the ordinary Chinese from everyday misery while at the same time tightening security, hoping to rapidly quell any violent protests putting in jeopardy the legitimacy of the Chinese Communist Party's leadership. While there appears to be a general sense of relief over the fact that the headwinds we've seen from emerging markets of late do seem to be abating, there is a degree of concern over the state of the Chinese economy.

China is fighting in a deliberately orderly fashion on four fronts:

- *The yuan's deliberate fall*: This might backfire, as the yuan depreciated more than 1 percent in a week against the dollar after appreciating almost 40 percent

---

[155] Julian Gewirtz, "Bury Zhao Ziyang, and Praise Him: Why We Should Remember the Contributions of China's Disgraced Former Leader," *Foreign Policy*, April 8, 2015, accessed January 17, 2018, http://foreignpolicy.com/2015/04/08/zhao-ziyang-china-ccp-deng-xiaoping-tiananmen/.

in the past few years, reaching a six-month low of 6.1192 against the dollar.

- *A flight to safety*: The bond spread has been widened between sovereign yield to interest-rate swap, hovering at 2007 levels.

- *A refi-risk increase*: Rising borrowing costs distress borrowers, bringing them closer to refi risk and hence default. Additionally, interbanking and swaps are being avoided.

- *Savers hoarding cash*: Gold prices are surging as savers and investors hoard cash and reinvest it in gold assets.

China's bark certainly seems worse than its bite. It shows China's weakness rather than strength. Had China been strong militarily (the PLA is still using old MiG-21s), it would not have needed all the circuses in the East and South China Seas. As is typical for a dictatorial regime in distress, it merely tries to distract its people from a deteriorating domestic situation with simplistic nationalistic rhetoric. The Chinese communist regime merely wants to garner explosive headlines about its so-called brave and daring actions across the Asia-Pacific region to distract a domestic audience disappointed by socioeconomic conditions.

Granted, the PLA and related security agencies have coast-guard ships pushing Filipino and Vietnamese fishing boats around and circling islands in the East China Sea, but it is all just a make-believe story. At least for the foreseeable future, in almost all cases, Beijing is not altering any strategic realities, for it cannot achieve this from a military perspective. And, unsurprisingly, the United States is mainly ignoring these Chinese actions.

It's almost pathetic to see China staging all this huffing and puffing solely because, under the current deteriorating socioeconomic conditions, the CCP leadership is afraid of losing its legitimacy and therefore prefers to resort to the cheapest tool—propaganda—to keep the nationalistic mind-set at a high volume to strengthen the illusion of rising Chinese power. Also, by having its PLA navy and coast guard antagonize countries such as the Philippines and Japan, China desperately wants to show its domestic audience that the regime is standing up to the United States, a treaty ally of both these countries.

It reminds me sadly of the movies *55 Days at Peking* and *The Sand Pebbles*, in which Chinese attack Western and Japanese troops with firecrackers and bows and arrows. While one should never underestimate the long-term strategic objectives of China, one also needs to remain pragmatic and refrain from playing panic soccer. For now, geopolitically speaking, ASEAN countries (without Laos and Cambodia, which are China's poodles) need to beef up their defenses and build a collective response against Beijing. But China cannot overpower any combination of countries that includes the United States.

What China is doing is merely testing the waters, as evidenced by how it has behaved in the South China and East China Seas over the past few years. Most likely, its next demonstrations will be geared toward Taiwan. Instead of shaking the cages of neighboring countries and potentially triggering a collective response that includes the United States, it should keep a lower profile and build relations through trade and culture.

One must not forget that China does not have a history of naval strategic thinking; it has mainly been a land power. If Beijing were smart (which it is not, as it is too preoccupied with deteriorating socioeconomic conditions that will ultimately lead to the fall of its house of cards, putting the CCP in the dungeon of history where it belongs), it would instead use the Deng Xiaoping approach. Concerning the West, we are at fault for feeding the dragon, naively believing that Beijing's power would be more benign if only China opened up, with public opinion playing a more significant role in shaping policy.

Asia is ruled by world economics, but world politics is ruled by Asia

Aside from journalistic dramatization, the issue is not a pan-Asian century or entity or movement of some kind. Granted, from 1965 onward, its twenty-three economies grew faster than those of all other regions, increasing their contribution to world GDP from 12 percent to nearly 50 percent today. Thus, if you unite their numbers, no one can deny their potential if, ceteris paribus, their growth continued. However, most of the tremendous global supply chains of which many of the Asian countries are a part do not end in Asia.

If we add up the populations of India, China, Southeast Asia, and Japan, we get an aggregate economy that is a huge percentage of world GDP—not least because it also equals nearly 50 percent of the world's population. But the math does not add up. Africa as a continent may be bouncing back (though not as a unified political and economic system), but every African country is very different. As for Asia, many of its countries have clashing interests, and they are thus unlikely to be allies in a loose sense. It is quite the opposite regarding the events unfolding in the East and South China Seas.

The focus in Asia is on China as it projects power both politically and economically. But being rich alone, as experience (notably Japan's in the late 1980s) amply reveals, does not mean anything. Does a bigger economy magically grant China an upgrade to all instruments of national power—military, political, and soft power? No. China bears large risk factors: economically speaking, a heavily indebted formal and informal banking sector combined with a real-estate bubble, while politically, as central authorities increase their security clampdown to address violent protests, lower and middle-class households start to question the legitimacy of the CCP's authority.

Now, again, no one can deny that the geostrategic balance in Asia is changing from that of a unipolar to a multipolar region. And with globalization and increased interconnectedness, when it rains in Asia, it pours in Europe and the United States. However, while Asia has been rising as a contributor to world GDP over the last fifty-plus years, given the nature of Beijing's foreign and domestic policies, there will be a growing coalition of local anti-CCP and anti-China sentiment overseas, potentially resulting in the downfall of Asia due to a domino effect.

When China is behaving in a roguelike manner, it doesn't usually end up augmenting its national power but quite the reverse. Look back in history, keeping in mind that until 1949, China had two political experiences in its history: a strong center or fissiparous provinces at war with one another. Today, because of Beijing's aggressive claims, the legitimacy of the CCP and its leadership look increasingly threadbare. We wouldn't bet on there being anything inevitable about Chinese supremacy, especially if we look at it by the numbers, let alone in five short years.

And when looking at the remainder of Asia outside Japan, Singapore, Taiwan, and Hong Kong, each of its countries is faced with daunting socioeconomic challenges, statistically evidenced by low GDP per capita. We will look at Asia through two geographic prisms: namely, East Asia and South Asia. However, first, we will take an overview. As of 2018, Asia relies on the rest of the world for growth, not vice versa. However, world politics is being determined by Asia.

Persistently loose monetary policy has fueled private credit booms across the Asian region, but, more than the degree, it is the speed at which credit is overtaking nominal GDP growth that is cause for concern. Remember that past financial crises in major economies were often preceded by the private-credit-to-GDP ratio rising sharply—by as much as 30 percent in the five years before a crisis. Many Asian countries have either breached or moved close to this mark since 2008. Asia needs to tighten policy and accelerate structural reforms, or it will become a breeding ground for future financial crises.

A debt-fueled asset-price boom incites development, but not forever. If policy makers decide to deflate the bubble for long-term sustainability slowly, then expected economic development will likely take a severe hit as the wealth effect, in which those who own assets feel wealthier and consume more, fades and debt-servicing costs mount.

In East Asia, the following tendencies are emerging as of 2018:

- Leaders: South Korea, Philippines, Malaysia, and Japan
- Followers: Vietnam, Myanmar, Taiwan, and Singapore
- Tailgaters: India, China, Indonesia, and Thailand

We will not analyze every one of these countries but focus on a couple of important ones, considering the changes that they are undergoing. China will struggle to implement reforms amid an economic slowdown, consolidate the new administration's power, and assert its influence in the region. The cautious, incremental implementation of changes over the year will be defined by the need to address widening regional and rural-urban economic imbalances to allow market forces to play a more crucial role in the allocation of capabilities and to streamline government bureaucracy.

However, severe risks to social and economic stability will persist, mainly from recent credit accumulation through shadow banking, threats to employment from slower growth, and rising public anxiety over corruption and environmental degradation. While the new leadership has signaled that it will tolerate a moderate economic slowdown (with a magic number for annual GDP growth set at 7 percent instead of at least 8, as in the past) and some increase in unemployment for the sake of reform, it will struggle to balance these goals against rising public expectations and increasing concerns about local-government debt.

Localized uprisings in property markets are likely this year and in the coming years, potentially making local-government debt woes worse. However, notwithstanding the risk of systemic financial crisis, the central government has the resources to manage these concerns. Obviously, reforms always come with more intense ideological debate, and there will be rising political expectations that go beyond the CCP's interests. Hence, the Chinese Communist Party will resort to tighter control over social media, dissent, and the ideological realm to ensure that further economic opening will not jeopardize its political authority and legitimacy as the events leading up to the bloody 1989 Tiananmen Square incident did.

Major powers will respond to China's growing influence, including the United States updating its engagements in the region and Japan reviving its international status. China will meanwhile refocus on development in the south and west, looking to open up land corridors to reach Central Asia (much to the annoyance of Russia), Eastern Europe, and the Middle East. Beijing will move beyond gas and oil to promote other commerce and investment transactions in these regions. Concomitantly, China will bolster its traditional foothold in Southeast Asia, seeking greater connectivity and market share in the face of growing competition. It will try to divide and conquer by, on one hand, remaining aggressive in North Asia about Japan while simultaneously courting, through trade and investments, Indonesia, Thailand, and Malaysia in the same way it did with Cambodia and Laos and, to a lesser extent, Myanmar. Overall, Beijing will try to utilize regional multilateral frameworks and its partner countries to divert US pressure while seeking to prevent competition with Washington from disrupting its delicate domestic transformation.

Meanwhile, Tokyo will maintain the recently increased tempo of economic diplomacy, focusing primarily on infrastructure exports and emerging markets. It will court states that offer both financial and strategic benefits especially—including India, Russia, and members of the ASEAN. As Japan tries to solidify its energy supply-chain security through arrangements in Russia, the Middle East, and elsewhere, the US-Iranian negotiations will give it the opportunity to pursue relations with Iran with fewer constraints but amid greater competition among energy clients in Asia. In light of history and the volatility of Japanese governments, it is paramount to emphasize that PM Abe's ruling party will remain broadly popular and firmly in control of policy, even after the hike in sales tax.

Several Asian states will experience more significant volatility as a result of China's slowdown, US monetary policy, and internal political dynamics. In particular, we have in mind Thailand, Indonesia, Myanmar, Vietnam, Cambodia, and Malaysia, where opposition pressure will spur the dominant ruling parties to try new ways of restoring support. These trends will require governments to use a range of tools—from public spending to security forces—to preserve their grip on power. Thus, while Southeast Asian states differ in their specific problems and capabilities, growing internal challenges will be a general trend in the region.

In South Asia, the principal actor is, of course, New Delhi as it gears up for national elections in 2019, and, as in many other countries including those in Western Europe, the Indian national elections are likely to illustrate the rising clout and popularity of parties on the local level, reflecting increasing frustration with the traditional duopoly of India's national politics. India's national political battle will take place at a time of near-unprecedented chaos in the Indian periphery. New Delhi will try to pursue its strategic interests in the broader Indo-Pacific basin, including Nepal, Sri Lanka, and Myanmar as well as through the ASEAN, while trying to restrict the risks of instability in Pakistan and Bangladesh and an Afghan state preparing for a US withdrawal. As New Delhi continues moving toward a more stable working accord with Beijing, it will also try to leverage its traditional relationships with the United States, Australia, and Japan to increase foreign investment and infrastructure development.

Bangladesh will again be caught amid violence and protests, while Sri Lanka will need to make a hard choice between India and China. Pakistan is also a source of headache as the growing uncertainty in Afghanistan will have the most direct consequences on its eastern neighbor, which already faces a strategic dilemma on how to manage its domestic jihadist insurgency. Pakistan Taliban rebels under a new leader based in eastern Afghanistan will try to take advantage of the power vacuum created by departing Western forces and the Afghan Taliban insurgency to launch a further offensive to the east of the Durand Line. Islamabad will have its hands full dealing with the uprisings next door and at home, as well as the new Afghan leadership.

Outlook for the Short and Long Term

Financial markets should watch out for Cold War 2.0

Figure 17: The Price of Gold

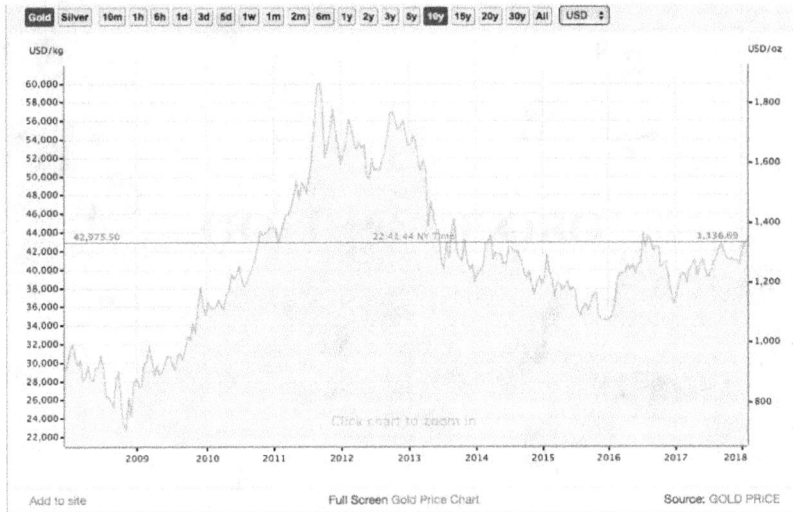

Source: Gold Price[156]

Russia and the West (that is, NATO) are in a standoff regarding the Crimea. Another flashpoint to keep high on the geofinancial radar is, again, the Tokyo-Beijing maritime tensions. To some degree, the increase in global political risk has roots in the GFC. The most significant cause, however, is the relative demise of the United States as the dominant superpower and, concomitantly, the more vocal rise of two regional powers, Russia and China.

---

[156] Gold Price, "The Price of Gold," accessed January 28, 2018, https://goldprice.org/gold-price-chart.html.

Figure 18: Arms Trade 2012–2016

The World's Arms Exports Since 1975

Worldwide arms exports (in US $ million)*

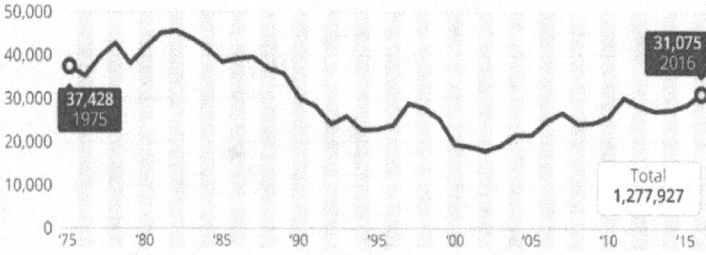

	USA	Russia	China	France
	Germany	United Kingdom	Others	

The biggest exporters 2012–2016 (in %)

| 33.0 | 23.0 | 6.2 | 6.0 | 5.6 | 4.6 | 21.6 |

* Figures are SIPRI Trend Indicator Values (TIVs)
expressed in US $ m at constant (1990) prices
Generated: February 20, 2017

©StatistaCharts   Source: SIPRI Arms Transfers Database

statista

Investors must get used to the notion that a continuously simmering pot of political unrest is the new reality for the global economy.

While in some states, political instability is nothing unusual and can be ignored, in the case of Ukraine, there is a need to pay attention to further developments because of the broader ramifications for emerging markets—for instance, in the Middle East with Iran (the nuclear deal and the spillover effect on Israel and Saudi Arabia) and Syria (the spillover effect of civil war on Lebanon, Iraq, Iran, and Turkey). Russia could suddenly become less accommodative with the West and spark anxiety, resulting in a rise in oil prices and fueling the appetite for US dollars and Swiss francs.

Investors should be taking a hard look at European banks, which have more than $10 billion invested in Ukraine, according to the BIS.[157] If the crisis continues to heat up, markets will also start reassessing financial institutions' investments in Russia, where European banks have a substantially more significant $120 billion exposure.[158]

With the Federal Reserve tapering off its monthly bond purchases, money has been flowing out of emerging markets, sending some currencies into a tailspin and forcing several central banks to respond with interest-rate hikes. Although Ukraine isn't a member of the MSCI emerging-markets index—it is considered an even less developed frontier market—the distinction between the two has begun to blur for some mutual-fund managers. Russia as well has a 5.6 percent weighting in the emerging-markets index and is a member of the BRIC nations—Brazil, Russia, India, and China—which have been seen as the bedrock of emerging-markets investing.

The Tokyo-Beijing tension remains a dangerous one: a belligerent China is looking to assert its position in the South China and East China Seas, alarming neighbors as well as the United States. Bluntly put, Beijing's long-term strategic intentions inspire deep anxieties. The Tokyo-Beijing relationship is one of the most critical bilateral tie-ups in the world because of its implications for regional and economic stability. And with two-way commerce between these Asian powers estimated at some $300 billion, any deterioration in relations would probably have significant repercussions for Asia's economy.

In Asia, the chances of a cold-war situation are high because of mutual recriminations and glowering. This is not an ideological conflict but more of an ongoing power change in Asia (in Beijing's

[157] Bank for International Settlements, "Consolidated Banking Statistics," accessed January 18, 2018, https://www.bis.org/statistics/b4-UA.pdf.
[158] Bank for International Settlements, "Consolidated Banking Statistics."

favor), and it involves how the Washington-Tokyo tandem tries to manage Beijing's increasing assertiveness and efforts to modify the status quo in its support. Still, strong economic ties between China and Japan could be one reason to expect cooler heads to prevail in any escalation in tensions. But the risk is that if China suffers socioeconomically from a hard landing, it will deflect national attention to the detriment of Japan.

Despite the current wintery dip between the White House and the Kremlin, if we put things into perspective, Washington's actual long-term geopolitical opponent will not be Russia but China, even though the White House is currently at risk of alienating both Beijing and Moscow. Interestingly, while the United States has been silent about China's annexation of Tibet and the subsequent cultural and human genocide by the Maoist regime, Washington is using more hostile language against the Kremlin due to recent events in Ukraine.

The reasons are 1) US trade interests are much more prominent in China than in Russia, and 2) several foreign-policy influencers, such as late Zbigniew Brzezinski, John McCain, or Condoleezza Rice, are stuck in Cold War rhetoric and unable to formulate a long-term strategic vision for the United States. The United States will face a tremendous challenge in Asia should China continue to rise economically, and in such a case, it is inevitable that the United States and China will engage in intense strategic competition much like the Soviet-American rivalry during the Cold War.

However, the US-China strategic rivalry lacks a single center of gravity.[159] Instead, there would be four potential hotspots over where Washington and Beijing might find themselves at war: the

[159] Zachary Keck, "US-China Rivalry More Dangerous Than Cold War?" *The Diplomat*, January 28, 2014, accessed March 4, 2018, https://thediplomat.com/2014/01/us-china-rivalry-more-dangerous-than-cold-war/.

Korean Peninsula, the Taiwan Strait, and the South and East China
Seas. Besides featuring more hotspots than the US-Soviet conflict,
Beijing and Washington might be more confident that they could
engage in a shooting war over one of these areas without it
escalating to the nuclear threshold.

Apparently, the West has been feeding the Chinese dragon, and
now that it has grown more significant, it is getting hungrier for
power. Strategic assessments have been blinded by money and
trade, and now the West and Asia will pay the price. On the other
hand, though Russia's actions in Ukraine are unacceptable, they
are not entirely surprising, as the West, with the United States in
the lead, has been putting Moscow in a geopolitical corner since
the end of the Cold War. Putin is far from the ideal freedom-loving
statesman, but from a realpolitik perspective, the West, including
the States, should have embraced Russia as it did Germany and
Japan after WWII. From a geostrategic perspective, the West's
relations with possible opponents should be such that its options
toward them are always more significant than their possibilities
toward each other. In other words, Washington should take steps
to make sure that its ties to both Beijing and Moscow are always
closer than those capitals' links to each other.

It was a good strategy during Kissinger's time, and it still is now.
But the former Obama administration's reluctant diplomacy
threatened to produce a different and much more unpleasant
result, and the current Trump policy might even push Russia and
China even closer together, causing them to mute their serious
differences and become much more than merely an axis of
convenience.

Ideally, the United States should seek to repair relations with both
countries. If the White House cannot bring itself to adopt that
approach, it should at least choose one dominant power to be the
designated adversary, not antagonize both governments. The last
thing to do is inadvertently help reverse the split between

Moscow and Beijing that began in the 1950s. That means setting policy priorities and making choices. Essential questions include which nation is more capable of harming critical Western interests and which country has the greater intention and capability to disrupt the status quo in its respective region. In both cases, the answer is China—not Russia.

Russia's official military doctrine, adopted in 2010, lists the expansion of NATO as its most significant external threat, and the bulk of Russia's defense as well as its foreign-policy budget is spent with that in mind. Over the past decade, that spending has managed to raise the armed forces from the disasters of the 1990s, with Chechnya as a clear illustration. Today, Russia has the third-largest military budget in the world—it was $90 billion in 2012—behind the United States and China. Even though it is not involved in any wars, it drafts hundreds of thousands of men into the armed forces every year, maintaining a standing army of more than eight hundred thousand soldiers, and spends the same proportion of its GDP—4 percent—on its military as the United States does.

Last year, as he prepared to begin his third term as president, Putin made the extravagant pledge to completely rearm the military at the cost of nearly $800 billion by the end of the decade. The windfall of high oil prices, which have been at historical peaks during the Putin era, just as Russia surpassed Saudi Arabia as the largest producer of both crude oil and natural gas in the world, underwrites such generosity. However, the West remains Russia's bogeyman, as evidenced by the fact that, for instance, in 2006, thanks to high energy prices, Russia repaid its external debt of $23.7 billion, not for the sake of improving its financial profile but solely to cut off the links of so-called dependency to Western creditors.

Also, in recent years, particularly during the Obama administration, Russia has opposed almost any initiative that might potentially challenge its influence or power, such as the expansion of NATO, the admission of the Baltic states into the European Union, the democratization of Ukraine, the war in Georgia, the civil war in Kosovo, relations with the United Kingdom, and more recently the diplomatic standoff around Edward Snowden and the civil war in Syria. Clearly, since reclaiming the presidency in May 2012, Putin has become the biggest impediment to the US White House's foreign-policy aims. That's undoubtedly played well with Moscow's yearning for the days when the nation was a superpower. Beneath Vladimir Putin's swagger, however, lie some weaknesses at the core of the Russian economy that threaten the Kremlin's future and his power-driven political base. And for that, Putin can blame a familiar nemesis: the United States and the West.

Putin's dream is to create a fifth Russian Eurasian empire constituted of the former Soviet states, possibly with the help of China. Moscow and Beijing have been developing relations over more than two decades. The two nations have long engaged politically; military cooperation is a more significant indicator of the degree of intimacy between states.

For example, the military alliance between the United States, Japan, and South Korea provides an adequate insight. Although Japan and South Korea argue over historical and territorial issues, under the broader framework of the alliance, they maintain a careful division of labor, work carefully, and stay in step on military matters. And Russia and China are aiming to develop a similar relationship.

In addition to bilateral relations, cooperation between Beijing and Moscow has a broader role in the global arena. China has had a vital role in the Shanghai Cooperation Organization (SCO) since the establishment of the Shanghai Five mechanism. The security organization is based in Shanghai, meaning that it is widely seen as representing Beijing's sphere of influence. In addition to China, other formal members of the SCO include Russia and certain other Commonwealth of Independent States (CIS) countries, making the organization the most effective platform for cooperation between China and the CIS. Central Asia also forms the innermost ring of Russian foreign policy, and for Moscow, China is an important international partner and external supporter. The cooperation of two major political entities—China and the CIS—through the SCO will very likely become the fulcrum of a quasi-alliance between Beijing and Moscow.

When trying to understand Russia's behavior, it is beneficial and exciting to put into perspective Putin's personality, as it is an essential driver behind the ultimate decisions being made by Moscow about foreign policy and defense. It is the basis for the whole Vladimir Putin cult.

From an introspectional perspective, Putin's anti-West and seemingly pro-China mind-set is apparently driven by his personality. Putin's state of mind is one of a former KGB colonel obsessed by the Cold War balance of power, emphasizing his intelligence training, which dates to the Soviet era. Understanding Putin requires exploring three core aspects of his political and personal character:

- The fighter—this is illustrated by his attitude during the Chechen conflict, where he showed that he is ferocious and even pitiless;

- The Chekist—he is a very good evaluator and interrogator and a cool, suspicious calculator thanks to the professional skills he acquired as a member of a Soviet security agency; and

- The believer—he is close with the Russian Orthodox Church, the soul of Russia.

These traits roughly correspond to Putin's instincts, his professional training and methods, and his religious and patriotic convictions.

Now, to take a "helicopter" view again, Russia's difficulty has nothing to do with intercontinental ballistic nuclear missiles and everything to do with natural gas transported on special shipping tankers to international markets around the world. Washington's surprising return to the world stage as an energy superpower is complicating life for the Russian petrostate. The emergence of a global, vibrant, and pipeline-free liquefied-natural-gas market is a direct threat to Moscow's interests in Europe, where Gazprom, the state-owned energy giant, supplies about 25 percent of the gas. And so is the shift in pricing power from suppliers to consumers as a result of the enormous supply shock emanating from North America.

Putin has long viewed the nation's natural resources as a foreign-policy lever. In price disputes, Moscow turned the gas taps off on its LNG pipelines to Ukraine from 2006 to 2009 in the middle of winter, resulting in critical shortages elsewhere on the European mainland. Gazprom has been able to obtain high prices, especially in the former Soviet states, by pegging its long-term contracts to the price of oil.

Russia renationalized the oil industry and dialed back the involvement of Western oil companies there. For example, after pressure from Moscow, the oil giant Shell gave up part of its stake in a Siberian LNG venture in Sakhalin to local interests. One of the other oil majors, British Petroleum, sold its share of a joint Anglo-Russian energy venture called TNK-BP to Rosneft after a conflict with investors in the country.

Taxes on the energy industry are critical to Moscow's patronage system. They provide it with the means to woo essential constituencies such as the security forces, the military establishment, and the political elites; to improve government pensions; and to spend more in impoverished regions in the Muslim North Caucasus and other rural areas. During his 2012 campaign, Putin promised to increase retirement benefits, improve wages for doctors and teachers, and invest in Russia's military arsenal. The former career KGB colonel is unlikely to loosen his grip on the state-owned energy industry, because that would weaken his tight grip on power.

The Kremlin's worry is twofold. An expanding supply of affordable LNG carried by ship compels Gazprom to either cut prices or lose market share.[160] Longer term, the Russians may even have to contend with shale-energy assets being developed by Western oil majors in Poland, Ukraine, and Lithuania, all Gazprom profit sanctuaries. The challenge for Putin is to revive the country's massive energy sector and then place Russia on a track to break free of its hydrocarbon dependency. The nation needs to make substantial infrastructure investments in the east and to expand nonenergy sectors where it has real potential, such as information technology, airplanes, helicopters, engines, turbines, and industrial pumps and compressors.

In addition to the NATO and energy pressure points, there are also some other issues that need to be mapped out, such as Russia's arm-twisting of ex-Soviet nations to join his Eurasian Customs Union. For most of them, that is an unattractive alternative to the European Union.

The second pressure point is Russia's privileged status at NATO, based on the assumption that Moscow is deemed to be a friend. And the last area is the dull but essential world of international organizations: in particular, Putin's record of obstruction in

---

[160] As a sidenote, a weird and surprising fact is that as American utilities shift to gas, displaced US coal is flooding European markets. The United States may supplant Russia as the world's number-three coal exporter by the end of 2018. Gazprom is under pressure to adopt spot-market pricing instead of tying its prices to oil. In June, the Russian gas giant agreed to revise its gas contracts with German utility RWE after losing an arbitration case; it's renegotiating supply contracts with other utilities, including Eni and EconGas.

institutions such as the Organization for Security and Cooperation in Europe, which handles sociopolitical issues like election rigging, media freedom, and minority rights. From a Western perspective, one should not underestimate Putin and his Russia for all the reasons mentioned above. The United States and Europe should not be comparing Putin and Russia to a "bored kid at the back of the classroom."[161]

This would be somewhat indicative of the West's lack of appreciation of who Vladimir Putin is. He's an old KGB colonel who has no illusions about the West's relationship with him and does not care about having a relationship with the West. Putin's aim, understandably, is to reestablish the former Soviet Union—the typical attitude of a person who has witnessed the demise of an empire and wants to take revenge. (As an analogy, see China's position of wishing to recover from the humiliation it suffered at the hands of Japan and the West for the past hundred years.) Despite the fact that most security and intelligence agencies are focused on Islamists as well as the China threat, they should keep a very close eye on Putin and his vast network of spies while pursuing engagement with Russia, thereby raising its awareness of a bigger existential threat: China.

From a Russian perspective, and bearing in mind Putin's psychological state of mind, Russian defense and foreign policies are geared toward fighting a nonexistent war. The West has never had any intention of invading or attacking Russia; clearly, the defeat and demise of both Napoleon and Hitler when they tried to conquer Russia remain highly valuable lessons to the West. Russia's biggest threat is not the West but China. The rise of China will represent an ever more critical political, economic, and security threat to Russia, employing the following avenues:

[161] Steve Holland and Margaret Chadbourn, "Obama Describes Putin as 'Like a Bored Kid'," Reuters, August 9, 2013, accessed March 4, 2018, https://www.reuters.com/article/us-usa-russia-obama/obama-describes-putin-as-like-a-bored-kid-idUSBRE9780XS20130809.

- Immigration: Russia and Siberia are very different from neighboring China, being sparsely populated with vast amounts of land and abundant resources. This is a massive attraction for China. The influx of legal and illegal Chinese immigrants is difficult to manage. Some scholars are worried that Chinese immigrants will outnumber Russian residents in the Far East and dominate its land.

- Economic expansion: Beijing's development in the Far East and Siberia is dangerous to Russia, which fears that the region will eventually be dominated by China economically. Some have even termed this a form of Chinese colonialism. The economic threat, along with the immigration threat, will eventually undermine Russia's control over this region and endanger Russia's sovereignty.

- Territorial risk: Despite a bilateral agreement signed by Moscow and Beijing in 2004 aimed at resolving disputes over the eastern sector of the 4,300-kilometer border, Russia's fear of China's territorial threat should remain. In dealing with border treaties between China and Russia from the mid-nineteenth century, China's attitude is that it recognizes the treaties' legal effect but at the same time considers them to have been imposed. But by Russia's logic, the fact that China believes these treaties are unequal hints at China's denial of the treaties' legitimacy.

- Expansion threat: China will unavoidably expand, and it will occupy Siberia and the Far East. Beijing's occupation of the region may not be reached through peaceful methods, such as immigration and economic expansion, but rather by force.

- Strategic security threat: In recent years, comparisons between Chinese and Russian military strength have not been in favor of Russia. China's conventional military forces have surpassed Russia's, and the gap between them in strategic nuclear weapons is narrowing. China's expenses have been twice those of Russia, and the room for Chinese military spending to grow is still quite massive, considering China's economic performance.

- China's threat to Moscow's sphere of influence: Russia sees the post-Soviet region as its sphere of influence, a part of the world where it has unique and historical interests, particularly in Central Asia and Eastern Europe. China's development in the region adds to Moscow's feelings of inferiority. It is a widespread view in Russia that Beijing has posed a challenge to the country. The Chinese are all over the world, and their business landscape is so vast that it covers the Baltic Sea region, Ukraine, Belarus, and Moldova.

China's strong rise should pose an essential question to Russia: How to cope with it? Many Russians believe that China will replace the United States shortly as the world's largest economy. And, bearing this in mind, there is a strong case advocating that competition and confrontation between China and Russia will become mainstream. So, which side should Moscow take, and what role will it play? It may consider the following:

- Aligning with China: This would be based on Russia strengthening its strategic ties with China and would call for alignment with China on the diplomatic front to counterbalance the United States. Politically, Russia would accept China's model as a physical resource for Russia's modernization. The setting up of the Shanghai Cooperation Organization (SCO) is indicative of this stance as well as the numerous military drills between both countries.

- Containing China: In this scenario, Russia would work with its former communist allies in Asia such as India, Vietnam, Indonesia, Cambodia, and Laos, as they also face a threat from China.

- Balancing China: Here, Russia would develop relations with China while making sure that it does not become a regional power. Such a balancing view is reflected in the way that Russia prefers to play mediation roles and hedge between China and the West to maximize outcomes while minimizing costs.

For a long-term strategy, Russia should aim at containing China and for the medium term, balance the rise of power in the Far East region. In the short term, from a tactical perspective, Russia could maintain its SCO alliance with China. Whatever combination of paths Russia chooses, the paramount milestone to achieve would be to rebalance the economy away from energy exports, creating a more stable and sustainable economic development.

The second milestone would be to reenergize the demography in Russia, thus stalling the reversal of the age pyramid. Third should be to normalize and strengthen relations with the West, as this would allow Russia to focus on China and the Far East territories entirely. But the economic challenge is the most important. In a nutshell, just as the West is pivoting to the East, Russia should do the same thing and aim at closing on China.

The West encourages the formation of a strategic Russia-China axis, as perceived inactions of the White House and Brussels (EU/NATO) are pushing the Kremlin into the arms of the Zhongnanhai. But the bolstered partnership between Moscow and Beijing is also the result of decade-long shortsighted Western calculations to drive a grudgeful Russia into a geopolitical corner instead of adopting a no-nonsense approach to post-1991 Moscow. Concomitantly, Russia's intimacy with China is the outcome of the impaired leading-from-behind US policy that has given preeminence to a back-seat projection of power.

While the West claims it has the high moral ground and righteousness on its side in the Ukraine crisis, the way it has managed the crisis so far and even, generally speaking, its relations with the Kremlin—all the more if we have the 1938 Munich events in the backs of our minds—will prove counterproductive in the medium term and eventually backfire, geopolitically speaking. First of all, the West does not have the high ground in morality or rectitude; we can easily point to the West's double standards when handling cases such as Israel, Kosovo, Iraq, and so on. Second, the EU, in the middle of a considerable legitimacy crisis that will be highlighted in the upcoming May elections, has stirred up the crisis in Ukraine first by proposing an EU adhesion agreement to Kiev without even consulting Russia, and later on by promising EU membership and billions of euros during the Kiev street protests.

The United States, through NATO, has hinted several times at making Ukraine a member of NATO, including in August 2013, when heralding the cooperation between Ukraine and NATO, knowing it would provoke Moscow. (Though Kiev passed legislation in 2010 that bars Ukraine from joining military alliances, legal frameworks can be changed politically.)

Apparently, both the EU's mismanagement and continuing voluntary miscalculations by the United States and NATO have made the Russian bear even angrier. As mentioned earlier, how would the United States feel if Russia or China suddenly signed a military alliance with Mexico or Canada? (Remember the Cuba crisis?) Russia, just as the United States in light of the Monroe Doctrine about North and South America, does not like foreign interference in its backyard.

And, quite frankly, what is this cynical Western policy of "What is good for us is fair and just by international law that we drafted, and those who don't like it can take a hike?" Realpolitik and pragmatism should be the order of the day—no more one-size-fits-all foreign policies.

Ever since the naively so-called end of history, the West, in its vanquisher's haughtiness, has continually looked down on Russia like a mighty lord would on a peasant. And ever since 1991, the White House has rejected every possibility of making the Kremlin an equal and respectful partner in a Euro-Atlantic alliance, instead using moral claims to push a resentful Kremlin into a geopolitical corner. Granted, 1) Russia has behaved wrongly in Georgia and some other neighboring regions; 2) Vladimir Putin is far from the ideal, freedom-loving political leader; and 3) no one can deny the allegation that Moscow intends to try rebuilding, in some shape or form, part of the former USSR. But the West, after outsmarting Russia during the Cold War, could have leveraged its victory in the 1990s by adopting a more no-nonsense approach, the way it did from 1945 to 1950 with Japan and Germany, in contrast to the 1919 Versailles Treaty, and by embracing Russia as a new full-blown member of Western security and economic architecture.

Presently, with the crisis in Ukraine, the West, as a result of its futile sanctions, is pushing Russia into the arms of China, further impaired by the lead-from-behind US foreign policy that President Obama implemented, particularly since 2012. And Donald Trump is not really shifting gears either. Consequently, Russia and China are now in the process of reinforcing their strategic partnerships through the Shanghai Cooperation Organization, the Collective Security Treaty Organization, and the Eurasian Union. And trade- and investment-wise, both capitals are sure to become even more unyielding business partners, as Moscow has negotiated a thirty-year deal with Beijing for rerouting its vast energy reserves away from Europe to the Chinese markets. Other investment deals have been made between the two giants, such as developing the Russian Far East together.[162]

If you think about it, in the spirit of the Cold War, when so-called capitalist, democratic forces fought communist regimes such as the USSR, one might wonder why the West has been treating Moscow—a former communist state that, after 1991 under Yeltsin, Medvedev, and Putin, embraced capitalist, Western-style values—with such contempt while at the same time courting and flirting intensely with Beijing, a dictatorial state that is still Mao-communist. Additionally, when the USSR collapsed in 1991, it did so in a relative absence of violence, unlike the Tiananmen massacre in the late 1980s, committed by the same Chinese communist regime that is still in power today.

Last but not least, geostrategically speaking and aside from trade and investment relations, ad hoc partnerships with Russia have proven more useful to the West than teaming up with the Chinese. To name just a few, there are international terrorism, nuclear nonproliferation, Afghanistan, Iran, Syria, North Korea, drug trafficking, developing the Arctic region, continued space exploration, and global warming. None of these challenges can be met by the West alone, and China so far has been geostrategically quasi-useless to the West. Now, unless NATO is prepared to go to war with Russia, Moscow will most likely annex some additional Eastern parts of Ukraine as well as of Moldova (Transnistria), knowing that both countries are on their own, as they are not part of NATO.

But the White House is not about to risk a conventional war over the Kremlin's non-NATO neighbors because its geostrategic interests there are limited, and the dispute might escalate to the

---

[162] Sputnik International, "Chinese Investments in Russia's Far East Increased by One-Third in 2016," September 8, 2017, accessed February 20, 2018, https://sputniknews.com/russia/201709081057218326-china-investment-russia-vladivostok-business/.

nuclear level. As a University of Miami professor specializing in US foreign policy once said, "Crimea isn't worth Charleston." And the White House has made clear that a military response is not on the table in Ukraine. But how much does that calculation change if NATO members such as Estonia or Latvia are in the crosshairs?

Therefore, in order to cut short any future Russian imperialistic initiatives in, for instance, the Baltic states (notably Estonia), the West needs to respond to the Ukraine crisis ASAP by redeploying NATO troops in Eastern Europe and to show Moscow that it should not dare to attack or violate the sovereignty and territorial integrity of any NATO member, including the Baltic states.

But that does not mean that NATO should fight for Ukraine as, fortunately, it has no military treaty with Kiev. And despite Europe's minimalist military efforts, its forces already far outrange Russia's reach.

However, Europe's relative military strength represents merely numbers, as without the United States being prepared to use force, no common European resolve will ever be found except popular rhetorical support. In other words, NATO's collective defense guarantee is sufficient only if Washington is prepared to use force. Eventually, of course, military numbers cannot tell us what will happen if a NATO member is attacked. Article 5 of the NATO charter, which requires the response of every member if one member is attacked, has remained virtually experimental. The only time it has ever been petitioned was at the request of the United States after the 9/11 attacks. And, as Syria has shown, the ghost of Iraq still stalks America's foreign policy, poisoning the debate over any intervention, no matter how "righteous."

As for Beijing, while it seems on the surface to have remained on the sidelines by abstaining during the March 15, 2014 UN Security Council vote on Ukraine, which mattered little, as Moscow had already vetoed the resolution, it is leveraging the geopolitical situation. Indeed, as Beijing sees that Washington is not undertaking any meaningful action against Russia, it is, maybe wrongly, postulating that in relation to the South and East China Seas maritime disputes, the United States—despite the official US-Asia pivot—will not want to intervene militarily to come to the rescue of the Philippines and/or Japan, despite existing mutual defense and security treaties.

Already, China feels emboldened enough to consider not only taking back the Senkaku Islands (known as the Diaoyu in China) but also potentially seizing the Ryukyu Islands (also known as the Okinawa prefecture). Obviously, strategically speaking, the stakes for the United States are higher in the East China Sea than in Ukraine, as the US Marines and Air Force have bases as well as tens of thousands of troops stationed on Okinawa. And occupying the Ryukyu would fracture the US strategic position in East Asia, isolating US forces based in Japan from those in the Gulf.

Hypothetically speaking, under these Chinese scenarios, once Okinawa was in the hands of the Chinese, the onus would fall on Washington to retake it—an unappealing prospect for conducting island fighting. Beijing is gambling on the fact that the States will lack leadership and avoid paying the hefty human and political price necessary to return to those islands.

Naturally, these geostrategic projections ignore not only the significant defense capabilities of the Japanese SDF but also that, with a Japanese population of 1.5 million based in Okinawa, Tokyo would fight to the death with its well-known fanaticism to protect the prefecture, as well as the fact that US forces on Okinawa, with the help of those in Korea, would pose a substantial fight against a Chinese takeover of Okinawa. But still, as China is growing more vocal and bullish, predominantly as it will face severe upcoming economic conditions (a potential economic hard landing), Beijing will be more than happy to deflect domestic anger toward Japan or the Philippines. Washington is concomitantly perceived as too compromising and unwilling to fight a war with a sophisticated regional power, unlike in the wars in Iraq and Afghanistan.

At a time when China's energy needs are growing stronger and to become less reliant on Gulf oil, which poses geostrategic maritime concerns to Beijing, the Russian partnership will be a highly welcoming platform that Xi Jinping will be eager to develop further. Therefore, in Asia, the United States needs to be very serious and firmly committed to defending Japan, as well as the Philippines, politically and militarily, thus providing no pretext to the Chinese for undertaking bolder unilateral actions. And in Europe, the United States must lead NATO in bolstering its defenses in the former Warsaw Pact countries, now mostly NATO members, to fend off Russian geopolitical temptations in the region.

If Washington fails to adjust its foreign and defense policy, its perceived inaction will probably further embolden the creation of the new strategic Russia-China axis. Had the West, and Washington in particular, treated Russia in a more no-nonsense way after 1991, Moscow would by now be on our side, ready to stand firm against China. But political shortsightedness and amateurism decided that things would be different. Granted, Moscow is not that naive either and will unquestionably maneuver with prudence to seal new deals with China. However, tactically speaking, both have significant advantages if they work closely together to fend off the West, the United States in particular.

The geofinancial outlook for 2018–2019

The most prominent risks to the systemic environment for the upcoming twelve months are twofold: geopolitical and financial. But these two threats will interact, with mutual negative effects. Intuitively, one can see how geopolitical events can hurt financial and commodity markets. There have been some cases in this past year that have illustrated how geopolitical incidents are fueling performance in these markets.

- Notwithstanding the fact that equity and currency markets fell right after the unexpected Brexit results, global equity markets rallied on the election of US president Donald Trump amid hopes of a probusiness agenda of tax reforms and less regulation. As of February 2018, US stock markets are up almost 35 percent since the 2016 election while the pan-European STOXX 600 is up nearly 10 percent. Pundits believe that geopolitical risk is here to stay and will continue to weigh down global markets. However, market volatility, measured by the VIX, has gone up steeply in recent weeks, doubling from 10 to 20.

- In North Asia, the critical geopolitical risk that markets will continue to focus on is the crisis on the Korean peninsula combined with the nuclear escalation that North Korea seems to want to unchain. In 2018, China will play a significant role in trying to tame the North Korean bully, although maybe not up to everyone's expectations. Some pundits believe that now that the resolutions of the recent Nineteenth National Congress of the Chinese Communist Party have been endorsed, Beijing will be more forcefully proactive, as Xi Jinping does not want North Korea to have nuclear weapons. But concomitantly, he also fears a shooting war that would result in refugees running across its borders. And finally, he hates the idea of the Korean Peninsula being reunited under the leadership of Seoul with Tokyo and Washington as patrons. As for Japan, PM Abe will further increase its military spending as well as Tokyo's diplomatic clout in the region on the back of a stronger economy.

- With a population of about 1.7 billion, South Asia is home to two nuclear-armed, mutually hostile neighbors; any misjudgment or miscalculation by either Pakistan or India could have disastrous effects, not only for the two nations but also for the region as a whole. In South Asia, there is not much hope of any enduring friendship between New Delhi and Islamabad or of their reaching an agreement on longstanding issues, such as border disputes, Islamic terrorism, and Kashmir. Already, the rivalry between the two most significant countries in South Asia has torpedoed regional cooperation. And the region continues to be one of the least integrated parts of the world, with trade among its nations not even totaling 5 percent of the global business that countries of the region conduct with the remainder of the world. But South Asia is a hostile ground not only between India and Pakistan but also between India and China. (Beijing and Islamabad are very close allies, as they both have an interest in containing India.) Sandwiched countries such as Bhutan and Nepal are ping-pong balls between the two regional powerhouses, with the Himalayan border disputes as the background to their rivalry. For example, in June, Chinese PLA troops started building a paved road toward India's border onto the Doklam plateau in Bhutan, which has been claimed by Beijing as its enclave. Thimphu, the capital of Bhutan, in turn requested help from neighboring India, which sent army troops across the border from the northeastern state of Sikkim. Beijing is likely to continue to poke into New Delhi's flank, testing whether the Indians are resolute in defending their hinterland.

- From Europe to Russia, the former Soviet satellite countries (Ukraine, the Baltic states, Georgia, and some Central European countries) as well as some Nordic countries will continue to feel more threatened by

Moscow and will likely engage in closer relations with NATO but not necessarily with the EU. For example, countries such as Sweden and Finland, which have been neutral since WWII, are seriously considering membership in the NATO alliance. Now that the war in Syria seems to be over, the Russians will refocus themselves on their hinterland in Europe. Europe, despite its harsh negotiating tactics with the United Kingdom regarding the Brexit terms, will remain weak. Populism, nationalism, and anti-EU-establishment right-wing as well as left-wing enthusiasm will continue to rise to the detriment of federalist EU policies. A particular note on Turkey: while the country is a bridgehead between Europe and the Middle East, President Erdogan will gradually shift toward its northern neighbor, the Moscow orbit. Illustrating this recent change of mind is, for example, the November 2017 Sochi conference on Syria to which only Russia, Iran, and Turkey, and not a single Western country, were invited. But Ankara still wants to maintain membership in NATO, at least for the sake of appearances but also as a joker in case of an unforeseen geopolitical event.

- In the Middle East, while the threat of ISIS has been contained to a certain degree in Syria and Iraq, the underlying threat of Islamic terrorism is ongoing. Granted, the likelihood of a confrontation between the West and Russia and Iran in the Middle East seems to be more remote than it has been during the past twenty-four months, although the rivalry between Iran and Saudi Arabia will continue to increase. But this competition will most likely not lead to a direct military confrontation between Tehran and Riyadh. The rivalry between Sunnis and Shiites will lead to small-scale proxy wars like the one in Yemen and maybe shortly in Lebanon, where Western and Russian militaries will not be directly involved but will instead use Saudi Arabia and Iran as their proxies in the overarching bitter Western-Russian (Chinese) conundrum. However, again, Riyadh and Tehran will not go into a full-blown conflict, as that would dry out their main source of revenues: oil exports. And then there is Israel. While the Palestinian conflict seems to have dipped in recent years, the decision by Trump to transfer the US embassy from Tel Aviv to Jerusalem, a de facto acknowledgment that the latter is the capital of Israel, will most likely put fuel on the fire of Palestinian discontent and could even widen it to the rest of the Middle East.

- In Africa, the coup d'état against Robert Mugabe in Zimbabwe took most of us by surprise, although not China, as the chief of the Zimbabwean armed forces was seen visiting Beijing officials a week before Mugabe's removal. With the military now in power in Harare, not much change should be expected, particularly since Beijing has a keen interest in keeping a stable regime in place. (Zimbabwe is a major source of commodities for China: raw tobacco, gold, nickel ore, ferroalloys, and diamonds.) Central and Eastern Africa, particularly the Congo and Sudan, remain a zone of war, chaos, and civilian distress. The western part of Africa will see the United States increase its military presence to fight the Islamic threat in Nigeria, Niger, and the other Sahel countries.

- As for South America and Central America, the Maduro economy in Venezuela will continue its recessionary course, with GDP forecasted to shrink by as much as a fifth and inflation hitting 2,500 percent. With a hypothetically competent government and more orthodox economic policies, Venezuela might have been able to handle its excessive indebtedness.

Although oil exports are falling, Venezuela still boasts the world's largest proven reserves, and oil prices have been at their peak for more than two years. But chronic mismanagement by governments under Hugo Chávez (and now Mr. Maduro), combined with the oil slump, has taken its toll. According to the IMF,[163] the economy has shrunk by a third over the past five years. After the default on the Venezuelan and PDVSA debt ($60 to $100 billion outstanding), it is likely that Caracas will not be able to restructure its debt successfully in an orderly fashion. The top five institutional holders of Venezuelan debt are Fidelity Investments ($572 million), T. Rowe Price ($370 million), BlackRock iShares ($222 million), Goldman Sachs ($187 million), and Invest PowerShares ($113 million), according to CNN.[164] The remaining countries in South America, including Brazil, Chile, and Argentina, will continue to witness a mild economic rebound (1 to 2 percent GDP growth per year). The outlook and risks for the Central American region as well as Mexico, according to the IMF, are being affected by their close business links to the United States through migration, trade, and direct foreign investment. Mexico's real annual GDP growth is forecasted to decelerate to 1.5 percent in 2018.[165] Uncertainty about future commerce relations with the United States, caused by NAFTA renegotiations, and higher borrowing costs are expected to neutralize the positive effect from stronger US growth.

[163] Valentina Romeil, "Hidden Numbers Reveal Scale of Venezuela's Economic Crisis," *Financial Times*, May 9, 2017, accessed February 20, 2018, https://www.ft.com/content/a6f7bdae-2f46-11e7-9555-23ef563ecf9a.

[164] Patrick Gillespie, "Venezuela Is in Default, and You May Own Its Debt," CNN Money, November 14, 2017, accessed February 20, 2018, http://money.cnn.com/2017/11/14/investing/venezuela-debt-401k/index.html.

[165] Trading Economics, "Mexico GDP Annual Growth Rate—Forecast," accessed February 20, 2018, https://tradingeconomics.com/mexico/gdp-growth-annual/forecast.

While the global economy will continue to gain pace during 2018 with the United States leading the charge, followed by the European Union, the United Kingdom, Japan, China, and the emerging markets, the fragile state of the financial markets could have geopolitical consequences. Too many pundits see blue skies ahead (mainly when paying attention to the bullish stock markets) without a sound risk awareness. These are the dark economic clouds on the horizon that could spell geopolitical disaster.

Here is a nonexhaustive list of such dark possibilities:

- A flattening yield curve in the bond markets can be an early warning for an upcoming recession; it can be the forerunner to an inverted curve, where the short end (in this case, a two-year yield), increases to above the long end, the ten-year yield. An inverted curve is the real warning of trouble and historically has indicated a recession. Historically, when the yield curve is flat or inverts, it's not a good sign for the upcoming twelve months. A flat curve tells you that twelve months from now, growth is going to be weaker. As I write this, the economy seems to be strengthening, and thus flattening may not mean what it has meant historically. However, there remains trepidation even though strategists point to very logical reasons behind the move.

- Shares from financial institutions are declining when rates are increasing, another potentially lousy sign. It is not good for financial institutions to see interest rates go up, even though they see their net interest margins and net interest income improving. However, the US tax reform that was recently passed will most likely compensate for the increased cost of funding and borrowing.

- Long periods of low volatility invariably signal a severe downturn. Those with eagle eyes might detect that the today's volatility lull is a bit deeper than the one from the first half of the early 2000s, while it's about the same as those in the 1950s, the 1960s, and the 1990s. So yes, volatility is weaker compared to average historical levels, but the volatility is at levels that are typical of the bottom of a quiet period between two crises.

- A rising US dollar and rising oil prices are both signs of cracks in the wall. When the USD is getting stronger, imports in the United States tend to rise and exports fall, resulting in an even more significant trade deficit. So, all other things remaining equal, as the US dollar gets stronger, Washington's trade deficit with the rest of the world will increase, which is not a good thing for the US economy. And the same goes for oil prices. While rising oil prices can provide support for the US oil industry, they also fuel inflation, which eats into corporate profit margins.

- Global debt is currently almost three times global GDP. In a McKinsey study, three areas of emerging risks are being pinpointed: 1) the steep increase in public (government) debt, which in some countries has reached close to or above 100 percent of GDP; 2) the continued rise in household debt to new peaks in Northern Europe and some Asian countries; and 3) the quadrupling of China's debt, fed by real estate and shadow banking, in just eight years.

- Notwithstanding massive QE measures, inflation remains unseen. Many feared that quantitative easing would lead to hyperinflation for the US economy following the economic crisis of 2008. The systemic crisis, however, was primarily a deflationary phenomenon, and the money injected into the system by QE, as seen by a spike in the M0 monetary base, was fundamentally restricted to the financial sector, with the more critical M2 money supply remaining relatively stable.

While it may not seem intuitive that financial markets (including commodity markets) can command geopolitical events, history is full of examples. When we go back in time, we can see that many military confrontations were rooted in economic triggers: Military Japan started WWII in Asia in a quest for land as well as for energy and mineral commodities. The ascent of Nazism in Germany and the start of WWII in Europe were rooted in the deep socioeconomic malaise that Germany was confronted with in the '20s and '30s. During WWI, Paris and London had old colonial vestiges, and Berlin wanted a new one. During WWII, London and Paris still had colonial empires, Berlin had always sought a new one, and America wanted to rid the world of realms and have free trade. And, in the case of the 2003 Iraq war, the control of Middle Eastern oil was at stake.

Additionally, in today's context of high indebtedness (both public and private—see the McKinsey report on the subject), an economy (for example, that of the United States) that bears a very heavy, unsustainable debt burden is fragilizing itself and therefore weakens its power-projection capacities. As a result, this weakened economy might decide to retreat and instead lead from behind (Obama's foreign policy and Trump's "America First" policy), thereby causing a power vacuum in some areas of the world: for example, Asia, the Middle East, and Eastern Europe. A rival geopolitical contender (e.g., China or Russia) might view this weakness as an opportunity to projects its own power more strongly. In turn, this could potentially result in a military escalation and eventually war with both countries.

Today's contemporary events are awash with examples of financial conditions that can trigger geopolitical changes. Here are some examples:

- Saudi Arabia and its acolytes are trying to keep oil prices low, not just in an attempt to break the back of the American fracking industry but foremost to punish Moscow and Tehran for their support of the Damascus regime. However, instead of this weakening the resolve of the leaders of Russia and Iran, both seem to be more adamant than ever in pursuing their geostrategies.

- In Venezuela, chronic mismanagement by governments under Hugo Chávez and now Mr. Maduro, combined with the oil slump, have taken their toll and could lead to a regime change in Caracas in the coming twenty-four months. However, hitting the current Maduro regime with crippling sanctions could backfire; instead, looking back at South Africa offers a better game plan. Additionally, Moscow seems interested in getting more involved in Venezuela; Putin recently renegotiated the restructuring of $3 billion of its debt.[166]

- In Zimbabwe, Robert Mugabe's removal from power found its causes not only in the deep bitterness between him and his former vice president, Mnangagwa, but foremost because of the mismanagement of the Zimbabwean economy under his thirty-seven-year authoritarian reign (inflation in the CPI of close to 100 percent and GDP −1.4 percent).[167]

---

[166] Andrey Biryukov and Ksenia Galouchko, "Russia Says Venezuela Accepts $3 Billion Restructuring Terms," *Bloomberg*, last modified November 8, 2017, https://www.bloomberg.com/news/articles/2017-11-08/russia-says-venezuela-accepts-terms-for-3-billion-restructuring.

- American economic anxiety and the growing gap between the rich and poor in the United States helped put Donald Trump in the White House. While monetary policy with super-low interest rates and quantitative easing provided necessary emergency medicine after the 2007–2008 financial crash and the 2010 euro-debt crisis, there have also been some adverse side effects. People with assets have gotten wealthier, while people without them have suffered with poor job prospects and no growth in wages. People with mortgages have found their debts cheaper, while people with savings have found themselves more impoverished. In other words, the massive scale of the quantitative easing that took place not only in the United States but also within the eurozone and the United Kingdom caused many distorted distributional effects. These collateral damages have exacerbated inequality amid uneven wage growth, thus fueling populist support for unconventional political challengers.

In conclusion, geopolitics and the sustainability of the bullish hype on today's stock markets are the most prominent risk concerns for investors over the next twelve months. North Korea, Iran, Russia, China, Saudi Arabia, Turkey, Qatar, and Venezuela are rising on the global radar screen as potential flashpoints. In essence, we cannot separate geopolitics and public policy from markets. The market can ebb and flow independently of the outside world for extended periods, but it cannot become a distinct entity. Think about what the markets consist of: assets that are intimately connected to what goes on in the real world. That is the inescapable reality.

---

[167] Trading Economics, "*Zimbabwe — Economic Indicators*," accessed February 20, 2018, https://tradingeconomics.com/zimbabwe/indicators.

Geofinancial risks on the horizon: 2018–2023

Some prophetically assert today that we are actually at a point at which everything we have known—international currencies, financial markets, the United States, the Western alliance, world governance, democracy, and more—is about to vanish. Granted, there is a heightened risk that financial crisis and impending military conflicts will converge as failed policies become self-fulfilling prophecies, but concomitantly, one cannot assert that we are on the eve of the destruction of an international order we have known since 1945.

First of all, no one should write history before it takes place, and Francis Fukuyama should know that. Second, no one can accurately predict the future—probably not even by looking into the mirror of the past (comparing today to 1914, the 1930s, etc.). However, this does not mean we should blind ourselves to the risks related to a potential upcoming perfect storm that would combine financial calamity with geopolitical disputes.

The issue is mostly that there is currently a power vacuum in the leadership of the United States, the European Union, and Japan, and it seems that they all have a too-conciliatory tone toward the rogues of China, Iran, ISIS, and Russia. Apparently, they have at heart their concern to avoid a military conflict with any of these out of fear of a full-blown escalation and instead prefer to lick the wounds afflicted by the recent and ongoing global financial crisis. But their keenness to appease rather than to alienate prompts questions and sends mixed signals about their will and capacity to cope with these disasters.

The years from 2008 to 2018 were a decade of uneasy calms interrupted by sudden bouts of abrupt market volatility. However, during those years, one might have been surprised how risk appetite remained so crucial, notwithstanding a high level of risk, especially from the geopolitical sphere. This irrationally exuberant risk appetite may continue in 2018 and beyond, but we believe that it is as likely to come to a sudden stop with renewed volatility in global financial markets.

Many unresolved threats that were present in 2017 and in recent years did not come to the forefront to affect global financial markets. As the case of Greece has shown, the eurozone debt crisis is far from being adequately addressed, and there remains an underappreciated threat of sovereign crises in other major developed nations. Other unresolved threats that are being ignored for now because of the panacea of cheap money and elevating asset prices include China's house of cards; the risk of another pandemic; the appalling fiscal positions of Japan, the United States, and the United Kingdom; threats posed by terrorism and the events in Syria and the Middle East; Ukraine and geopolitical tensions with Russia; and the East and South China Seas disputes involving China and its neighbors.

To summarize, there are long-term fundamentals that I believe will affect us through 2025:

- Macroeconomic risk is significant, as there is a critical threat of a debt crisis in major industrial nations with weak public-finance data emanating from the debt-laden eurozone, the United States, China, and Japan. Even the economic recoveries in the United Kingdom and the States, while substantial, remain vulnerable at best. A significant terrorist incident, another war, too-big-to-fail banks, or some other eruption could badly affect weak consumer and investor sentiment.

- Systemic risk remains high as few of the lingering problems in the banking and financial systems have been adequately addressed, and there is a real risk of another new Grexit or Lehman Brothers moment seizing up the global financial system once again. The massive risk from the unregulated shadow-banking system continues to be underappreciated. There are many Lehman Brothers look-alikes out there in the eurozone, the United Kingdom, and the United States.

- Geopolitical risk remains high, particularly in the Middle East, North Asia, Southeast Asia, and Russia. This is notable in the continuing significant tensions in North Korea, the South and East China Seas, and the Mashriq and between Iran and Saudi Arabia. There is the real threat of conflict and the consequent effect on the global economy and oil prices. Many pundits believe that the deepening economic, political, and military flashpoints between Japan and China could evolve into an actual war. There are also simmering tensions between the United States and its Western allies, primarily the United Kingdom, not to mention with Russia and the resurgent and increasingly dominant China.

- Notwithstanding some rate increases in the United States, overall monetary risk is high as the policy responses of the US Federal Reserve, the Bank of England, the Bank of Japan, the European Central Bank, and the majority of central banks continue to be ultra-loose monetary policies, negative interest-rate policies (NIRP), nearly zero-interest-rate policies (ZIRP), the debasement of paper and electronic currencies, and the printing and creation of electronic coins.

Should these systemic macroeconomic and geopolitical risks increase even further in the coming months, the central banks' response will likely again be more cheap-money policies. This will result in further currency debasement, and there is a risk of currency wars deepening. Indeed, notwithstanding conflicting claims in the United States, ultra-accommodative monetary policies are set to remain for the foreseeable future.

Indeed, the narrative that the States is tightening its monetary policy continues to be false but has been heard for many years now. Any meaningful increase in US interest rates would likely severely affect already stressed and stretched asset markets and push the United States and the world into an economic depression. Ever since 1694 and the ensuing three centuries of Bank of England history, the key interest rate has never been this low and never at all in the advanced economies.

A reversion to the mean average—at around 5 to 6 percent— would cause a collapse in real estate and equity markets. While America's massive bond-buying program has been halted, it continues in the United Kingdom and has intensified to a very significant degree in Japan and the eurozone.

Since the 2007–2008 crash, the US Federal Reserve has created more than $4.3 trillion to prop up financial institutions and the broader economy. While the Fed ended its bond-buying program in 2014, its balance sheet has been destroyed, and it is unable to sell large volumes of bonds for fear of interest rates moving higher again. The massive levels of indebtedness at all levels of US and Western society make any significant recovery highly vulnerable.

This possibility is also illustrated by the bearish price conditions on energy and other vital commodities, such as copper. A reversion back to a debt-monetization program seems possible. America and the advanced economies are now dangerously addicted to easy money and the attendant debasement of the US dollar and all paper currencies. The US Federal Reserve Bank will continue pushing the drug of easy money, much of which falls into the pockets of the Wall Street banks and the global markets.

Central banks are persisting in the attempt to inflate their way out of the lingering public-finance crisis instead of the more prudent option, which is to avoid a deflationary collapse by downsizing the massively oversize and overleveraged financial system. This could be done—with difficulty, admittedly—through a process of downsizing, debt write-offs, deleveraging, and consolidation.

With the Federal Reserve's balance sheet having deteriorated significantly, at some stage, this will lead to the dollar having a sustained period of weakness. A monetary crisis centering on the dollar remains likely—a frightening vista that most cannot bring themselves to consider, let alone comprehend. Currency debasement will end in financial tears as it has done throughout history. The question is not if but when. And currency wars look set to heat up again in 2018. The latest salvo is Tokyo's radical decision to further debase the yen through significant monetary easing.

A new global currency war is possible in 2018 as nations seek to maintain jobs and exports through currency devaluation. China and Japan may be set to be the most aggressive in this regard. Japan is devaluing the yen, and China will be reluctant to allow that to happen. China will devalue the yuan to maintain export competitiveness. We may see the further weakness of the euro currency, especially against the US dollar. Concomitantly, the United States cannot afford to have its dollar strengthen much more against the euro, as this would affect exports to one of its most significant commerce partners.

A particular note on the risk of bail-ins: indeed, bail-ins are among the most unappreciated threats for 2018 and in the coming years. Most Western countries are putting in place the framework for bail-in regimes. Preparations for bail-ins are being put in order by the international monetary and banking authorities, including the Bank of England, the Federal Reserve, and the ECB. Canada, Australia, the United Kingdom, the EU, New Zealand, and the United States have plans in place for bail-ins in case banks and other large financial institutions get into difficulty.

Now, in the event of bank bankruptcy, the deposits of corporations and individuals can be taken away by the government. A couple of years ago, some credit-rating agencies warned that Europe's banks were vulnerable due to weak public-finance conditions, unfinished regulatory hurdles, and the risk of bail-ins. Assessing sovereign and counterparty risk remains essential. And what about the eurozone debt crisis? Well, over the past few years, the eurozone debt crisis raised its ugly head again as concerns mounted about Grexit—Greece leaving the monetary union and reverting to the drachma.

Germany continues to try to calm markets and EU households by claiming that Berlin would be "comfortable" with a Greek exit and that any fallout would be manageable. Alas, this is a frequent refrain by politicians before economic dislocations. Germany likely fears the precedent of reopening negotiations between the Troika and Greece, lest other countries upon whom very onerous conditions were placed, such as Ireland, follow their example. The assertion that the EU could comfortably manage the exit of Greece is irresponsible, particularly at this very delicate and uncertain time for the European economy. The Troika, and the EU members in particular, should consider the debt-swap proposals made by the new far-left Greek government, whereby the outstanding debt would be swapped for new growth-linked bonds. Intrinsically, it makes sense, as the only way to help a sick country to recover economically is by providing it with fiscal hormones aimed at reigniting the economic engine and thus safeguarding future debt-service payments.

Index

Bibliography

Albrow, Martin, and Elizabeth King, eds. *Globalization, Knowledge, and Society*. London: Sage, 1990.

Aliber, Robert Z., and Charles P. Kindleberger. *Manias, Panics, and Crashes: A History of Financial Crises*. Hoboken, NJ: Wiley, 2001.

Allison, Graham. *Lee Kuan Yew: The Grand Master's Insights on China, the United States, and the World*. Cambridge, MA: MIT Press, 2013.

ADVFN. "NASDAQ Company Listings." Accessed February 20, 2018. http://www.advfn.com/nasdaq/nasdaq.asp.

Baartman, Marcel. "Geopolitical Tensions and Carefree Financial Markets." *Clingendael Magazine*, July 13, 2017. https://www.clingendael.org/publication/geopolitical-tensions-and-carefree-financial-markets.

Bank for International Settlements. Consolidated Banking Statistics, January 18, 2018. https://www.bis.org/statistics/b4-UA.pdf.

Baud, Celine, and Cedric Durand. "Financialization, Globalization and the Making of Profits by Leading Retailers." *Socio-Economic Review* 10 (2011): 2–26. Accessed February 20, 2018. http://cemi.ehess.fr/docannexe/file/2483/3._baud.durand.pdf.

BBVA Research. "Big Data to Track Geopolitical and Social Events." December 2015. Accessed January 23, 2018. https://www.bbvaresearch.com/wp-content/uploads/2015/12/DEO_Dec15_Cap4.pdf.

Beck, Julie. "How 'Quantum Cognition' Can Explain Humans' Irrational Behaviors." *The Atlantic*, September 17, 2015. https://www.theatlantic.com/health/archive/2015/09/how-quantum-cognition-can-explain-humans-irrational-behaviors/405787/.

Bergmann, Gustav. *Philosophy of Science*. Madison: University of Wisconsin Press, 1957.

Bernard, Henri J., and Joseph Bisignano. "Information, Liquidity and Risk in the International Interbank Market: Implicit Guarantees and Private Credit Market Failure." BIS Working Paper 86, March 2000.

Biryukov, Andrey, and Ksenia Galouchko. "Russia Says Venezuela Accepts $3 Billion Restructuring Terms," *Bloomberg*. Last modified November 8, 2017. https://www.bloomberg.com/news/articles/2017-11-08/russia-says-venezuela-accepts-terms-for-3-billion-restructuring.

Blackwill, Robert D., and Jennifer M. Harris. *War by Other Means: Geoeconomics and Statecraft*. Cambridge, MA: Harvard University Press, 2017.

Robert D. Blackwill, "America Must play the Geoeconomics Game," *The National Interest*, June 26, 2016, accessed January 29, 2018, http://nationalinterest.org/feature/america-must-play-the-geoeconomics-game-16658

Blalock, Hubert M. Jr. *Theory Construction*. Englewood Cliffs, NJ: Prentice Hall, 1969.

Bloomfield, Arthur A. *Short-Term Capital Movements under the Pre-1914 Gold Standard*, Princeton Studies in International Finance 11. Princeton, NJ: International Finance Section, Department of Economics, Princeton University, 1963.

Blouet, Brian. *Global Geostrategy: Mackinder and the Defence of the West*, Geopolitical Theory. London: Routledge, 2013.

Bohm, David. *Causality and Chance in Modern Physics*. London: Routledge & Kegan Paul, 1957.

Bonizzi, Bruno. "Financialization in Developing and Emerging Countries." *International Journal of Political Economy* 42(4) (2013): 83–107. Accessed February 20, 2018. https://www.researchgate.net/publication/269488087_Financialization_in_Developing_and_Emerging_Countries.

Boot, Arnoud, and Matej Marinc. "Financial Innovations, Marketability, and Stability in Banking." Research Handbook on International Banking and Governance, 2011. doi: 10.4337/9781849802932.00035.

Bordo, Michael D., Barry Eichengreen, and Jongwoo Kim. "Was There Really an Earlier Period of International Financial Integration Comparable to Today?" NBER Working Paper 6738, National Bureau of Economic Research, Cambridge, September 1998. Accessed February 20, 2018. http://www.nber.org/papers/w6738.

Bremmer, Ian. *The Fat Tail: The Power of Political Knowledge in an Uncertain World*. New York: Oxford University Press, 2010.

Brousseau, Vincent, and Fabio Scacciavillani. "A Global Hazard Index for the World Foreign Exchange Markets." European Central Bank Working Paper, Series 1, 1999.

Brzezinski, Zbigniew. *The Grand Chessboard: American Primacy and Its Geostrategic Imperatives*. New York: Basic Books, 1997.

Burns, Nicholas, Jonathon Price, Zoe Baird, Robert Blackwill, James Cartwright, JDowdy ohn , Peter Feaver, Stephen

Hadley, Christopher Kirchhoff, Jane Holl Lute, Thomas Pritzker, Kirk Rieckhoff, John Sawers, Schwab Susan, Julianne Smith, James Steinberg, Stuart Douglas, Dov Zakheim, Leah Joy Zell, Ferguson Niall, Jennifer Harris, Joseph S. Nye, and the Aspen Strategy Group. America's National Security Architecture: Rebuilding the Foundation. Cambridge, MA: The Belknap Press, 2016.

Butcher, Mike. "EQLIMN Startup Aims to Surface Geopoitical Big Data in the Middle East." TechChrunch, September 3, 2014. Accessed January 5, 2018. https://techcrunch.com/2014/09/03/eqlim-startup-aims-to-surface-geopolitical-big-data-in-the-middle-east/.

Carter, Barry E., and Ryan Farha. "Overview and Operation of U.S. Financial Sanctions, Including the Example of Iran." Georgetown University Law Center, 2013. Accessed February 20, 2018. https://scholarship.law.georgetown.edu/cgi/viewcontent.cgi?article=2267&context=facpub.

Cochrane, John H. "Eugene F. Fama, Efficient Markets, and the Nobel Prize." Chicago Booth Review, May 20, 2014. Accessed February 20, 2018. http://review.chicagobooth.edu/magazine/winter-2013/eugene-fama-efficient-markets-and-the-nobel-prize.

Cohen, Samuel Bernard. Geopolitics: The Geography of International Relations, 2nd ed. Lanham, MD: Rowman & Littlefield, 2008.

Collins, Mike. "Wall Street and the Financialization of the Economy." Forbes, February 4, 2015. https://www.forbes.com/sites/mikecollins/2015/02/04/wall-street-and-the-financialization-of-the-economy.

Davis, Robert, "British Slaves on the Barbary Coast," BBC History, February 17, 2011. Accessed March 4, 2018. http://www.bbc.co.uk/history/british/empire_seapower/white_slaves_01.shtml

de Blij, Harm. *Why Geography Matters: More Than Ever*. Oxford, UK: Oxford University Press, 2012.

Dobbs, Richard, Susan Lund, Jonathan Woetzel, and Mina Mutafchieva. "Debt and (Not Much) Deleveraging." McKinsey & Company, February 2015. Accessed February 20, 2018. https://www.mckinsey.com/global-themes/employment-and-growth/debt-and-not-much-deleveraging.

Dugin, Alexander. *The Fourth Political Theory*. Seattle: Amazon Digital Services, 2012.

Duisenberg, Willem F. "The Role of Financial Markets for Economic Growth." Speech delivered to the economics conference The Single Financial Market: Two Years into EMU, Vienna, May 31, 2001. Accessed February 18, 2018. https://www.ecb.europa.eu/press/key/date/2001/html/sp010531.en.html.

Dupuy, Jean-Pierre. *Le Sacrifice et L'envie: Le Libéralisme aux Prises avec la Justice Sociale*. Paris: Calman-Levy, 1992.

Edwards, Sebastian. "Crisis Prevention: Lessons from Mexico and East Asia." NBER Working Paper 7233, July 1999. doi:10.3386/w7233.

Dell'Ariccia, Giovanni, Enrica Detragiache, Gian Maria Milesi-Ferretti, A. J. Tweedie, and Barry J. Eichengreen. "Liberalizing Capital Movements: Some Analytical Issues." *Economic Issues* 17 (1999): 1–21.

FDIC, Historical Statistics on Banking (HSOB),
http://www2.fdic.gov/hsob/index.asp

Fell, Andy. "Does Probability Come from Quantum Physics?" *UC
Davis Newsletter*, February 5, 2013.
https://www.ucdavis.edu/news/does-probability-come-
quantum-physics/.

Ferguson, Niall. *The Square and the Tower*. New York: Penguin
Press, 2018.

Fligstein, Neil. *The Architecture of Markets: An Economic Sociology
of Twenty-First Century Capitalist Societies*. Princeton, NJ:
Princeton University Press, 2002.

Fonseca, Goncalo L. "Evolutionary Economics." The History of
Economic Thought, March 1, 2014. Accessed January 29,
2018. http://www.hetwebsite.net/het/school/evol.htm.

Foster, John Bellamy. "The Financialization of Capitalism."
Monthly Review 58(11) (2007). Accessed February 18,
2018. https://monthlyreview.org/2007/04/01/the-
financialization-of-capitalism/.

Friedman, George. *The Next 100 Years: A Forecast for the 21st
Century*. New York: Anchor, 2010.

Funke, Jayson J. "Geography of Finance." Oxford Bibliographies.
Last modified September 30, 2013. Accessed February 20,
2018.
http://www.oxfordbibliographies.com/view/document/o
bo-9780199874002/obo-9780199874002-0024.xml.

Gewirtz, Julian. "Bury Zhao Ziyand and Praise Him: Why We
Should Remember the Contributions of China's Disgraced
Former Leader." *Foreign Policy*, April 8, 2015. Accessed

January 17, 2018. foreignpolicy.com/2015/04/08/zhao-ziyang-china-ccp-deng-xiaoping-tiananmen.

Giles, Lionel. *Sun Tzu on The Art of War*. London: Luzac & Co., 1910.

Gillespie, Patrick. "Venezuela Is in Default, and You May Own Its Debt," CNN Money, November 14, 2017. Accessed February 20, 2018. http://money.cnn.com/2017/11/14/investing/venezuela-debt-401k/index.html.

Giordano, Luca, and Claudia Guagliano. "Financial Architecture and the Source of Growth: International Evidence on Technological Change." *Quaderni di Finanza* (2014). doi:10.2139/ssrn.2474991.

Gold Price. "The Price of Gold." Accessed January 28, 2018. https://goldprice.org/gold-price-chart.html.

Goldfinger, Charles. *La Géofinance: Pour Comprendre la Mutation Financière*. Paris: Collection Odysée, 1986.

Goldman, Minto F. *Rivalry in Eurasia: Russia, the United States, and the War on Terror*, Praeger Security International. Santa Barbara, CA: ABC-CLIO, LLC, 2009.

Greenspan, Allan. "Do efficient financial markets mitigate financial crises?" Speech delivered to the Financial Markets Conference of the Federal Reserve Bank of Atlanta, Sea Island, Georgia. October 19, 1999. Accessed March 4, 2018. https://www.federalreserve.gov/boarddocs/speeches/1999/19991019.htm

Greer, Scott A. *The Logic of Social Enquiry*. Chicago: Aldine Atherton, 1969.

343

Grenville, Stephen. "Financial Crises and Globalisation from an Australian Perspective." Paper delivered to the Reinventing Bretton Woods Committee Conference on International Capital Mobility and Domestic Economic Stability, Canberra, July 15, 1999.

Griffith-Jones, Stephany. *A BRICS Development Bank: A Dream Coming True?* New York: United Nations Conference on Trade and Development, 2014. Accessed February 20, 2018. http://unctad.org/en/PublicationsLibrary/osgdp20141_en.pdf.

Guillén, Mauro F., and Sandra L. Suárez. "The Global Crisis of 2007–2009: Markets, Politics, and Organizations." In *Markets on Trial: The Economic Sociology of the U.S. Financial Crisis*, edited by Michael Lounsbury and Paul M. Hirsch, 257–79. Bingley, UK: Emerald Group Publishing Limited, 2010. http://citeseerx.ist.psu.edu/viewdoc/download?doi=10.1.1.702.1072&rep=rep1&type=pdf.

Gulhan, Aziz. "Financial Literacy Matters." *Sanford Journal of Public Policy*, November 8, 2013. https://sites.duke.edu/sjpp/2013/financial-literacy-matters/.

Hammana, Sama. "Geofinance: Financialities of the Anthropocene." PhD thesis, Goldsmiths University of London, 2017. Accessed January 29, 2017. https://schizoaesthetic.org/images/geofinance.pdf.

Handfield, Rober Beaudoin, and Steve A. Melnyk. "The Scientific Theory-Building Process: A Primer Using the Case of TQM." *Journal of Operations Management* (1998). Accessed February 20, 2018. https://www.researchgate.net/publication/222225902_T

he_Scientific_Theory-
Building_Process_A_Primer_Using_the_Case_of_TQM. July
1998.

Hanes, W. Travis. "Kingdoms and City-States in Southwest Asia."
World History Now, 2009. Accessed February 20, 2018.
https://historyonlinenow.weebly.com/section-4-
kingdoms-and-city-states-in-southwest-asia.htm
http://www.historyonlinenow.com/worldhistory/WorldH
istoryNowSplashPage.htm.

Hart, Michael L., David Lamper, and Neil F. Johnson. "An
Investigation of Crash Avoidance in a Complex System,"
Physica A: Statistical Mechanics and its Applications,
316(1–4) (2002): 649–61. Accessed February 20, 2018.
https://www.sciencedirect.com/science/article/pii/S037
843710201381X?via%3Dihub.

Haushofer, Karl. "Geopolitik des Pazifischen Ozeans." *The
Canadian Historical Review* 5 (1925): 268–9.

Hens, Thorsten, and Klaus Reiner Schenk-Hoppé. "Survival of the
Fittest on Wall Street." *Evolutionary Finance.* Last modified
February 2, 2004.
http://www.evolutionaryfinance.ch/papers/surv_of_the_fi
ttest.pdf.

Hens, Thorsten, Klaus Reiner Schenk-Hoppé, and Martin Stalder.
"An Application of Evolutionary Finance to Firms Listed in
the Swiss Market Index." *Zeitschrift für Volkswirtschaft und
Statistik* 138(4) (2002): 465–87.
http://citeseerx.ist.psu.edu/viewdoc/download?doi=10.1.
1.312.1290&rep=rep1&type=pdf.

Holland, Steve and Margaret Chadbourn, "Obama Describes Putin
as 'Like a Bored Kid'," Reuters, August 9, 2013. Accessed
March 4, 2018. https://www.reuters.com/article/us-usa-

russia-obama/obama-describes-putin-as-like-a-bored-kid-idUSBRE9780XS20130809

Hovi, Jon, Robert Huseby, and Detlef F. Sprinz. "Are Targeted Sanctions More Effective Than Comprehensive Sanctions?" The Graduate Institute of Geneva, 2013.

Hufbauer, Gary Clyde, Kimberly Ann Elliott, Tess Cyrus, and Elizabeth Winston. "US Economic Sanctions: Their Impact on Trade, Jobs, and Wages." Peterson Institute for International Economics, Working Paper Special, April 1997. Accessed February 20, 2018. https://piie.com/publications/working-papers/us-economic-sanctions-their-impact-trade-jobs-and-wages.

International Monetary Fund. "Globalization: A Brief Overview." May 1, 2008. Accessed February 20, 2018. https://www.imf.org/external/np/exr/ib/2008/053008.htm.

———. "Globalization: Threat or Opportunity?" Last modified April 12, 2000. Accessed January 2, 2018. https://www.imf.org/external/np/exr/ib/2000/041200to.htm.

———. "The End of the Bretton Woods System." Last modified January 25, 2018. Accessed January 25, 2018. https://www.imf.org/external/about/histend.htm.

Investopedia. "Globalization." April 1 2015. Accessed February 20, 2018. https://www.investopedia.com/terms/g/globalization.asp.

Issing, Otmar. "The Globalisation of Financial Markets." European Central Bank, September 12, 2000. Accessed February 20, 2018.

https://www.ecb.europa.eu/press/key/date/2000/html/sp000912_2.en.html.

Ju, Hailong. *China's Maritime Power and Strategy: History, National Security and Geopolitics.* Singapore: World Scientific, 2015.

Kahn, Charles M., and William Roberds. "The CLS Bank: A Solution to the Risks of International Payments Settlement." *Carnegie-Rochester Conference Series on Public Policy* 54(1) (2001): 191–226.

Kaplan, Abraham. *The Conduct of Inquiry: Methodology for Behavioral Science.* San Francisco: Chandler, 1964.

Kaplan, Robert D. *Asia's Cauldron: The South China Sea and the End of a Stable Pacific.* New York: Random House, 2014.

Keck, Zachary. "US-China Rivalry More Dangerous Than Cold War?" *The Diplomat*, January 28, 2014. Accessed March 4, 2018. https://thediplomat.com/2014/01/us-china-rivalry-more-dangerous-than-cold-war/

Kennedy, Paul. *The Rise and Fall of the Great Powers.* New York: Random House, 1987.

Kersten, Andrew E., and Lindenmeyer Kriste , eds. *Politics and Progress: American Society and the State since 1865.* Santa Barbara, CA: Praeger, 2001.

Khanna, Parag. "Want to Understand How Trump Happened? Study Quantum Physics." *Quartz*, November 11, 2016. Accessed January 27, 2017. https://qz.com/834735/want-to-understand-how-trump-happened-study-quantum.

Klare, Michael. "The New Geopolitics." *Monthly Review* 55 (03) (2003). Accessed January 29, 2018.

https://monthlyreview.org/2003/07/01/the-new-geopolitics/.

Krippner, Greta R. "The Financialization of the American Economy." *Socio-Economic Review* 3 (2008): 173–208. https://papers.ssrn.com/sol3/papers.cfm?abstract_id=811461.

Levin, Simon. *Fragile Dominion: Complexity and the Commons.* New York: Perseus Publishing, 1999.

———, "What Can Mother Nature Teach Us about Managing Financial Systems?" Christian Science Monitor, August 22, 2016, https://www.csmonitor.com/Science/Complexity/2016/0822/What-can-Mother-Nature-teach-us-about-managing-financial-systems.

Levine, Ross. "Finance and Growth: Theory and Evidence." NBER Working Paper 10766, September 2004. doi: 10.3386/w10766.

———. "Financial Development and Economic Growth: Views and Agenda." *Journal of Economic Literature* 35(2) (1997): 688–726.

Levine, Ross, and Sara Zervos. "Stock Markets, Banks, and Economic Growth." *The American Economic Review* 88(3) (1998): 537–58.

LeVine, Steve. "The 14 Rules for Predicting Future Geopolitical Events." *Quartz*, January 7, 2013. Accessed January 23, 2018. https://qz.com/40960/the14-rules-for-predicting-geopolitical-events/.

Lucas, Robert E. "On the Mechanics of Economic Development." *Journal of Monetary Economics* 22 (1988): 3–42. Accessed

February 18, 2018.
https://www.parisschoolofeconomics.eu/docs/darcillon-thibault/lucasmechanicseconomicgrowth.pdf.

Lund, Susan, and Hans-Helmut Kotz. "Financial Globalization 2.0."
McKinsey & Company, September 5, 2017. Accessed
January 21, 2018.
https://www/mckinsey.com/mgi/overview/in-the-news/financial-globalization-2.

Lund, Susan, Ekart Windhagen, James Manyika, Phillipp Harle,
Jonathan Woetzel, and Diana Goldshtein. "The New
Dynamics of Financial Globalization." McKinsey &
Company, August 2017. Accessed February 20, 2018.
https://www.mckinsey.com/industries/financial-services/our-insights/the-new-dynamics-of-financial-globalization.

Machiavelli, Niccolò. *The Prince*. Rome: Antonio Blado d'Asola,
1532. Accessed July 2017.
https://www.gutenberg.org/files/1232/1232-h/1232-h.htm.

Mackinder, Halford J. "The Geographical Pivot of History." *The
Geographical Journal* 23(4) (1904): 421–37.

Macro Trends. "Crude Oil Prices—70 Year Historical Chart."
Accessed January 29, 2018.
http://www.macrotrends.net/1369/crude-oil-price-history-chart.

Magdoff, Harry, and Paul Sweezy. *The Dynamics of U.S. Capitalism*.
New York: Monthly Review Press, 1965.

Mahan, Alfred T. *The Influence of Sea Power Upon History*. New
York: Little, Brown & Company, 1890.

Mahbubani, Kishore. *The Great Convergence: Asia, the West, and the Logic of One World*. New York: PublicAffairs, 2013.

Marshall, Tim. *Prisoners of Geography*. New York: Scribner, 2016.

McGinn, Jeffrey. *Tail Risk Killers: How Math, Indeterminacy, and Hubris Distort Markets*. New York: McGraw-Hill, 2011.

Mionel, Oana. "The Globalization of Financial Markets and the Main Actors." *Knowledge Horizons–Economics* 5(3) (2013): 66–8. Accessed February 20, 2018. http://orizonturi.ucdc.ro/arhiva/2013_khe_3_pdf/khe_vol _5_iss_3_66to68.pdf.

Mountain Math Software. "The Uncertainty Principle." January 16, 2015. Accessed January 22, 2018. http://www.mtnmath.com/whatrh/node72.html.

Muñoz, Katja. "The Role of Big Data in Early Warning Conflict Monitoring." LinkedIn, September 5, 2016. Accessed January 21, 2018. https://www.linkedin.com/pulse/role-big-data-early-warning-conflict-monitoring-dr-katja-mu%C3%B1oz.

NASDAQ. "End of Day Commodity Futures Price Quotes for Crude Oil WTI (NYMEX)." Accessed January 29, 2018. http://www.nasdaq.com/markets/crude-oil.aspx?timeframe=10y.

Nasr, Vali. *The Dispensable Nation: American Foreign Policy in Retreat*. New York: Anchor Books, 2013.

NATO. "Defence Expenditure of NATO Countries (2010–2017)." June 29, 2017. Accessed January 29, 2018. https://www.nato.int/cps/en/natohq/news_145409.htm.

NYSE. "Shares Outstanding and Market Capitalization of Companies Listed." Accessed February 20, 2018. http://www.nyxdata.com/nysedata/asp/factbook/viewer_edition.asp?mode=tables&key=333&category=5.

Parenti, Fabio M., and Umberto Rosati. *Geofinanza e Geopolitica Copertina Flessibile*. Milan: EGEA, 2016.

Patton, Mike. "Who Owns the Most US Debt?" *Forbes*, October 28, 2014. https://www.forbes.com/sites/mikepatton/2014/10/28/who-owns-the-most-u-s-debt/#6a85ffc3819c.

Paul, Karamjeet. *Managing Extreme Financial Risk: Strategies and Tactics for Going Concerns*. Waltham, MA: Academic Press, 2014.

Payscale. "Average Salary in New York, New York." Accessed February 20, 2018. https://www.payscale.com/research/US/Location=New-York-NY/.

Persaud, Avinash. "The Liquidity Puzzle." Risk.net, June 1, 2000.

Popper, Karl. *The Poverty of Historicism*. Oxford, UK: Routledge & Kegan Paul, 1957.

———. *The Logic of Scientific Discovery*. New York: Science Editions, 1961.

Porter, Michael E. "The Competitive Advantage of Nations." *Harvard Business Review*, March–April 1990. Accessed January 29, 2018. https://hbr.org/1990/03/the-competitive-advantage-of-nations.

Reinhart, Carmen M., and Kenneth S. Rogoff. "Growth in a Time of Debt." *American Economic Review* 100(2) (2010): 573–8.

Romei, Valentina. "Hidden Numbers Reveal Scale of Venezuela's Economic Crisis." *Financial Times*, May 9, 2017. Accessed February 20, 2018. https://www.ft.com/content/a6f7bdae-2f46-11e7-9555-23ef563ecf9a.

S&P Global RatingsDirect. "2016 Annual Global Structured Finance Default Study and Rating Transitions." Standard and Poors, May 9, 2017. https://www.capitaliq.com/CIQDotNet/CreditResearch/RenderArticle.aspx?articleId=1846067&SctArtId=424868&from=CM&nsl_code=LIME&sourceObjectId=10070711&sourceRevId=2&fee_ind=N&exp_date=20270511-00:49:05.

Savin, Leonid. "India and Its Strategic Culture." Katehon. Accessed February 20, 2018. katehon.com/article/india-and-its-strategic-culture.

Schenk-Hoppé, Klaus Reiner. "Evolutionary Finance: A Tutorial." University of Leeds, July 13, 2008. Accessed February 20, 2018. http://www.optirisk-systems.com/papers/KlausReinerSchenkHoppe.pdf.

Schoenmaker, Dirk. "What Happened to Global Banking after the Crisis?" Bruegel, March 14, 2017. Accessed February 20, 2018. bruegel.org/2017/03/what-happened-to-global-banking-after-the-crisis.

Silver, Nate. *The Signal and the Noise: Why So Many Predictions Fail—But Some Don't*. New York: Penguin Press, 2013.

Smith, Adam. *The Wealth of Nations*. London: William Strahan and Thomas Cadell, 1776.

South, Andrew H., and Zev R. Gurwitz. "2016 Annual Global Structured Finance Default Study and Rating Transitions." S&P Global Ratings Direct, May 9, 2017.

https://www.spratings.com/documents/20184/774196/
2016+Annual+Global+Structured+Finance+Default+Study
+And+Rating+Transitions.pdf/dd0ac65e-b3ff-4da6-b399-
65b8aba5be74.

Sputnik International. "Chinese Investments in Russia's Far East
Increased by One-Third in 2016," September 8, 2017.
Accessed February 20, 2018.
https://sputniknews.com/russia/201709081057218326-
china-investment-russia-vladivostok-business/.

Statista. "Percentage Added to the Gross Domestic Product (GDP)
of the United States of America in 2016, by Industry (as a
Percentage of GDP)." Accessed February 20, 2018.
https://www.statista.com/statistics/248004/percentage-
added-to-the-us-gdp-by-industry/.

Stern New York University. "Measured Spread from Treasury."
1997. Accessed February 20, 2018.
http://pages.stern.nyu.edu/~eelton/working_papers/cor
p%20bonds/all%20tables%20and%20figures%201.pdf.

Stinchcombe, Arthur L. *Constructing Social Theories*. New York:
Harcourt, Brace & World, 1960.

Stockhammer, Engelbert. "Financialisation and the Slowdown of
Accumulation." *Cambridge Journal of Economics* 28(5)
(2004): 719–41.

Strandskov, Jesper. "Sources of Competitive Advantage and
Business Performance." *Journal of Business Economics and
Management* 7(3) (2006): 119–29. Accessed January 20,
2017.
http://www.tandfonline.com/doi/pdf/10.1080/16111699
.2006.9636132.

Styer, Daniel F. *The Strange World of Quantum Mechanics.* Cambridge, UK: Cambridge University Press, 2000.

Sunday, Christopher E. "The Role of Theory in Research." University of the Western Cape, 2015. Accessed February 20, 2018. https://www.uwc.ac.za/Students/Postgraduate/Documen ts/The%20role%20of%20theory%20in%20research.pdf.

Sweezy, Paul M. "More (or Less) on Globalization." *Monthly Review* 49(4) (1997). Accessed January 28, 2018. https://monthlyreview.org/1997/09/01/more-or-less-on-globalization.

Thakor, Anjan. "International Financial Markets: A Diverse System is the Key to Commerce." Center for Capital Markets Competitiveness, February 10, 2015.

"Theory, Fact and the Origin of Life." *Nature: Structural & Molecular Biology* 12 (2005): 101. Accessed February 20, 2018. https://www.nature.com/articles/nsmb0205-101.

Tomaskovic-Devey, Donald, and Ken-Hou Lin. "Financialization: Causes, Inequality Consequences, and Policy Implications." *North Carolina Banking Institute Journal* 18 (2014): 166–94. Accessed February 20, 2018. http://scholarship.law.unc.edu/cgi/viewcontent.cgi?articl e=1365&context=ncbi.

Trading Economics. "Mexico GDP Annual Growth Rate—Forecast." Accessed February 20, 2018. https://tradingeconomics.com/mexico/gdp-growth-annual/forecast.

———. "Netherlands GDP." Accessed February 20, 2018. https://tradingeconomics.com/netherlands/gdp.

———. "Turkey GDP." Accessed February 20, 2018. https://tradingeconomics.com/turkey/gdp.

———. "Zimbabwe—Economic Indicators." Accessed February 20, 2018. https://tradingeconomics.com/zimbabwe/indicators.

United States Department of Labor. "Current Employment Statistics—CES (National)." Accessed March 23, 2017. https://www.bls.gov/ces/.

United States Federal Reserve. "Large Commercial Banks." Federal Statistical Release. Accessed February 20, 2018. https://www.federalreserve.gov/releases/lbr/current/.

Useem, Michael. *Investor Capitalism: How Money Managers Are Changing the Face of Corporate America*. New York: Basic Books, 1996.

vander Straeten, Pascal. *Tail Risk Management: Building a Resilient Financial Business in a Volatile World*. Dallas: Value4Risk, 2017.

Wallace, Walter L. *The Logic of Science in Sociology*. Chicago: Aldine Atherton, 1971.

White, Hugh. *The China Choice: Why We Should Share Power*. Oxford, UK: Oxford University Press, 2013.

———. *The Revenge of Geography: What the Map Tells Us about Coming Conflicts and the Battle against Fate*. New York: Random House, 2012.

Wildau, Gabriel. "Foreign Bank Lending to China Hits Record High." *Financial Times*, November 8, 2017. Accessed March 4, 2018. https://www.ft.com/content/64e14e70-c510-11e7-a1d2-6786f39ef675

Wilensky, Harold L. "The Professionalization of Everyone?" *American Journal of Sociology* 70(2) (1964): 137–58. Accessed January 2, 2017. http://www.journals.uchicago.edu/doi/abs/10.1086/223 790.

Witko, Christopher. "How Wall Street Became a Big Chunk of the US Economy—And When the Democrats Signed On." *Washington Post*, March 29, 2016. Accessed January 28, 2018. https://www.washingtonpost.com/news/monkey-cage/wp/2016/03/29/how-wall-street-became-a-big-chunk-of-the-US-economy.

Woods, Sam. "Geofinance." Speech given at the Mansion House City Banquet, London, October 4, 2017. Accessed January 29, 2017. https://www.bankofengland.co.uk/speech/2017/geofinan ce-speech-by-sam-woods.

World Trade Organization. "Report on G20 Trade Measures: Mid-October 2016 to Mid-May 2017," June 30, 2017. Accessed February 20, 2018. https://www.wto.org/english/news_e/news17_e/g20_wt o_report_june17_e.pdf.

XE.com. "XE Currency Charts: USD to EUR." Accessed January 30, 2018. https://www.xe.com/currencycharts/?from=USD&to=EU R&view=10Y.

Yates, Robin D. S. *The City State in Ancient China*. New York: Columbia University, 1958.